CYBER 2020

The Fifth International Conference on Cyber-Technologies and Cyber-Systems

October 25 - 29, 2020

CYBER 2020 Editors

Steve Chan, Decision Engineering Analysis Laboratory, USA

Manuela Popescu, IARIA, EU/USA

Khurram Bhatti, Information Technology University (ITU), Lahore, Pakistan

Maria Mushtaq, LIRMM –CNRS, University of Montpellier, France

Xing Liu, Kwantlen Polytechnic University, Surrey, B.C., Canada

Printed from e-media with permission by:

Curran Associates, Inc.
57 Morehouse Lane
Red Hook, NY 12571

Some format issues inherent in the e-media version may also appear in this print version.

International Academy, Research, and Industry Association (IARIA)
412 Derby Way
Wilmington, DE 19810

Phone: (408) 893-6407
Fax: (408) 527-6351

petre@iaria.org

Additional copies of this publication are available from:

Curran Associates, Inc.
57 Morehouse Lane
Red Hook, NY 12571 USA
Phone: 845-758-0400
Fax: 845-758-2633
Email: curran@proceedings.com
Web: www.proceedings.com

Table of Contents

CYBER 2020

Forward

The Fifth International Conference on Cyber-Technologies and Cyber-Systems (CYBER 2020), held on October 22-29, 2020, continued the inaugural event covering many aspects related to cyber-systems and cyber-technologies considering the issues mentioned above and potential solutions. It is also intended to illustrate appropriate current academic and industry cyber-system projects, prototypes, and deployed products and services.

The increased size and complexity of the communications and the networking infrastructures are making it difficult the investigation of the resiliency, security assessment, safety and crimes. Mobility, anonymity, counterfeiting, are characteristics that add more complexity in Internet of Things and Cloud-based solutions. Cyber-physical systems exhibit a strong link between the computational and physical elements. Techniques for cyber resilience, cyber security, protecting the cyber infrastructure, cyber forensic and cyber crimes have been developed and deployed. Some of new solutions are nature-inspired and social-inspired leading to self-secure and self-defending systems. Despite the achievements, security and privacy, disaster management, social forensics, and anomalies/crimes detection are challenges within cyber-systems.

The conference had the following tracks:

- Cyber security
- Cyber infrastructure
- Cyber Attack Surfaces and the Interoperability of Architectural Application Domain Resiliency
- Embedded Systems for the Internet of Things
- Cyber resilience

We take here the opportunity to warmly thank all the members of the CYBER 2020 technical program committee, as well as all the reviewers. The creation of such a high quality conference program would not have been possible without their involvement. We also kindly thank all the authors that dedicated much of their time and effort to contribute to CYBER 2020. We truly believe that, thanks to all these efforts, the final conference program consisted of top quality contributions.

We also gratefully thank the members of the CYBER 2020 organizing committee for their help in handling the logistics and for their work that made this professional meeting a success.

We hope that CYBER 2020 was a successful international forum for the exchange of ideas and results between academia and industry and to promote further progress in the domain cyber technologies and cyber systems.

CYBER 2020 General Chair

Steve Chan, Decision Engineering Analysis Laboratory, USA

CYBER 2020 Steering Committee

Carla Merkle Westphall, Federal University of Santa Catarina (UFSC), Brazil
Rainer Falk, Siemens AG, Corporate Technology, Germany
Anne Coull, University of New South Wales, Australia
Daniel Kästner, AbsInt GmbH, Germany
Barbara Re, University of Camerino, Italy
Soultana Ellinidou, Cybersecurity Research Center | University Libre de Bruxelles (ULB), Belgium
Patrik Österberg, Mid Sweden University, Sundsvall, Sweden
Steffen Fries, Siemens, Germany

CYBER 2020 Publicity Chair

Daniel Andoni Basterrechea, Universitat Politecnica de Valencia, Spain

CYBER 2020

COMMITTEE

CYBER 2020 General Chair

Steve Chan, Decision Engineering Analysis Laboratory, USA

CYBER Steering Committee

Carla Merkle Westphall, UFSC, Brazil
Rainer Falk, Siemens AG, Corporate Technology, Germany
Anne Coull, University of New South Wales, Australia
Daniel Kästner, AbsInt GmbH, Germany
Barbara Re, University of Camerino, Italy
Soultana Ellinidou, Cybersecurity Research Center | University Libre de Bruxelles (ULB), Belgium
Patrik Österberg, Mid Sweden University, Sundsvall, Sweden
Steffen Fries, Siemens, Germany

CYBER 2020 Publicity Chair

Daniel Andoni Basterrechea, Universitat Politecnica de Valencia, Spain

CYBER 2020 Technical Program Committee

Aysajan Abidin, imec-COSIC KU Leuven, Belgium
Khalid Alemerien, Tafila Technical University, Jordan
Usman Ali, University of Connecticut, USA
Ghada Almashaqbeh, CacheCash Development Company, Inc., USA
Mohammed S Alshehri, University of Arkansas, Fayetteville, USA
Marios Anagnostopoulos, Critical Infrastructure Security and Resilience group - Norwegian University of Science & Technology, Norway
Abdullahi Arabo, University of the West of England, UK
A. Taufiq Asyhari, Coventry University, UK
Pranshu Bajpai, Michigan State University, USA
Morgan Barbier, ENSICAEN, France
Samuel Bate, Intertek NTA, UK
Vincent Beroulle, Univ. Grenoble Alpes, France
Khurram Bhatti, Information Technology University (ITU), Lahore, Pakistan
Davidson R. Boccardo, Clavis Information Security, Brazil
Ravi Borgaonkar, SINTEF Digital / University of Stavanger, Norway
Nicola Capodieci, University of Modena and Reggio Emilia (UNIMORE), Italy
Pedro Castillejo Parrilla, Technical University of Madrid (UPM), Spain
Steve Chan, Decision Engineering Analysis Laboratory, USA
Christophe Charrier, Normandie Universite, France
Bo Chen, Michigan Technological University, USA
Anne Coull, University of New South Wales, Australia

Monireh Dabaghchian, Morgan State University, USA
Vincenzo De Angelis, University of Reggio Calabria, Italy
Lorenzo De Carli, Worcester Polytechnic Institute, USA
Christos Dimopoulos, European University Cyprus, Cyprus
Soultana Ellinidou, Cybersecurity Research Center | University Libre de Bruxelles (ULB), Belgium
Rainer Falk, Siemens AG, Corporate Technology, Germany
Yebo Feng, University of Oregon, USA
Khan Ferdous Wahid, Airbus Digital Trust Solutions, Germany
Eduardo B. Fernandez, Florida Atlantic University, USA
Steffen Fries, Siemens, Germany
Steven Furnell, University of Plymouth, UK
Kambiz Ghazinour, SUNY Canton, USA
Uwe Glässer, Simon Fraser University - SFU, Canada
Chunhui Guo, San Diego State University, USA
Amir M. Hajisadeghi, AmirkabirUniversity of Technology, Iran
Ehsan Hesamifard, University of North Texas, USA
Zhen Huang, DePaul University, USA
Christos Iliou, Information Technologies Institute | CERTH, Greece / Bournemouth University, UK
Georgios Kambourakis, University of the Aegean - Karlovassi, Samos, Greece
Daniel Kästner, AbsInt GmbH, Germany
Basel Katt, Norwegian University of Science and Technology (NTNU), Norway
Mazaher Kianpour, Norwegian University of Science and Technology, Norway
Maria Krommyda, Institute of Communication & Computer Systems (ICCS), Greece
Fatih Kurugollu, University of Derby, UK
Petra Leimich, Edinburgh Napier University, Scotland, UK
Rafał Leszczyna, Gdansk University of Technology, Poland
Jing-Chiou Liou, Kean University - School of Computer Science and Technology, USA
Hao Liu, University of Cincinnati, USA
Xing Liu, Kwantlen Polytechnic University, Canada
Qinghua Lu, CSIRO, Australia
Mahesh Nath Maddumala, Mercyhurst University, Erie, USA
Louai Maghrabi, University of Business & Technology, Jeddah, Saudi Arabia
Yasamin Mahmoodi, Tübingen University | FZI (Forschungszentrum Informatik), Germany
David Maimon, Georgia State University, USA
Mahdi Manavi, Mirdamad Institute of Higher Education, Iran
Sayonnha Mandal, St. Ambrose University, USA
Sathiamoorthy Manoharan, University of Auckland, New Zealand
Michael Massoth, Hochschule Darmstadt - University of Applied Sciences / CRISP – Center for Research in Security and Privacy, Darmstadt, Germany
Vasileios Mavroeidis, University of Oslo, Finland
Carla Merkle Westphall, UFSC, Brazil
Yasir F. Mohammed, University of Arkansas, USA
Lorenzo Musarella,University Mediterranea of Reggio Calabria, Italy
Maria Mushtaq, LIRMM | Univ. Montpellier | CNRS, Montpellier, France
Roberto Nardone, University Mediterranea of Reggio Calabria, Italy
Klimis Ntalianis, University of West Attica, Greece
Jason Nurse, University of Kent, UK
Patrik Österberg, Mid Sweden University, Sundsvall, Sweden

Copyright Information

PCache: Permutation-based Cache to Counter Eviction-based Cache-based Side-Channel Attacks

Muhammad Asim Mukhtar
Department of Electrical Engineering
Information Technology University
Lahore, Pakistan
Email: asim.mukhtar@itu.edu.pk

Muhammad Khurram Bhatti
Department of Computer Engineering
Information Technology University
Lahore, Pakistan
Email: khurram.bhatti@itu.edu.pk

Guy Gogniat
Lab-STICC Laboratory, CNRS
Université Bretagne Sud
Lorient, France
Email: guy.gogniat@univ-ubs.fr

Abstract*—Eviction-based cache-based Side-Channel Attacks (SCAs) are continuously increasing confidentiality issues in computing systems. To mitigate these attacks, randomization-based countermeasures have raised interest because these have the potential to achieve strong security and high performance while retaining the cache features such as high-associativity and operate without the involvement of system software. However, existing countermeasures are proved to be less secure because of the small eviction set size or weak indexing functions used in them. To cope with this issue, we propose a novel randomization-based architecture, called PCache, which introduces hidden members in the eviction sets to enlarge their size, which makes it difficult for an attacker to launch eviction-based cache-based SCAs. PCache replaces cache lines in multiple steps by passing through different permutation functions, which consider bits of tag and index part of the memory address in the replacement process and result in strong indexing function. Experimental evaluations show that PCache provides high security. For a 10MB cache, an attacker needs 2 years to find the eviction set and can launch eviction-based cache-based SCAs with only 28% confidence level. Moreover, PCache performance overhead is only 1.6% at maximum as compared to classical set-associative caches.

Keywords–Cache-based side-channel attacks; Randomization; Prime+Probe attack.

I. INTRODUCTION

Caches are the main component of a computer that contributes significantly to performance and purposefully each aspect of them is designed to achieve maximum performance. However, performance-based designs raise confidentiality issues. These designs enable cache-based Side-Channel Attacks (SCAs) such that a process can extract the memory access-patterns that indirectly reflect the secrets of co-running processes [1]–[4].

Various cache-based SCAs have been proposed. The prominent one is eviction-based cache-based side-channel attack, where an attacker intentionally fills cache lines with the memory blocks, called eviction set, so that eviction triggers on victim accesses. Recent research works have shown that these attacks can recover keys of cryptographic algorithms [1]–[4], detect user keystrokes [5], and combining with other side-channel can read unauthorized address space of system software or applications [6] [7]. Moreover, these attacks can exploit widely used architectures especially Intel and ARM, and can also extract the secret information of application executing in hardware-assisted trusted execution environments like Intel-SGX and ARM-TrustZone [8].

Numerous countermeasures have been proposed these recent years, which can broadly be categorized into partitioning and randomization approaches. Partitioning-based techniques [9]–[11], which statically divide the cache into multiple non-interference domains, provide strong security but degrade performance, which is the main purpose of caches. Randomization-based techniques [12]–[14], which make eviction set confidential by random memory-to-cache mapping, provide better performance but lead to weak security. Recent research works showed that the eviction set can be revealed using the Prime-Prune-Probe attack in a practically feasible time [15] [16]. However, we observe that the randomization-based techniques can provide security by making eviction set large and introducing new type of member called hidden members, which are relocated as a result of accommodating memory block in cache, making eviction process confusing for the attacker. This greatly increases the effort of the attacker such that the eviction-based cache SCAs become impractical.

The goal of this work is to reduce the limitation of randomization-based techniques to improve security. We propose PCache an architecture that evicts a cache line via a series of relocation using already stored content. This introduces hidden members in an eviction set, which cannot be learned using the Prime-Prune-Probe attack. Moreover, relocated members explore all their possible cache locations where they can reside in cache. These all cache locations become members of eviction set, which exponentially increases the number of members in eviction set. We show that PCache provides strong security and high performance without reducing the associativity and involvement of system software. Our main contributions are:

- We propose PCache, which achieves strong security against eviction-based cache-based SCAs by a novel approach of making eviction set size large and introducing hidden members in the replacement process.
- We evaluate the security of PCache by estimating the effort required by an attacker to learn the eviction set.
- We find new approaches that can be used to launch eviction-based cache-based SCAs on PCache. These are *Exclude-Prime-Probe*, which is an approach to find the hidden members of the eviction set, and *Eviction Distribution Estimation*, which is an approach to launch eviction-based cache-based SCAs without the need of learning hidden members of eviction set.
- We build PCache in Champsim simulator, which is a

trace-driven simulator, and compare the performance of PCache with the set-associative cache using SPEC CPU2017 benchmark.

Section II presents the background and related work. Section III presents the PCache architecture and operation. Section IV discusses the security perspective of PCache and new approaches to attack PCache. Sections V and VI present the experimental evaluation of security and performance, respectively. Section VII concludes the work.

II. Background and Related Work

A. Conventional Cache

Caches are a type of memory that is faster and smaller than the main memory. Caches buffer the memory blocks for the near future so that if the processor demands those blocks, they will be bring from cache rather than the main memory, resulting in reduced memory access latency. A basic storage cell of cache is called the cache line, and a group of cache lines is called a cache set. The cache line typically stores contiguous 64 bytes of main memory, which we call a memory block. Each memory block maps to one cache set but can be placed in any cache line in the cache set. The memory blocks that map to the same cache set are the conflicting blocks and cause replacement in case of cache set in full. The memory address is divided into three parts: offset, index and tag. The offset indicates the byte in the cache line. The index indicates the cache set where memory block can be stored. The tag differentiates the identity of one memory block from others in a cache set.

B. Eviction-Based Cache-Based SCAs

Numerous eviction-based cache-based SCAs have been proposed [1]–[4]. Using these attacks, an attacker finds the cache locations (lines or sets) that are shared with a victim's program, which usually has control flow dependency with secret information. Then, the attacker initializes these cache locations of its interested state (by evicting or flushing them). These cache locations will be changed if the victim accesses them. For example, in Prime+Probe attack [1], the attacker fills cache-sets by its memory lines and observes evictions of these cache-sets after the victim's execution. Evict+Reload [2] is same as Prime+Probe attack except it could be launched in case of attacker and victim share memory lines. Flush+Reload [3] is similar to Evict+Reload except the attacker initializes cache state by flushing cache-sets instead of evicting cache-sets. The Flush+Flush [4] attack is a variant of Flush+Reload attack that attacker perceives the state of cache-sets by measuring time required to flush these cache lines instead time required to access these cache lines.

C. Secure Cache Architectures

A range of countermeasures against cache-based SCAs have been proposed by modifying the cache architecture [9] [12]–[14] [17]. All of these countermeasures either partition the cache capacity or randomize the memory-to-cache mapping. The disadvantages of partitioning-based countermeasures are that these require invasive changes in software and degrade performance because of under-utilization of cache. Randomization-based countermeasure appears to be more promising. The state-of-the-art on randomization-based countermeasures are RPCache [12], NewCache [17], CEASER [14] and ScatterCache [13]. RPCache and NewCache randomize the mapping of memory lines to cache sets using permutation tables. The drawback of these countermeasures is that they require storage-intensive permutation tables, which limits the cache scalability. CESAR has proposed the concept of encrypting the memory-to-cache mapping using DES. The main drawback of CEASER is that it uses a set-associative cache that limits the encrypted space, which can be learned by an adversary in a few seconds [16]. Moreover, CEASER proposed key remapping to overcome the learning issue but this approach incurs performance degradation. ScatterCache uses hashing over skew-associative caches to randomize the memory-to-cache mapping. ScatterCache has extended the time to learn the mapping by an adversary. However, ScatterCache is proved to be less resilient to eviction-based cache-based SCAs [15].

D. Prime-Prune-Probe Attack

In this section, we present the Prime-Prune-Probe attack [15], which is used to learn the eviction set of recent randomization-based countermeasures, i.e. CEASER and ScatterCache. We explain this attack as we use it to show the security of our countermeasure. In Prime-Prune-Probe attack, the attacker chooses group, say it g, of addresses at random and fills the cache with g addresses. Then, attacker prunes the self-collision by again accessing the group addresses and removing the address from group g on observing longer access latency, which means it is evicted as a result of a collision with other members of groups. After pruning, g group contains fewer addresses, say it g'. The attacker then calls the victim program to execute, which may evict cache lines filled with g' addresses. Then, the attacker observes eviction, and if it finds eviction of g' address from cache line as a result of victim accesses, it considers evicted address as a member of the eviction set. The attacker repeats the Prime-Prune-Probe attack until it learns all members of the eviction set.

III. PCache: Permutation Based Cache

PCache achieves security against eviction-based cache-based SCAs by making large eviction set to deprive attackers of initializing cache lines with the required confidence, and it introduces cache lines in replacement process that relocate in the cache to achieve indirect eviction of another cache line, increasing the effort of the attacker to find relocating cache lines.

The objective of PCache is to mitigate eviction-based cache-based SCAs that share cache lines such as Prime+Probe and Evict+Reload attacks. We consider that an attacker has access to user-level privilege instructions except cache management related instructions such as $clflush$ and $prefetchtx$. Because of no access to $clflush$ instruction, Flush+Flush and Flush+Reload attacks cannot be launched. Moreover, physical attacks are not considered in the threat model of PCache. In addition to achieving security, we also focus to retain the fundamental design features of cache such as transparent to the user and less reliance on system software.

Structurally, each way in PCache is indexed by different permutation functions. Permutation functions compute the values using incoming address to find cache locations in each way. PCache operates differently on hit and miss operation. On hit, incoming address goes through all permutation functions and completes in single lookup to all ways. However, on miss, ways of PCache are seen as multiple groups and incoming address goes through permutation functions of first group only, as shown in Figure 1.

On event of cache miss, the replacement process completes in multiple steps and requires multiple lookups to ways. To understand the miss operation, we use an example, given in Figure 1, which shows PCache having 6 lines and 6 ways. Alphabets A-Z indicate the address stored in cache line and PF indicates the permutation function of each way. $G1$ and $G2$ indicate the groups of cache-ways, each group contains 3 cache-ways. V is the incoming address that triggers the process of replacement, which completes in multiple steps. First, incoming address V goes through permutation functions of $G1$ and replaces one cache-line at random from $G1$. let us assume the replaced cache line is C. Instead of evicting C, the replaced cache line C is moved to next group $G2$. let us assume the second replacement is P. Lastly, the replaced cache line in $G2$, which is P, will be evicted. In this example, there are only two groups, therefore, only one relocation happened, that is, from $G1$ to $G2$. In the case of more than two groups, the process of relocation continues until last group and evicts cache line from it.

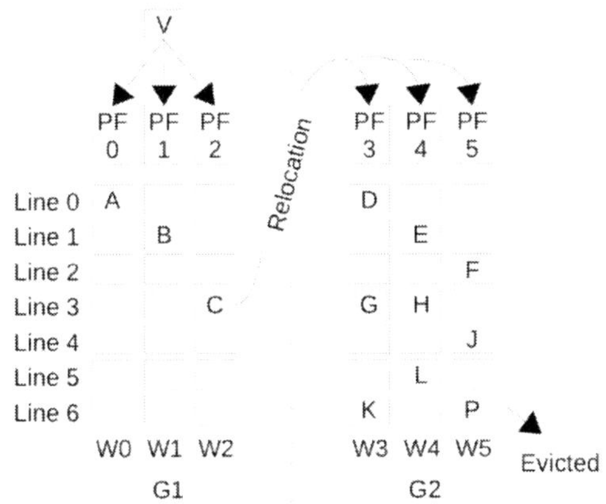

Figure 1. PCache having 6 ways, 6 lines and 2 groups. PF: Permutation function, Wx: Ways

While explaining the PCache operation, we have discussed only one path ($V \rightarrow C$ and $C \rightarrow P$) of relocations but other paths are also possible, as in each group one cache line is selected at random. Figure 2 shows all possible paths represented in tree diagram. The numbers 0-5 indicate the permutation functions used to index the ways. Alphabets A-P indicate the address stored in cache-lines selected by each permutation function. In the replacement process, there are two types of members. First, members that get evicted by incoming address, which are shown at the last level in Figure 2, we call them evicting members. Second, members that relocated to other cache lines as a result of accommodating incoming address, we call them hidden members. Note that, all cache lines belonging to path need to be filled to cause eviction of a specific line in PCache. In the perspective of security, hidden members are unknown to the attacker, and finding these require great effort. We discuss in detail the security perspective in Section IV. Note that, we refer PCache ways and groups configuration as ways/groups, for example, PCache given in Figure 1 refers as $6/2$ Pcache.

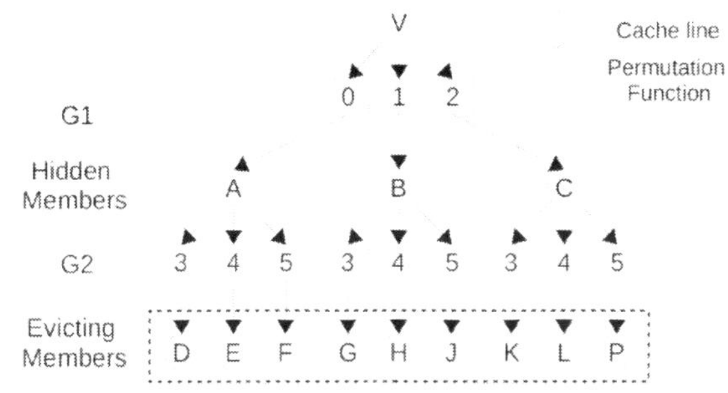

Figure 2. Cache-lines involved in replacement process represented in tree diagram.

A. *Permutation Function*

Selection of indexing function is critical in terms of both security and performance. In terms of security, it should not be predictable and in terms of performance, it comes in the critical path of memory access, therefore, it should be a low latency circuit. As PCache evicts the cache lines before relocating them multiple times, the attacker is limited to learn index function using cache collisions because of no direct relation of eviction between incoming and evicted cache lines. We have used a simple permutation function as an indexing function. This is better in terms of performance as it requires few gates to implement and incurs low latency. We have designed permutation functions to achieve the following objectives. First, memory addresses select different cache lines in each group, so that the member in one group does not conflict in other groups. Second, we consider tag and index bits of memory address to take part in the whole replacement process. As the system software remaps the physical mapping of application frequently, this changes the member of eviction set frequently and makes it impractical for an attacker to execute eviction-based cache-based SCAs.

IV. Security Perspective

Eviction-based cache-based SCAs have three phases. First, attacker *finds* members of eviction sets. Second, attacker *fills* cache with members of eviction sets. Third, attacker *observes* state of eviction sets in cache. PCache makes each step of attacker difficult. Because of hidden members in evicting sets, attacker's effort of learning eviction sets is greatly increased. Because of large eviction sets, filling and observing eviction sets becomes difficult while attack.

A. *Finding Members of Eviction sets*

Prime-Prune-Probe attack, which is an approach to learn members of eviction sets in random memory-to-cache mapping, can find the evicting members of eviction sets only. In case of PCache, this approach fails to learn the hidden members in eviction sets. This is because most of the hidden members does not evict as a result of victim access but relocate to another way. Moreover, there are members that only become a member of eviction set against interested victim address if they are placed in a specific way. In other cache-ways, these memory addresses may become a member of other eviction set.

To launch eviction-based cache-based SCAs, we find that attacker may adopt two approaches. First, the attacker tries to learn hidden members indirectly by breaking the path in replacement candidate tree, we call *exclude-prime-probe*. Second, the attacker does not find hidden members but tries to estimate the eviction distribution against all possible victim accesses, we call *eviction distribution estimation*. We discuss both approaches in the following sections.

1) Exclude-Prime-Probe Method: Eviction of cache lines as a result of victim access indicates the presence of all hidden members in the Pcache, which can be seen as a branch of the tree. To launch eviction-based cache-based SCAs, the attacker needs to know each member of the branch to cause eviction on victim access. let us assume that the attacker has found the evicting members using a g', as discussed in Section II-D. Then, to find hidden members, the attacker again places memory addresses belonging to g' in the PCache excluding the randomly selected addresses from them, which attacker expects that these may be the parents (or hidden members) of evicting members. The number for excluded addresses depends on the number of relocations, which defines how much parents are of evicting members. After placing members again, the attacker calls victim and observes the eviction of the evicting members. Lastly, if any evicting member remains un-evicted or its probability of eviction is small relative to all turns, the attacker considers the excluded address of g' as a parent of it. We used this approach to find the hidden members of the eviction set and estimate the attacker's effort required to show the security of PCache.

2) Eviction Distribution Estimation: Another approach that the attacker can adopt is to estimate the evictions of each location in the PCache against each victim's access. For this, the attacker randomly fills whole PCache and then allows the interested victim program to access PCache, which causes eviction of attacker's filled cache lines. The attacker observes these evictions and relates the cache lines having high eviction probability with the interested victim access. The attacker has to access as many times to ensure that all possible evicting cache lines should be selected multiple times for eviction. The number of access required by the attacker indicates the effort required to learn eviction distribution. The number of memory accesses can be modeled as *coupon collector's problem*, which gives the expected number of accesses (n_{access}) needed such that β portion of the evicting members of a replacement tree is evicted. This can be obtained using $E[n_{access}] = -n_{em} \cdot ln(1-\beta)$, where as n_{em} is the number of evicting members in tree. For 32/4 PCache, which has 2^{12} evicting members per tree, would require $\approx$ 18.86k victim calls to evict $\beta = 99\%$ of the eviction members of tree. This gives the eviction estimation cache lines against one victim address. However, for a successful attack, the attacker needs to know against all vulnerable victim address space. For example, in the case of AES, the attacker has to learn against all cache lines belonging to AES tables, which are 128. Therefore, the attacker needs 2.4 million victim calls to estimate the eviction distribution. Moreover, in case of multiple accesses to PCache, in Section V-B, we show that estimation of eviction distribution become indistinguishable because of all cache lines are selected for eviction and different victim memory accesses evict the same cache lines.

B. Filling and Observing Complexity

Assuming that the attacker has learned the eviction sets, to launch the attack, it needs to place learned memory addresses in the cache at the right cache-way to get evicted on victim access. As there is a random replacement policy, so the number of accesses required to place a memory address in the right way cannot be done in one access but multiple accesses. The number of accesses required by the attacker to place in an interesting cache way can be viewed as the bin-and-ball problem and can be given using the following equation.

$$n_{access} = \frac{log(1-confidence)}{log(1-p)} \quad (1)$$

Where n_{access} is the number of accesses required by the attacker to fill interested cache way, $confidence$ indicates the probability by which event of filling can be fulfilled, and p indicates the probability with which a memory address can successfully be placed at the right location in PCache. p defines the worst case and best case for the attacker, it can vary form $1/w$ (worst case) to 1 (best case), where w is the number of ways. Worst case is case when attacker selects a memory address that is a part of eviction set only if it is placed at one specific cache way. Inversely, the best case is the case when attacker selects a memory address that is a part of eviction set irrelevant to cache ways. As attacker has no information about that the memory address belongs to best or worst case, practically attacker has to assume worst case for every address to launch attack successfully with 99% confidence.

Depending on n_{access}, the attacker has to fill all lines of PCache that are involved in the replacement process, which is shown in replacement candidate tree in Figure 2. We will use the word tree to refer to the PCache in following discussion for simplicity. To fill first level of tree, attacker has to access $n_{access} \cdot w$. This number of accesses will guarantee the filling of first level of tree but which memory accesses are placed at the right cache ways is unknown to the attacker. Therefore, on next level attacker has to fill child of each memory address accessed for filling of first level of tree. This exponentially raises the number of memory accesses required on each level. Total number of accesses for filling of cache belongs to one replacement candidate tree can be given by

$$T[n_{access}] = \sum_{i=0}^{l} n_{access}^{i} \cdot w^{i} \quad (2)$$

$T[n_{access}]$ is the total number of accesses required by the attacker to attack, whose value varies depending on n_{access}. The attacker has to consider the worst-case to derive n_{access} for a successful launch of eviction-based cache-based SCAs but $T[n_{access}]$ becomes greater than cache capacity and limits the attacker from filling the PCache with 99% confidence. Figure 3 shows the maximum confidence level with which the filling of PCache can be fulfilled in 32/4 PCache. This shows that the attacker can fill PCache with maximum of 17%, 26% and 28% confidence level for 1MB, 8MB and 10MB, respectively. Attacker can use n_{access} at maximum of 1 for 1MB and 2 for 8MB and 10MB PCache.

V. SECURITY EVALUATION

Security of PCache is based on the fact that members of eviction sets greatly increase the effort of attacker. In this section, we evaluated effort required by the attacker to find evicting members using Prime-Prune-Probe method and hidden members using Exclude-Prime-Probe method, discussed in Sections II-D and IV-A1, and using Eviction Distribution Estimation, discussed in Section IV-A2.

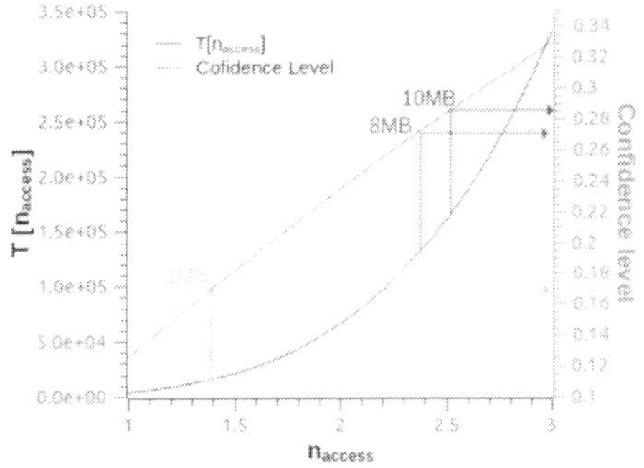

Figure 3. Confidence level required for filling of 32/4 PCache

A. *Evaluation Using Prime-Prune-Probe and Exclude-Prime-Probe Method*

We have made a model of PCache using Python. In experiment, we have taken the following assumptions. First, we have assumed noise-free model that the attacker and victim are running only. Second, we have filled the cache with attacker addresses using random function. Third, we have randomly selected the permutation function of each level. Lastly, we have evaluated the attacker effort on 1MB, 8MB and 10MB cache with 4 and 8 groups of ways.

We have measured the turns required to reveal 1000 hidden members. Then, we have multiplied the number of total addresses required by attacker with the average turns measured using experiment. For time calculation, same setting is used as in research work [15], which compromised security of ScatterCache, that is, flush time 0.5ms, victim execution time 3ms, cache hit time 9.5ns and cache miss time 50ns.

TABLE I. TIME REQUIRED TO LEARN EVICTION SET IN 32/4 PCACHE.

Capacity (MB)	n_{ve} (k)	T_E (hours)	n_{vh} (k)	T_H (hours)
1	301	0.39	113.03	613.6
8	411	1.04	919.52	12605.8
10	491	1.17	1150.68	18497.1

Results of experiment is shown in Table I. In this table n_{ve} and n_{vm} indicate the number of victim call against one evicting and hidden member respectively, and T_E and T_H indicate the time required to find evicting and hidden members,respectively, in eviction set for $n_{access} = 2$. Results show that time required by the attacker to find hidden members of one replacement candidate tree becomes difficult as cache capacity is increased or the number of ways are increased in a group. The attacker would need $\approx$ 25 months (or 2 years) to learn eviction set against one memory address in 10MB cache with 32 ways and 4 groups. Even after learning the whole eviction set attacker can launch attack with only 28% confidence. As permutation is tag dependent, the attacker has to again find the hidden members once the physical mapping is changed by operating system. Moreover, we have assumed fixed permutation mapping, security can be improved by making them configurable permutation functions so that these functions should be changed once before time given in Table I for specific cache configurations.

B. *Evaluation Using Eviction Distribution Estimation*

To estimate eviction distribution, we have executed experiment as discussed in Section IV-A2 and extracted number of evictions per each cache line in 8MB cache with 4 groups per way by accessing memory accesses 18.86k times. Result in Figure 4 shows the number of evictions per each cache line against single memory access. This result shows that the number of evictions per cache lines against one memory addresses may be distinguishable.

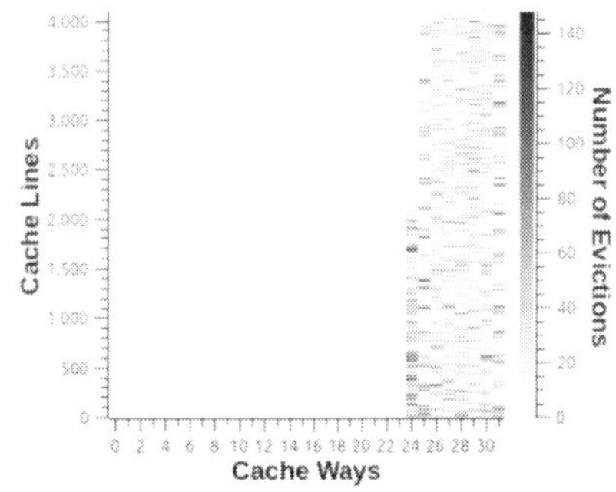

Figure 4. Number of Evictions per cache lines as a result of 18.86k accesses using one victim memory address.

As evictions occur from the last group of PCache, so probability of evicting same cache lines by different memory addresses is high. This increases the difficulty for an attacker if multiple memories are accessed by victim, which is practical assumption that there are always multiple memory accesses by program. We have extracted the eviction per cache lines using 100 memory addresses, which is shown in Figure 6. This result shows that each cache line is selected at-least-once for eviction and makes it impractical for an attacker to distinguish memory addresses from Eviction Distribution Estimation.

VI. PERFORMANCE EVALUATION

We have performed microarchitectural simulation using trace-based simulator ChampSim. Table II shows the configuration used in our study. The L3 cache is 8MB shared between 2 cores. For PCache, we have taken Permutation function latency of 1 cycle.

We have used 20 SPEC CPU2017 benchmarks as workloads for performance evaluation. For each benchmark, we have used a representative slice of 1 billion instructions and built 19 groups of workload where each group contains 2 benchmarks. We have performed simulation until all workloads in group finish executing 1 billion instructions. For measuring aggregate performance, we have measured the weighted speedup metric of proposed cache and normalized it to the baseline.

TABLE II. BASELINE CONFIGURATION

Component	Specification
Core	2 cores
L1 cache	Private, 32kB, 8-way set-associative, split D/I
L2 cache	Private, 256kB, 8-way set-associative
L3 cache	Shared, 8MB, 32-way set-associative or 32/4 PCache

Figure 5 shows the performance of 32/4 PCache with random replacement policy. As performance is normalized to the baseline, so bar higher than 100% is better. PCache with LRU is competitive to set-associative cache with LRU policy (or baseline) on most of the workloads. Moreover, results in Figure 5 show that PCache also outperforms the baseline

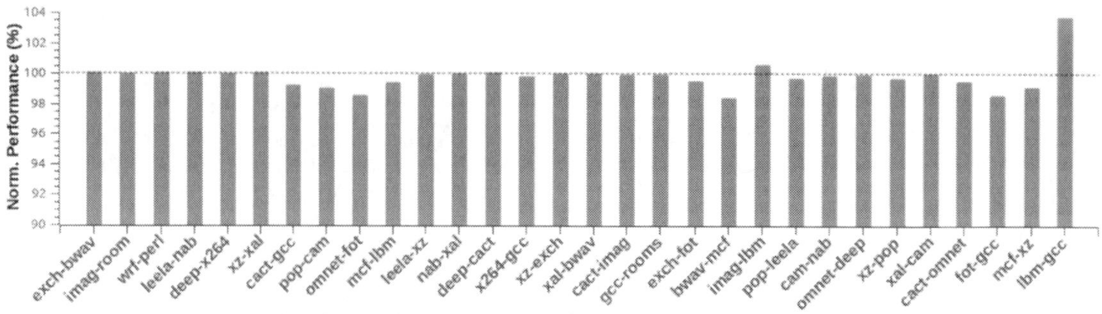

Figure 5. Normalized Performance of 8MB 32/4 PCache over SPEC CPU2017 workloads.

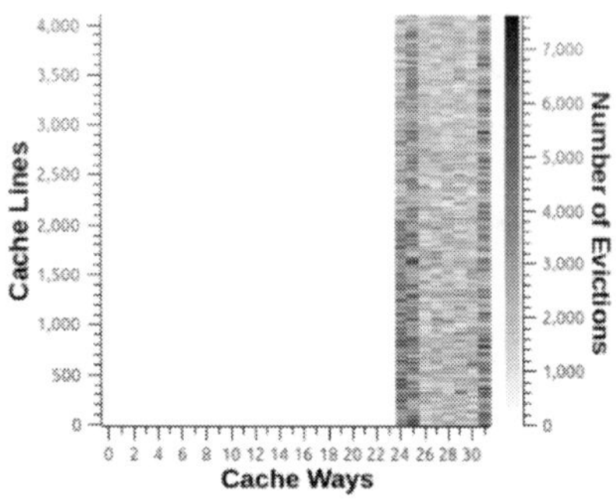

Figure 6. Number of Evictions per cache lines as a result of 18.86k accesses using 100 sequenced victim memory addresses.

of about 3% on $lbm - gcc$ because of conflict misses are reduced. However, PCache with random replacement policy shows degradation as compared to baseline on some workloads but a maximum of 1.6%, and performance loss is between 1.4% to 1.6%. Overall, the performance loss is only 0.002% on average as compared to the set-associative cache over SPEC CPU2017.

VII. Conclusion and Future Work

We have presented PCache, a cache design that provides security against eviction-based cache-based SCAs by making large eviction sets and introducing hidden members in the replacement process. PCache divides the cache into multiple groups and relocates a cache-line to multiple groups before eviction. In each group, relocated line passes through different permutation functions, resulting in difficulty for an attacker to find these relocated lines (or hidden members) in practically feasible time. Our evaluation shows that, for 10MB cache, the attacker needs 2 years to learn eviction set against one memory address. Moreover, a large eviction set and random replacement policy limit the attacker to launch eviction-based cache-based SCAs with only 28% confidence. Along with strong security, PCache has low-performance overhead of about 1.6% at maximum as compared to set-associative cache with LRU policy. While we have analyzed PCache as last-level-cache, this idea can also be extended on other shared structures like Translation Lookaside Buffers, which are also vulnerable to SCAs.

References

[1] F. Liu, Y. Yarom, Q. Ge, G. Heiser, and R. B. Lee, "Last-level cache side-channel attacks are practical," in 2015 IEEE Symposium on Security and Privacy, May 2015, pp. 605–622.

[2] M. Lipp, D. Gruss, R. Spreitzer, C. Maurice, and S. Mangard, "Armageddon: Cache attacks on mobile devices," in 25th USENIX Security Symposium, 2016, pp. 549–564.

[3] Y. Yarom and K. Falkner, "FLUSH+RELOAD: A high resolution, low noise, L3 cache side-channel attack," in 23rd USENIX Security Symposium (USENIX Security 14), 2014, pp. 719–732.

[4] D. Gruss, C. Maurice, K. Wagner, and S. Mangard, "Flush+Flush: A fast and stealthy cache attack," in Proceedings of the 13th International Conference on Detection of Intrusions and Malware, and Vulnerability Assessment, 2016, pp. 279–299.

[5] D. Wang et al., "Unveiling your keystrokes: A cache-based side-channel attack on graphics libraries," in NDSS, 2019.

[6] P. Kocher et al., "Spectre Attacks: Exploiting speculative execution," in 40th IEEE Symposium on Security and Privacy (S&P'19), 2019, pp. 1–19.

[7] M. Lipp et al., "Meltdown: Reading kernel memory from user space," in 27th USENIX Security Symposium (USENIX Security 18), 2018, pp. 973–990.

[8] M. A. Mukhtar, M. K. Bhatti, and G. Gogniat, "Architectures for Security: A comparative analysis of hardware security features in Intel SGX and ARM TrustZone," in 2019 2nd International Conference on Communication, Computing and Digital systems (C-CODE), 2019, pp. 299–304.

[9] T. Kim, M. Peinado, and G. Mainar-Ruiz, "STEALTHMEM: System-level protection against cache-based side channel attacks in the cloud," in Presented as part of the 21st USENIX Security Symposium (USENIX Security 12), 2012, pp. 189–204.

[10] V. Kiriansky, I. Lebedev, S. Amarasinghe, S. Devadas, and J. Emer, "DAWG: A defense against cache timing attacks in speculative execution processors," in 2018 51st Annual IEEE/ACM International Symposium on Microarchitecture (MICRO), Oct 2018, pp. 974–987.

[11] F. Liu et al., "CATalyst: Defeating last-level cache side channel attacks in cloud computing," in 2016 HPCA, March 2016, pp. 406–418.

[12] J. Kong, O. Aciicmez, J.-P. Seifert, and H. Zhou, "Deconstructing new cache designs for thwarting software cache-based side channel attacks," in Proceedings of the 2Nd ACM Workshop on Computer Security Architectures, ser. CSAW '08. ACM, 2008, pp. 25–34.

[13] M. Werner et al., "ScatterCache: Thwarting cache attacks via cache set randomization," in 28th USENIX Security Symposium (USENIX Security 19), 2019, pp. 675–692.

[14] M. K. Qureshi, "CEASER: Mitigating conflict-based cache attacks via encrypted-address and remapping," in 51st IEEE MICRO, 2018, pp. 775–787.

[15] A. Purnal and I. Verbauwhede, "Advanced profiling for probabilistic Prime+Probe attacks and covert channels in ScatterCache," ArXiv, vol. abs/1908.03383, 2019.

[16] R. Bodduna et al., "Brutus: Refuting the security claims of the cache timing randomization countermeasure proposed in CEASER," IEEE Computer Architecture Letters, vol. 19, no. 1, 2020, pp. 9–12.

[17] F. Liu, H. Wu, K. Mai, and R. B. Lee, "Newcache: Secure cache architecture thwarting cache side-channel attacks," IEEE Micro, vol. 36, no. 5, Sep. 2016, pp. 8–16.

Efficient AES Implementation for Better Resource Usage and Performance of IoTs

Umer Farooq
Department of Electrical Engineering
Dhofar University
Salalah, Oman
Email: ufarooq@du.edu.om

Maria Mushtaq
LIRMM-CNRS
Univ Montpellier
Montpellier, France
Email: maria.mushtaq@lirmm.fr

Muhammad Khurram Bhatti
Department of Computer Engineering
Information Technology University
Lahore, Pakistan
Email: khurram.bhatti@itu.edu.pk

Abstract—**The research on Internet of Things (IoT) devices has advanced tremendously over the past few years. IoT-based systems have their applications in almost every sphere of human life. Modern IoT devices are of quite heterogeneous nature and they are going to be involved in every thing from turning home lights ON/OFF to handling life critical data of a patient in smart health system. Because of the amount and nature of the data handled by IoT devices, they are a lucrative target for various kinds of security attacks. Among the many countermeasures against the security threats, Advanced Encryption Standard (AES) is a popular cryptographic scheme as it offers robust and platform independent implementation. In this work, keeping in view of the heterogeneous nature of the target IoT devices, we explore five different implementations of AES algorithm. These implementations use different algorithmic and architecture optimizations. The results obtained through these implementations reveal that some of them are very suitable for resource constrained edge IoT devices while others are useful for performance hungry middle layer gateways of an IoT-based system. Experimental results reveal that in an IoT-based system, a uniform cryptographic implementation should not be considered and that the implementations should be altered as per the nature of the target device.**

Keywords–Cryptography; Embedded Security; AES.

I. INTRODUCTION

Over the past few years, the research in embedded systems, especially their miniaturized form i.e. the Internet of Things (IoTs) devices has made huge progress. The IoT devices are going to be part of human life for a long time to come and they are speculated to change the way humans perceive about their life [1]. The IoT devices powered by high performance embedded systems have their applications in almost every sphere of human life like smart vehicles, homes, health systems, environmental monitoring, supply chains, etc. [2]. The aforementioned applications of IoT devices indicate that they have to handle enormous amounts of critical data. The handling of the data means processing, transmission, and storage of data. The critical nature of the data handled by IoT devices makes them a lucrative target for potential security attacks. The potential security threats can result in the compromise of integrity and the availability of data. A compromised IoT-based system can put even lives in danger [3] [4]. Hence, a secured IoT-based system, where the integrity and authenticity of the data is ensured through proper security measures becomes of paramount importance [5].

The importance of security for an IoT-based system is clear from the discussion presented above. However, there is no one standard way to make an IoT-based system secure [6]. This is because of the fact the IoT-based systems are normally multi-layered systems and different layers require different measures to make them secure. For example, the top layers like application and network layer are made secure easily through well established firewalls and security protocols. But the security of edge side layer is a hugely challenging task because of the varying nature of the edge side IoT devices and different types of security threats [7]. The edge side nodes of an IoT-based system are normally quite heterogeneous in nature. They have different hardware resources with varying performance requirements. These nodes are normally subjected to a range of security attacks like hardware trojans, side channel attacks, denial of service attacks [8]. All the aforementioned attacks compromise the authenticity, integrity, or the availability of the data in an IoT-based system. A number of countermeasures to these attacks like side channel analysis, isolation, blocking, and implementation of cryptographic algorithms have been proposed in the past [9] [10]. Among these countermeasures, the cryptographic schemes are of particular importance as they offer robust and hardware independent solutions. There are many cryptographic schemes that have been used in the past to secure embedded systems. Some of the most commonly used techniques include Data Encryption Standard (DES), 3-DES, and Advanced Encryption Standard (AES) techniques. AES is a cryptographic technique that uses symmetric cipher and offers highest possible security level. Standard implementation of AES on the hardware is quite challenging in terms of resource and performance requirements and it is not normally suited for resource constrained and performance critical IoT devices.

A lot of work has been done in the recent past to improve the efficiency of AES algorithm in embedded system. The improvement in efficiency means mainly reduced resource requirement with improved performance. Most of the work in the state-of-the-art considers the implementation of AES on FPGA. For example, the authors in [11] implement the AEs algorithm in a completely sequential manner. The sequential implementation results in a design that requires fewer resources as compared to existing solutions and this kind of implementation is well suited for resource constrained embedded systems. Similarly, the authors in [12] present the power efficient implementation of AES algorithm that is well suited for power constrained devices. Authors in [13] present another efficient implementation of AES that uses concepts of loop unrolling and parallelism to achieve high performance. This kind of implementation is well suited for applications requiring high speed and where the resources are not a constraint. Moreover, authors in [14]–[16] explore further high speed implementations of AES algorithm that provide very low delay numbers but require high number of resources on the target architecture. Although these implementations give good results in terms pf performance, they are not well suited for resource constrained IoT devices as they require huge amount of resources. To address this problem, authors in [17] present a version of AES implementation that is well suited for resource constrained IoT devices. Moreover, the authors in [9] propose another version of AES implementation that is well suited for IoT devices. It is important to mention here that both aforementioned works target only a single AES implementation and they do not take into account the heterogeneous nature of IoT devices. This kind of implementations might be useful in certain scenarios. However, this kind of static approach cannot be applied across a group of heterogeneous devices.

In this work, we explore five different implementation techniques of AES algorithm. We apply different types of optimizations and based on those optimizations, we obtain different area and performance results for each technique. For example, some of the proposed techniques require very small resources which is very suitable for resource constrained IoT devices. However, their execution speed is also low. On the other hand, there are some other techniques which have very high performance and they can satisfy the requirements of performance constrained IoT devices. But at the same time, they require higher number of resources as well. So, the main contribution of this paper is the provision of a pool of AES implementation techniques that are well suited for the target IoT device. The implementation results of the proposed techniques show that by carefully optimizing the algorithms and by exploiting the resources of target architecture, better area and speed results can be obtained. In the remainder of the paper, Section II gives an overview of AES encryption algorithm. Section III discusses the five implementation techniques and also highlights how these techniques can result in good area and delay trade-offs. Experimental results are discussed in Section IV and the paper is finally concluded in Section V.

II. Overview of AES Algorithm

AES was selected by National Institute of Standards and Technology (NIST) [18] as a replacement of old DES. The main reason behind its selection was its agility and simple iplementation. At the same time, it provided robust security against all kinds of security threats. AES is an iterative algorithm that is implemented over multiple rounds and it supports key sizes of 128, 192, and 256 bits. Larger the key size, better the security. However, larger key sizes require more resources. In this work, we focus on the AES implementations with 128 bit key size. However, the results obtained with this key size can be extrapolated to larger key sizes as well. In the remaining part of this section, an overview of the AES algorithm is presented.

An overview of the implementation of AES algorithm is shown in Figure 1. It can be seen from this figure that AES implementation in hardware can mainly be divided into two parts: one is called the cipher module and the other is called the key expansion module. Both modules run in parallel where key expansion module generates the key and the cipher module uses that key to encrypt or decrypt the text under consideration. Normally, for 128 bit key size implementation, cipher module performs 10 rounds of operations. In the first nine rounds,

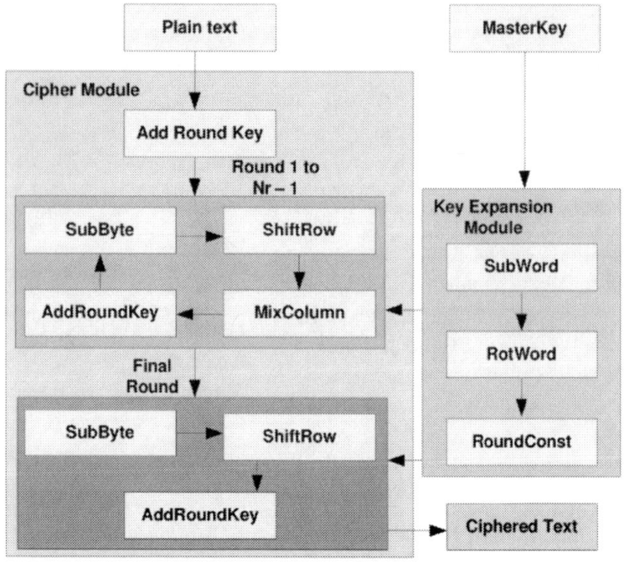

Figure 1. Standard Overview of AES Algorithm

the cipher module performs SubByte, ShiftRow, MixColumn, and AddRoundKey operations. In the final round, MixColumn operation is removed and only SubByte, ShiftRow, and AddRoundKey operations are performed. During each of the ten rounds, key expansion module provides the cipher module with the expanded key through its SubWord, RotWord, and RoundConst operations. It can be seen from Figure 1 that the AES algorithm acts on the input data in an iterative manner to give the encrypted data. Further discussion on the individual operations of two modules of AES algorithm is provided next.

It can be seen from Figure 1 that the cipher module starts with ***SubByte*** operation. This operation takes the input data one byte at a time and replaces it with a byte from the substitution box (also called as S-box). S-box is constructed through two transformations. In the first transformation, multiplicative inverse is taken while in the second part, affine transformation is performed. In this transformation, the input data is multiplied by constant matrix M and the result is then added to an eight bit vector C given below.

$$M = \begin{bmatrix} 1 & 0 & 0 & 0 & 1 & 1 & 1 & 1 \\ 1 & 1 & 0 & 0 & 0 & 1 & 1 & 1 \\ 1 & 1 & 1 & 0 & 0 & 0 & 1 & 1 \\ 1 & 1 & 1 & 1 & 0 & 0 & 0 & 1 \\ 1 & 1 & 1 & 1 & 1 & 0 & 0 & 0 \\ 0 & 1 & 1 & 1 & 1 & 1 & 0 & 0 \\ 0 & 0 & 1 & 1 & 1 & 1 & 1 & 0 \\ 0 & 0 & 0 & 1 & 1 & 1 & 1 & 1 \end{bmatrix}, C = \begin{bmatrix} 1 \\ 1 \\ 0 \\ 0 \\ 0 \\ 1 \\ 1 \\ 0 \end{bmatrix}$$

After the SubByte operation, as the name implies, the ***ShiftRow*** operation performs the circular shift on the rows of the input data. It is important to mention here that the input data is represented as 4x4 matrix where each entry is a byte. The ShiftRow operation performs circular shifting on last three rows while leaving the first row unchanged. This function rotates the second row by one byte, third row by two bytes, and fourth row by three bytes.

TheShiftRow operation operates on the rows of input data whereas the ***MixColumn*** function operates on each of the four columns of the input data. In this function, each column of the input data is considered as polynomials and given by

$$a(x) = \{03\}x^3 + \{01\}x^2 + \{01\}x + \{02\} \qquad (1)$$

Finally, the ***AddRoundKey*** is the operation that mixes the key with the data using a bit-wise XOR operation and gives the output of the round.

As described earlier, the main purpose of key expansion module is to give the expanded key for each round. In this module, ***SubWord*** function applies S-box to perform substitution and give the output. The ***RotWord*** function performs cyclic permutation and ***RoundConst*** performs bit-wise XOR operation.

III. Proposed AES Algorithm Implementation

It is clear from the discussion presented in Section II that the implementation of AES algorithm can mainly be divided into two parts: one is the implementation of cipher module and the other is the implementation of key expansion module. The cipher module is mainly an iterative process and its implementation can be paralleled by applying the concept of loop unrolling. In loop unrolling, the N iteration of cipher module are unrolled and they are executed in parallel. The parallelism obtained in cipher module is further aided through splitting in the key expansion module. So, the loop unrolling in cipher module and splitting in key expansion module completely parallelize the implementation of AES algorithm on hardware. This parallel implementation of AES algorithm has the potential to significantly increase the performance of AES algorithm. However, it can also severely increase the resource requirement of the AES algorithm.

Apart from the algorithmic optimizations like loop unrolling and splitting, the decision to choose appropriate resources of the target architecture also plays a significant role in the final performance of the implemented algorithm. For example, in this work, we choose Spartan-6 FPGA of Xilinx. This FPGA mainly uses Configurable Logic Blocks (CLBs) for the implementation of computing operations. The CLBs are generic computation blocks. Apart from CLBs, Spartan-6 FPGAs also have some dedicated blocks, which if chosen wisely can give significant advantages is performance and the overall resources requried for the implementation. Careful analysis of the different computation operation of AES algorithm indicates that operations like AddRoundkey, MixColumn, etc. can be implemented using CLBs only. However, the SubByte operation that involves S-box can either be implemented using CLBs or Block RAMs (BRAMs). It is clear from the discussion presented in previous section that the S-box values are predefined and they can be stored in BRAMs at the configuration time or they can also be stored in CLBs as CLBs can act both as computation blocks or the storage blocks. The usage of CLBs as storage blocks for S-box values can significantly shift the balance of AES algorithm implementation either in favor of performance or the resource requirements. In the following part of this section, we use different combinations of the algorithmic and architecture optimizations and explore their effect on the design of different implementation techniques.

Based on the discussion presented above, we have explored five different implementation techniques for AES algorithm. Due to the different algorithmic and architecture optimizations, these techniques give different resource and performance results. An overview of the implementation of these techniques is provided next.

Technique 1: In the first technique, the S-Box for both cipher module and key expansion module is implemented in the BRAMs of target architecture. Moreover, the both the key expansion module and cipher module are executed in a serialized manner. In this manner, first the key is expanded and next the cipher module is executed. In terms of implementation, this is the simplest of the five techniques that we explore in this work. As the whole implementation is executed in a serialized manner, this technique gives us the best results in terms of resource requirement. However, the performance of this technique is quite low. This kind of technique is well suited for embedded devices with low resource availability and no performance constraints. But, it is not suitable for devices who are performance critical.

Technique 2: Just like the first technique, in this technique, the S-box for both cipher module and key expansion module is implemented in BRAMs. However, contrary to first technique, here the two modules are executed in parallel. The parallel execution is achieved through loop unrolling in cipher module where N iterations of cipher module are unrolled and key generation through key expansion module is performed online through splitting. Because of the parallel execution, this technique greatly improves the critical path delay of the implementation. however, it may require significantly more resources as compared to the serialized implementation.

Technique 3: In this technique, the S-box for cipher module is implemented in BRAMs whereas the entire key expansion module is implemented using CLBs. Moreover, the execution if the implementation is performed in a serialized way. That means, first the key expansion module is executed and they key is generated and next the cipher module is executed where generated keys are used for encryption/decryption. Compared to the first two techniques, this technique requires smaller number of BRAMs because of the key expansion module's S-box implementation in CLBs. This fact may also lead to better delay results as less number of BRAMs are involved in the critical path of the implementation.

Technique 4: In this technique, the S-box for cipher module is implemented in BRAMs whereas the entire key expansion module is implemented using CLBs. Compared to technique 3, this technique is executed in a parallelized manner. The parallelism is achieved through loop unrolling and online key generation. Compared to technique 3, this techniqu gives better delay results but poor area results.

Technique 5: In the last technique that we explore, both the cipher module and key expansion modules are implemented entirely using CLBs. Furthermore, both modules are executed in a serialized manner. Implementation of S-box in CLBs leads to very good delay results. However, this implementation results in very high number of CLBs that are required for the implementation.

In this section, we have given an overview of the different optimizations used for the exploration of different implementations. Further discussion on the results obtained for these implementation techniques is presented in Section IV.

IV. Results and Analysis

A. Experimental Setup

The five exploration techniques described in previous section are implemented on a Spartan-6 FPGA from Xilinx. For

TABLE I. EXPERIMENTAL RESULTS

Technique	Number of Slice Register	Number of Slice LUTs	Frequency (MHz)	Throughput (Gb/S)	Efficiency
Technique 1	278	3315	137.29	17.57	4.85
Technique 2	1547	3253	223.03	28.54	5.89
Technique 3	280	4307	207.74	26.6	5.78
Technique 4	1589	4530	214.96	27.51	4.51
Technique 5	256	9375	886.64	113.49	11.78

this purpose, we have used xc6slx150-3-fgg900 platform and the techniques are implemented using Xilinx's Vivado design suite. The VHDL core of each technique is synthesized, placed, and routed using this suite where explicit directives are used to ensure the implementation of S-box in either BRAMs or in CLBs. Moreover, parallel processes are used to ensure where parallel execution is needed. The synthesized implementation was used to measure a number of parameters pertaining to each implementation. These parameters include number of slice registers, slice LUTs (a term used alternatively for CLBs here), maximum frequency, and critical path delay etc. Moreover, theoretical throughput and efficiency of each implementation technique are also calculated using (2) and (3) respectively. Although the results presented in this work are based on a Xilinx FPGA, the optimization techniques are generic in nature and they are applicable to any underlying hardware. A thorough discussion on the results of each technique is provided next.

$$T_{\text{put}} = \frac{Processed\ bits}{Delay} \tag{2}$$

$$Efficiency = \frac{T_{\text{put}}}{Resources} \tag{3}$$

B. Experimental Results

Experimental results obtained after the implementation of five exploration techniques are given in Table I. In this table, the first column corresponds to the technique while next five columns indicate the number of slice registers, slice LUTs, frequency, throughput, and efficiency values obtained for each technique.

It can be seen from second column of Table I that the techniques using parallelism (i.e., Technique 2 and 4) require significantly more slice registers as compared to the techniques that are implemented in a serialized manner. This is because of the fact that while parallelizing the implementation, significantly more registers are required for each stage of cipher module and key expansion module. These registers are used to keep the two modules in complete synchronization and without them it will not possible to parallelize the implementation. The next column gives a comparison of slice LUTs for different exploration techniques. It is clear from the results presented incolumn three that the techniques using BRAMs for their S-box implementation require less number of slice LUTs as compared to the techniques using CLB (or LUTs) for the implementation of S-box. Furthermore, it can also be observed from third column that technique 5 requires significantly more slice LUTs than any other technique. This is because of the reason that this technique is implementing the S-box of both cipher module and key expansion module in LUTs.

The routing of each exploration technique also gives its

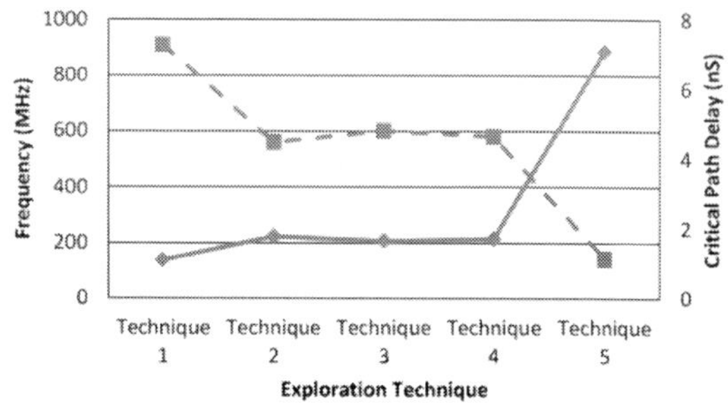

Figure 2. Frequency-Delay Comparison

corresponding operating frequency. The frequency numbers of each technique are given in the fourth column of Table I. It can be seen from this table that in general the techniques employing parallelism have higher frequency and the techniques implemented in a serialized manner have a lower operating frequency. There is one exception however. Technique 5 is implemented entirely in a serialized manner, but still it reports high frequency results. This is because of the fact that complete absence of BRAMs reduces the internal delay of BRAMs and also eliminates the communication delay between CLBs and BRAMS eventually resulting in better frequency results as compared to all other techniques. We further consolidate the frequency and critical path delay in the form of Figure 2. In this figure, solid and dashed lines indicate the frequency and critical path delay results respectively. It is clear from this figure that the techniques with high frequency results hav lower critical path delay and vice versa.

We have also computed the theoretical throughput results using (2) and these results are depicted in the column 5 of Table I. It can be seen from these numbers that in general the techniques with higher frequency have better throughput as compared to the techniques with lower frequency. The efficiency results of each technique are also computed using (3) and they are depicted in column 6 of Table I. It can be seen from this table that technique 5 gives the best efficiency results. This is mainly because of the reason that this technique uses less number of registers and almost no BRAMs. Moreover, this technique gives significantly better frequency results as compared to all other techniques which eventually leads to the best efficiency results for this technique.

Finally, to have a complete overview of the quality of an implementation, we perform a comparison between the total resource requirement and the critical path delay numbers of all the techniques under consideration. In this comparison, the resource requirement gives an overview of the area and critical path delay number gives an overview of the performance of

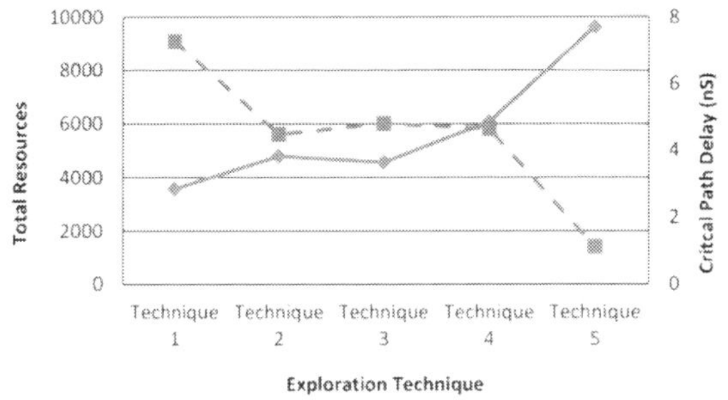

Figure 3. Area-Delay Comparison

the technique. These results are shown in Figure 3. In this figure, the resources are shown as solid line while critical path delay values are shown as dashed line. It can be seen from this figure that technique 1 requires smallest number of resources; hence it is suitable for area constrained IoT devices. However, it should be noted that this technique also has the poorest critical path delay value. So, this kind of technique is suitable to secure edge side nodes. On the other hand, technique 5 requires highest number of total resources but at the same time it gives the best delay results as well. From these numbers, it can be concluded that this kind of technique is well suited for devices that are performance constrained and where number of resources is not an issue for them.

V. Conclusion

IoT devices have gained tremendous popularity over the past few years and they are now the driving force of a multi-billion dollar industry. Modern IoT devices are quite heterogeneous in nature and they are subject to all sorts of security threats. In this work, based on various algorithmic and architecture optimizations, we explore five different implementations of AES cryptographic scheme. We consider AES as it is quite robust and its five different implementations are well suited for the varying requirements of heterogeneous IoT devices. Experimental results of these implementations reveal that the serialized implementation of cipher and key expansion modules of AES algorithms leads to the best area results; hence making the serialized implementation suitable for resource constrained edge IoT devices. However, this kind of implementation is not suitable for high performance IoT devices. For such devices, the experimental results reveal that the implementations using parallelism are more suitable. Although such implementations are quite resource hungry, they give very good performance results.

References

[1] D. Singh, G. Tripathi, and A. J. Jara, "A survey of internet-of-things: Future vision, architecture, challenges and services," in 2014 IEEE World Forum on Internet of Things (WF-IoT), March 2014, pp. 287–292.

[2] A. Mosenia and N. K. Jha, "A comprehensive study of security of internet-of-things," IEEE Transactions on Emerging Topics in Computing, vol. 5, no. 4, Oct 2017, pp. 586–602.

[3] M. Zhang, A. Raghunathan, and N. K. Jha, "Trustworthiness of medical devices and body area networks," Proceedings of the IEEE, vol. 102, no. 8, Aug 2014, pp. 1174–1188.

[4] K. E. Psannis, C. Stergiou, and B. B. Gupta, "Advanced media-based smart big data on intelligent cloud systems," IEEE Transactions on Sustainable Computing, vol. 4, no. 1, 2018, pp. 77–87.

[5] Y. Cherdantseva and J. Hilton, "A reference model of information assurance amp; security," in 2013 International Conference on Availability, Reliability and Security, Sept 2013, pp. 546–555.

[6] S. Vashi, J. Ram, J. Modi, S. Verma, and C. Prakash, "Internet of things (iot): A vision, architectural elements, and security issues," in 2017 International Conference on I-SMAC (IoT in Social, Mobile, Analytics and Cloud) (I-SMAC), Feb 2017, pp. 492–496.

[7] M. M. Kermani, M. Zhang, A. Raghunathan, and N. K. Jha, "Emerging frontiers in embedded security," in 2013 26th International Conference on VLSI Design and 2013 12th International Conference on Embedded Systems, Jan 2013, pp. 203–208.

[8] H. Salmani and M. M. Tehranipoor, "Vulnerability analysis of a circuit layout to hardware trojan insertion," IEEE Transactions on Information Forensics and Security, vol. 11, no. 6, June 2016, pp. 1214–1225.

[9] H. Suo, J. Wan, C. Zou, and J. Liu, "Security in the internet of things: A review," in 2012 International Conference on Computer Science and Electronics Engineering, vol. 3, March 2012, pp. 648–651.

[10] K. Hu, A. N. Nowroz, S. Reda, and F. Koushanfar, "High-sensitivity hardware trojan detection using multimodal characterization," in 2013 Design, Automation Test in Europe Conference Exhibition (DATE), March 2013, pp. 1271–1276.

[11] G. Rouvroy, F. X. Standaert, J.-J. Quisquater, and J. Legat, "Compact and efficient encryption/decryption module for fpga implementation of the aes rijndael very well suited for small embedded applications," in Information Technology: Coding and Computing, 2004. Proceedings. ITCC 2004. International Conference on, vol. 2, April 2004, pp. 583–587 Vol.2.

[12] J. Van Dyken and J. G. Delgado-Frias, "Fpga schemes for minimizing the power-throughput trade-off in executing the advanced encryption standard algorithm," J. Syst. Archit., vol. 56, no. 2-3, Feb. 2010, pp. 116–123. [Online]. Available: http://dx.doi.org/10.1016/j.sysarc.2009.12.001

[13] T. Hoang and V. L. Nguyen, "An efficient fpga implementation of the advanced encryption standard algorithm," in Computing and Communication Technologies, Research, Innovation, and Vision for the Future (RIVF), 2012 IEEE RIVF International Conference on, Feb 2012, pp. 1–4.

[14] M. I. Soliman and G. Y. Abozaid, "{FPGA} implementation and performance evaluation of a high throughput crypto coprocessor," Journal of Parallel and Distributed Computing, vol. 71, no. 8, 2011, pp. 1075 – 1084.

[15] A. Gielata, P. Russek, and K. Wiatr, "Aes hardware implementation in fpga for algorithm acceleration purpose," in Signals and Electronic Systems, 2008. ICSES '08. International Conference on, Sept 2008, pp. 137–140.

[16] S. Qu, G. Shou, Y. Hu, Z. Guo, and Z. Qian, "High throughput, pipelined implementation of aes on fpga," in Information Engineering and Electronic Commerce, 2009. IEEC '09. International Symposium on, May 2009, pp. 542–545.

[17] S. Kulkarni, S. Durg, and N. Iyer, "Internet of things (iot) security," in Computing for Sustainable Global Development (INDIACom), 2016 3rd International Conference on. IEEE, 2016, pp. 821–824.

[18] J. Daemen and V. Rijmen, The Block Cipher Rijndael, ser. Lecture Notes in Computer Science, J.-J. Quisquater and B. Schneier, Eds. Springer Berlin Heidelberg, 2000, vol. 1820.

Challenges of Using Performance Counters in Security Against Side-Channel Leakage

Maria Mushtaq
LIRMM-CNRS, Univ Montpellier
Montpellier, France
Email: maria.mushtaq@lirmm.fr

Pascal Benoit
LIRMM-CNRS, Univ Montpellier
Montpellier, France
Email: Pascal.Benoit@lirmm.fr

Umer Farooq
Dhofar University
Salalah, Oman
Email: ufarooq@du.edu.om

Abstract—**Over the past few years, high resolution and stealthy attacks and their variants such as Flush+Reload, Flush+Flush, Prime+Probe, Spectre and Meltdown have completely exposed the vulnerabilities in modern computing architectures. Many effective mitigation techniques against such attacks are also being proposed that use system's behavioral parameters at run-time using *Performance Counters* (PCs) coupled with machine learning models. Although PCs, both in hardware and software, have shown promising results when used in the context of security, this paper provides experimental evaluation and analysis of the potential challenges, perils and pitfalls of using these counters in security.**

***Keywords*–Performance Counters; Side-Channel Attacks (SCAs); Cryptography; Detection; Mitigation; Machine Learning; Security; Privacy.**

I. Introduction

One of the biggest challenges in modern computing infrastructure today is that security is not regarded as a system-wide issue and, therefore, preventive measures are vulnerability-specific, limited in scope, and even create new attack surface. To put things in perspective, the two computing legends of modern RISC (Reduced-Instruction Set Computing) architecture, David A. Patterson and John H. Hennessy, stated during their Turing award lecture in 2018 that, "The state of computer security is embarrassing for all of us in the computing field" [1]. The primary reason behind these comments is the fact that, almost everything in modern computing architectures today –from computational optimizations to storage elements and interfaces, from end-user applications to the operating system & hypervisor, and from microarchitecture to underlying hardware –is leading to the discovery of new attack vectors. This is a trend getting further momentum, and worse, a complete attack surface is not known yet. Hardware, which is often considered as an abstract layer that behaves correctly –executing instructions and giving a logically correct output, is leaking critical information as a side effect of software implementation and execution.

Today, computing systems are going through the trough of disillusionment related to the prevailing security. The revelations of security and privacy vulnerabilities in microprocessors, both at software and hardware level, have been appalling. These vulnerabilities affect almost every processor, across virtually every operating system and architecture. We believe that the fundamental reason for existence of these vulnerabilities is that the evolution of computing architecture under Moore's law has been focused almost entirely on the performance enhancement and optimization over the past many decades. To this end, the gains are tremendous as many software and hardware optimization tools and techniques have been proposed to boost performance, such as: hierarchical and shared-memory architectures, pipelining, out-of-order and speculative execution, branch prediction, data/instruction de-duplication, shared libraries, compiler optimizations, use of virtual memory and use of specialized hardware accelerators etc. Security, however, has been often an afterthought all along. But the latest security vulnerabilities, like Spectre and Meltdown along with a large number of sophisticated and stealthy attacks like Flush+Reload, Flush+Flush and Prime+Probe, have demonstrated that security cannot be considered as an afterthought anymore. These vulnerabilities span across multiple levels, from execution units to caches, DRAMs (Dynamic Random Access Memory) and interconnect networks. Thus, security has earned its position as a first-order design constraint today alongside performance, area and power consumption.

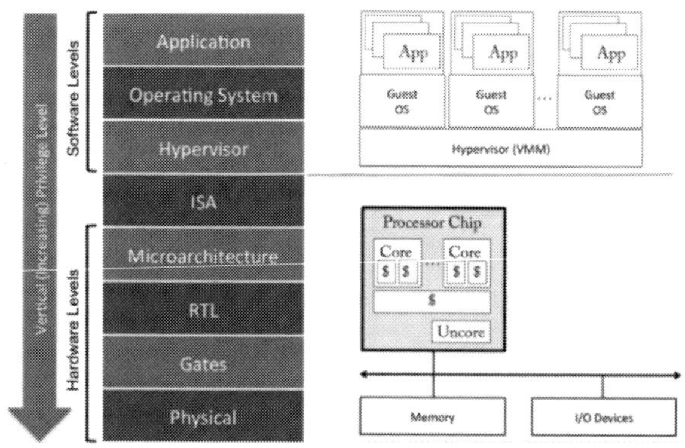

Figure 1. An abstract representation of the full computing stack, covering both software and hardware levels, in a modern general-purpose processor.

Current research in computing architectures is focused on *threat-based design* [2]. For instance, novel architectures like Intel's SGX [3], ARM's TrustZone [4], Bastion [5], AMD's SEV [6] and IBM's 4758 [7] Secure co-processor are a few attempts by major vendors to incorporate security in the design-level specifications. A common characteristic in these novel architectural designs, however, is that they are incremental designs built on top of general-purpose processor architectures, and expand them with new security features. Thus, they use more or less the same levels of privilege across various layers of computing stack as illustrated in Figure 1.

While it makes perfect sense that a sustainable security can only be achieved by removing the vulnerabilities at the design-time through the proposition of safe software and hardware, researchers are far from achieving that goal. Recent research work suggests that no architecture, new and old alike, is completely immune to information leakage attacks that target all levels (OS, hypervisor, ISA (Instruction Set Architecture), microarchitecture, physical etc.) of computing stacks as shown in Figure 1. In this backdrop, many attempts have been made in recent years to detect, and subsequently mitigate, information leakage attacks using various approaches. The scope of this work, however, is limited to the security solutions against access-driven cache side- and covert-channel attacks. Cache side-Channel attacks are strong cryptanalysis techniques that break cryptographic algorithms by targeting their implementations [8].

Some of the most promising approaches against side-channel information leakage in contemporary architectures to-date are using either hardware and software performance counters or machine learning or a combination of both. Though these approaches have shown promising results in detecting and mitigating a large number of attacks that exploit existing vulnerabilities, the attack vector is still expanding and these approaches need to scale every time a new vulnerability is discovered. Moreover, they rely heavily on the authenticity, determinism, run-time overheads, precision and availability of information that is leveraged through hardware/software performance counters. We believe that, With sophisticated and stealthy attacks appearing everyday, it is just a matter of time that these defenses will not be very effective and the attacker will find a way around such defenses by either manipulating the PCs' information or completely by-passing them undetected.

In this work, we analyze the effectiveness of hardware and software performance counters in security against side-channel attacks. We provide analysis on their benefits, limitations, perils and pitfalls when used to perform detection and mitigation. We validate our analysis with practical results against a large attack vector. The rest of this paper is organized as following. Section II provides related work on the use of HPCsv& SPCs in security. Section III elaborates various PCs and their monitoring tools in existing architectures. Section IV discusses the core limitations of these counters along with experimental data. Section V concludes this paper.

II. Related Work

This section provides the state-of-the-art on various security mechanisms being proposed in recent research work that utilise PCs to perform real-time detection and mitigation of side-channel attacks. Side-channel attack detection techniques are divided into two basic categories; signature-based and anomaly-based detection. Some techniques use a combined approach as well, *i.e.*, signature + anomaly-based detection. Some of the recent research works belonging to the category of *signature-based* detection are reported in [9], [10], [11], [12], [13]. Similarly, in the category of *anomaly-based* detection techniques, many recent research works are reported in [14], [15], [16], [17], [18].

Allaf *et al.* [9] propose a mechanism to inspect Prime+Probe and Flush+Reload attacks targeting AES cryptosystem. Their mechanism uses ML models and HPCs. The proposed mechanism shows good accuracy under isolated conditions, where the attacker and victim are the only load on the system. Another work proposed by Mushtaq *et al.* [10] targets stealthier CSCAs (Cache Side Channel Attacks) like Flush+Flush (F+F). Authors proposed *NIGHTs-WATCH* to detect cache-based side-channel attacks at run-time using ML models coupled with different hardware performance counters that are used to profile victim cryptosystems like RSA (Rivest Shamir and Adleman) and AES (Advanced Encyption Standard) under attack and no-attack scenarios. *NIGHTs-WATCH* being a run-time detection mechanism is evaluated using a variety of metrics like detection accuracy, speed and overhead. Evaluation of the proposed detection technique shows that it can achieve a high detection accuracy with little performance overhead for both attacks even under noisy conditions. Later, this work was extended by Mushtaq *et al.* [12] to include Prime+Probe and other variant attacks under both RSA and AES crypto-systems using the same approach. Their experimental results show consistency for Flush+Flush attack on different implementations of AES as well. Another technique named as *WHISPER* [8] uses multiple machine learning models in an *Ensemble* fashion to detect SCAs at runtime using behavioral data of concurrent processes, that are collected through hardware and software performance counters (HPCs & SPCs). *WHISPER* presents experimental evaluation against Flush+Reload, Flush+Flush, Prime+Probe, Spectre and Meltdown attacks and reports high detection accuracy and low False Positives & False Negatives.

Some of the signature-based detection techniques do not rely on Machine Learning to learn attack signatures. Rather they use thresholds of particular PCs to determine if an attack is in place. One of these works presented in [16], utilizes the values of cache miss rates and page faults of processes to detect an attack. Payer *et al.* in [16] proposed an attack detection framework *HexPADS*, which can detect cache-based side-channel attacks along with Rowhammer [19] and CAIN [20] attacks. *HexPADS* reads status of different performance counters like total executed instructions, total LLC (Last Level Cache) accesses and total LLC misses. It also uses kernel information of processes like total page faults. The proposed detection mechanism basically continuously monitors the cache accesses and misses of all processes. If cache miss rate of a process is found to be higher than 70%, i.e., greater than 70% of cache accesses results into misses, and the same process has a low number of page-faults, the process is reported an attack.

Bazm *et al.* [21] relied on *Intel Cache Monitoring Technology (CMT)* [22] and hardware performance counters and used Gaussian Anomaly detection [23] for detection of cache based side-channel attacks at the level of VMs in IAAS (Infrastructure as a Service) Cloud platforms. Briongos *et al.* [14] proposed *CacheShield* to detect cache side channel attacks on legacy software (victim applications) by monitoring hardware performance events during their execution. The proposed method is implemented at user level and does not require any help from the OS/hypervisor and would be applicable in cloud environments. As indicated by the authors, this effort is motivated by two main problems of the other detection mechanisms: high detection performance overheads for VMs and requirement of monitoring of both attacker and victim at the same time.

Multiple mitigation techniques have also been proposed against cache-based side-channel attacks in the last decade. These techniques can be categorized into logical & physical isolation techniques, noise-based techniques, scheduler-based techniques and constant time techniques (referring to different cache levels in the cache hierarchy). For instance, logical physical isolation techniques include Cache Coloring [24], CloudRadar [25], STEALTHMEM [26], NewCache [27] and Hardware Partitioning [28]; noise-based techniques include fuzzy times [29], bystander workloads [30]; and scheduler-based techniques include obfuscation [30] and minimum times-lice [31]. Most of these detection and mitigation techniques rely on the low-level behavioral information of the system during execution that is being leveraged for a high-level interpretation and usage through PCs. In Sections III and IV, this paper discusses key benefits and challenges associated with such use of PCs.

III. Performance Counters and Their Use in Security

Performance counters, both software and hardware, have been available in modern processors for more than a decade now with a primary objective to measure the performance of the software when it's being written.

Software Performance Counters (SPCs) are bits of code that monitor, count, or measure events in software, which allow to see patterns from a high-level view. They are registered with the operating system during installation of the software, allowing anyone with the proper permissions to view them. Performance counters can help measure key parts of the software by monitoring the code paths being taken by the software during execution. Like all software, the reliability of SPCs depends on the quality of code and environmental factors. In addition, virtualization in modern computing systems can skew the measurements of processor related counters not because of bad code, but due to how threads are scheduled between the virtual machine, the hypervisor, and the hardware. Almost all operating systems support SPCs such as; page faults, major page faults, minor page faults and invalid page faults. The SPCs are not architecture specific events, but specific to operating systems.

Hardware Performance Counters (HPCs) are special purpose registers built in the microarchitecture of modern processors. HPCs are available as hardware registers that monitor certain events that take place at the CPU level, like the number of cycles and instructions that a program has executed, its associated cache misses and hits, number of accesses to off-chip memory, total number of CPU cycles, number of retired instructions, branch predictions, among several other things. These HPCs are both fixed and programmable in nature. Fixed HPCs are used to measure only specific native events and they cannot measure any other types of event. Programmable HPCs, however, can be programmed to monitor many different events.

Almost all operating systems provide tools to monitor SPCs. There are many high-level libraries and APIs that can be used to configure and read HPCs as well such as: PerfMon [32], OProfile [33], Perf [34], Perftool [35], Intel Vtune Analyzer [36] and PAPI [37] etc. The research work in security reported so far in the state-of-the-art in Section II uses these libraries to access performance counters.

The events that can be tracked with these software and hardware performance counters are usually simple ones, but combined in the right way, they can provide extremely useful insights of a program's behavior and, therefore, constitute a valuable *tool* for run-time analysis. This is the primary motivation behind their recent use in security domain, particularly in the run-time detection and mitigation against various side- and covert-channel attacks that target the execution or the implementation of security-sensitive applications like cryptosystems. Section II details most of such research works.

As an illustrative example of what kind of useful information can be retrieved using performance counters, we consider the case of Prime+Probe cache-based side-channel attack [38], which is a last level cache-based cross-core attack. Like most of such attacks, as shown in Figure 2, this is a three-phase attack in which the attacker fills the cache line(s) with its own content at first, as shown in part (a). This is called the Prime phase. In the second phase, usually a wait phase, the attacker lets the victim program to execute and access whichever memory locations the victim intends to access as shown in part (b). In the third phase, called the Probe phase, attacker accesses the same cache line(s) again, only to find out which particular memory addresses have been touched upon by the victim program. Since there is a significant difference in the amount of time taken to process an instruction if it is supplied to the CPU from cache (i.e., a cache hit) compared to when it is not found in the cache (i.e., a cache miss) and therefore being fetched from main memory.

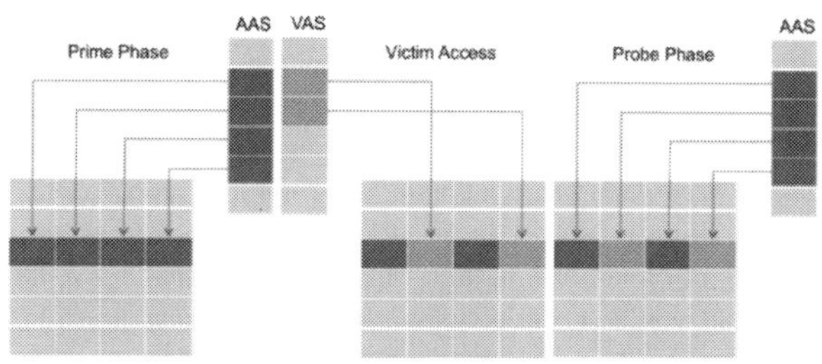

(a) Attacker's prime phase (b) Victim's memory accesses (c) Attacker's probe phase

Figure 2. Working principal of Prime+Probe Cache Side-Channel Attack. Here, AAS refers to the Attacker Address Space, whereas VAS refers to the Victim Address Space.

For a computing system under Prime+Probe attack, a careful analysis of the number of total CPU cycles, combined with the cache misses and hits by using performance counters, can reveal a lot of useful information about the system's run-time behavior under attack. Thus, it can be used to subsequently protect the system as well as shown in many recent research works (Section II).

IV. Challenges in using Performance Counters for Security

Although performance counters, both SPCs and HPCs, have shown promising results when used in the context of security, in this paper, we intend to warn the readers/users about the potential challenges, perils and pitfalls of using these counters in security based on our experiments. Information leakage attacks are becoming stealthy and sophisticated over time. Moreover, they target all layers in computing stack, from logical to physical layers. It is only a matter of time that these attacks will find a way to either *bypass* such detection and mitigation mechanisms that are based on performance counters or find a way to *fool* their measurements. In this section, we provide some experimental evidence and analysis to support this argument. Table I lists the attacks against which we have analyzed the robustness of various performance counters. We have run these attacks alone as well as in various combinations and under variable system load conditions on Intel's x86 architecture to determine whether the information reported by the performance counters is still useful from security perspective. We have experimented with a large set of performance counters with their application scope all layers of computing stack. We then shortlisted only the most relevant counters, as shown in Table II, with respect to the attacks mentioned in Table I for further analysis.

TABLE I. List of Cache-based SCAs that are used as use-cases for the analysis of performance counters on Intel's core i7 machine.

#	Cache SCAs	Attack's Target
1	Flush+Reload	AES & RSA Cryptosystem
2	Flush+Flush	AES & RSA Cryptosystem
3	Prime+Probe	AES & RSA Cryptosystem
4	Spectre	Speculative Execution
5	Meltdown	Out-of-Order Execution

TABLE II. Selected performance counters related to cache-based SCAs mentioned in Table I

Scope of Counter	Performance Counter	Counter ID
L1 Caches	Data Cache Misses	L1-DCM
	Instruction Cache Misses	L1-ICM
	Total Cache Misses	L1-TCM
L2 Caches	Instruction Cache Accesses	L2-ICA
	Instruction Cache Misses	L2-ICM
	Total Cache Accesses	L2-TCA
	Total Cache Misses	L2-TCM
L3-Caches	Instruction Cache Accesses	L3-ICA
	Total Cache Accesses	L3-TCA
	Total Cache Misses	L3-TCM
System-wide	Total CPU Cycles	TOT_CYC
	Branch Miss-Predictions	BR_MSP
	Total Branch Instructions	TBI
	Page Faults	PF

In the following, we provide insights on the discrete challenges that any security mechanism would face while using performance counters. Our analysis is based on extensive experiments that we have performed with a set of PCs being used in existing state-of-the-art security mechanisms and under a large attack vector comprising of most recent side- and covert-channel attacks as shown in Table I.

A. *Discernible Information*

The PCs allow leveraging a lot of interesting information for high level visualisation and usage in real-time that cannot be observed otherwise. However, our experiments show that their ability to reveal such information gets limited very quickly. For instance, Figures 3–5 illustrate the measured results on the count of L1 data cache misses that were obtained by running various attack (shown in red) and no attack (shown in green) scenarios. Figure 3 shows the L1 data cache misses for P+P attack, while Figure 4 shows the same feature for F+F attack. These two measurements show that, although the PC provides distinguishable information in case of P+P attack, the information is not easily discernible in case of F+F attack due to overlapping behavior despite the same experimental settings. Thus, stand alone, the same PC does not help determining whether a system is under attack or not in case of F+F attack (Figure 4). The situation escalates rather quickly if multiple attacks are running simultaneously, as shown in Figure 5, where we performed experiments with six attacks running in parallel. As illustrated in Figure 5, the information collected on L1 data cache misses is no more discernible and limits the ability of any detection or mitigation mechanism to report an attack scenario based on PC's data alone. Therefore, despite their availability and ability to leverage low-level execution information in real-time, the PCs may not always be helpful in extraction of useful information.

B. *Non-deterministic Behavior*

Non-determinism is another issue with PCs. Non-determinism refers to a situation where two identical runs of the same program with exactly the same inputs may not produce the same results of monitored events. For applications that are time- and security-critical, determinism is an essential property. However, our experiments show that PCs produce deterministic results only in a strictly controlled environment, which is not always possible to maintain. Deterministic results of PCs also depend on the measuring tools. Authors in [39] report that non-determinism varies the measurements of PCs from $1-10\%$. Non-determinism is more an issue of HPCs compared to SPCs. Only few HPCs can produce deterministic results like *retired instruction* when measurements are taken with good tools that can remove sources of contamination from HPCs measurements. Most potentially deterministic events on Intel x86 are affected by the hardware interrupt count [39]. Many important hardware events, such as the ones which measure cache performance and execution cycle counts, are not deterministic on modern out-of-order machines. This severely limits the usefulness of PCs in situations where exact deterministic behavior is necessary. Our experiments show that some of the major sources of non-determinism are linked to the operating system's activities, context switching between concurrently running processes, hardware interrupts, performance overhead of measurements and the precision of the measuring tools. Hardware counters like cache accesses, total execution cycles are non-deterministic on modern out-of-order processors. Therefore, to use HPCs for security applications, one needs to find deterministic HPCs from available counters. In order to avoid false positive and false negatives from the defense mechanisms in security, the sources of contamination must be removed or limited to make the tools reliable.

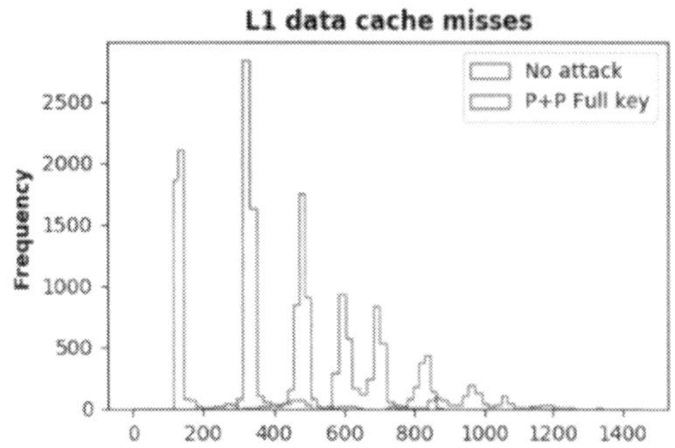

Figure 3. Experimental results measured through performance counters on the effect of P+P attack on L1 data cache misses

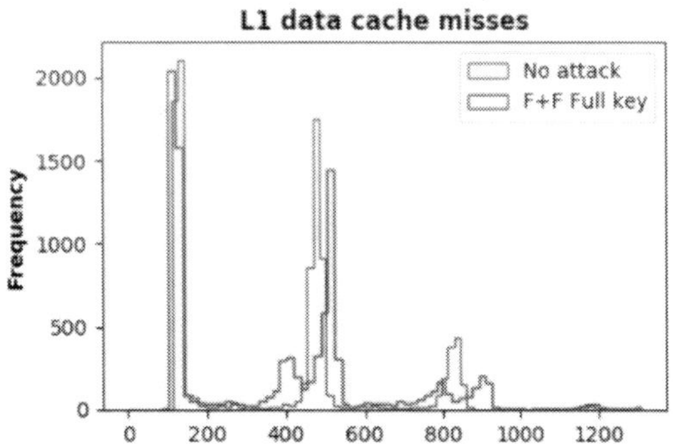

Figure 4. Experimental results measured through performance counters on the effect of F+F attack on L1 data cache misses.

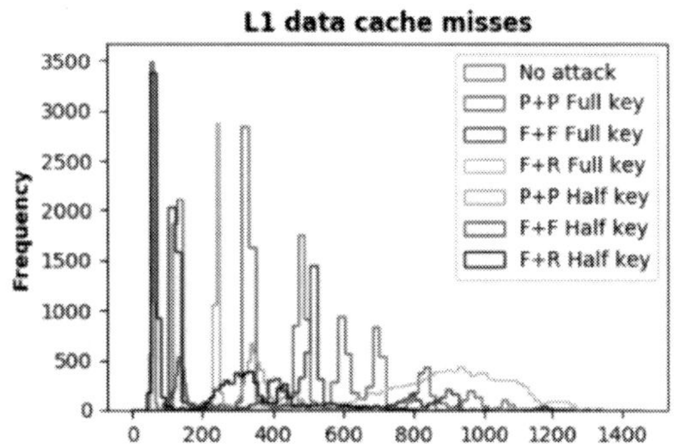

Figure 5. Experimental results measured through performance counters on the effect of multiple attacks running simultaneously on L1 data cache misses.

C. *Multiplexing Issues*

Although there are hundreds of logical PCs available in modern computing systems to measure various aspects of system's behavior at run-time, physically, there is a limited number of counters that are used to measure and leverage low-level information. Multiplexing allows more counters to be used simultaneously than are physically supported by the hardware. With multiplexing, the physical counters are time-sliced, and the counts are estimated from the measurements. In order to increase the degree of confidence in attack detection and mitigation, many recent techniques use multiplexing of features. In our experiments, we observed that multiplexing can lead to many issues. A naive use of multiplexing could lead to erroneous results in the measurements of PCs that would not be detected by the user. Such errors in measurement occur when the sampling time for these PCs in insufficient to permit the estimated counter values to converge to their expected values. Authors in [40] have also reported similar issues. In such cases, sometimes the PCs do not update their measurement and keep reporting the last sampled/collected data. Another issue with the accuracy of measurements done by multiplexed PCs. Due to lack of sampling granularity under a time-sliced multiplexing model, sometimes the PCs lack accuracy even though they measure and report the events. Such inaccurate or imprecise measurement generate a lot of false positives and negatives by the security mechanisms using multiplexed PCs. Thus, based on our experiments, it is highly recommended to carefully select the minimum number of PCs as features and avoid multiplexing as much as possible. Authors in [40] also mention potential sources of inaccuracy in counter measurements. They point out issues such as the extra instructions and system calls required to access counters, and indirect effects like the pollution of caches due to instrumentation code, but they do not present any experimental data.

D. *Performance Overhead*

One of the key challenges faced by PC-based security mechanisms is the cost of their sampling/measurement at run-time. The overhead comes from collecting data of PCs during their start and stop and reading of data. The PCs' interface necessarily introduce overhead in the form of extra instructions, including system calls, and the interfaces cause cache pollution that can change the cache and memory behavior of the monitored application. The cost of processing counter overflow interrupts can be a significant source of overhead in sampling-based profiling. A lack of hardware support for precisely identifying an event's address may result in incorrect attribution of events to instruction addresses on modern superscalar, out-of-order processors, thereby making profiling data inaccurate. The performance overhead issue can only be dealt with at the design level of measuring tools in order to keep their run-time overhead and memory footprint as small as possible. Moreover, hardware support for interrupt handling and profiling should be used if possible. Performance overhead can be linked to two distinct usage models of the PCs, namely; counting and sampling. The performance overhead of counting usage model comprises of costs associated with starting and stopping of a PC and reading its values. Whereas, the overhead of sampling usage model comprises of the frequency of sampling or sampling granularity. Though the overhead varies on different platforms and under different measuring tools, it is still a major limitation in the use of PCs in real-time detection and mitigation tools and techniques. Authors in [41] and [42] have reported overheads for various computing architectures.

V. Conclusions

High resolution & stealthy attacks have completely exposed the vulnerabilities in modern computing architectures in recent years. Many effective mitigation techniques against such attacks are being proposed that use Performance Counters coupled with machine learning models. In this work, we analyze the effectiveness of hardware and software performance counters in security against side-channel attacks. We provide analysis on their benefits, limitations, perils and pitfalls when used to perform detection and mitigation. We validate our analysis with practical results against a large attack vector.

References

[1] J. L. Hennessy and D. A. Patterson, "A new golden age for computer architecture: Domain-specific hardware/software co-design, enhanced security, open instruction sets, and agile chip development," Turing Lecture, 2018.

[2] Rube B. Lee, Security Basics for Computer Architects, ser. Synthesis Lectures on Computer Architecture. Morgan & Claypool Publishers, September 2013, vol. 8, pp. 1–111.

[3] I. Anati, S. Gueron, S. Johnson, and V. Scarlata, "Innovative technology for cpu based attestation and sealing," in Proceedings of the 2nd international workshop on hardware and architectural support for security and privacy, vol. 13. ACM New York, NY, USA, 2013.

[4] J. Winter, "Experimenting with ARM TrustZone–or: How I Met Friendly Piece of Trusted Hardware," in 2012 IEEE 11th International Conference on Trust, Security and Privacy in Computing and Communications. IEEE, 2012, pp. 1161–1166.

[5] D. Champagne and R. B. Lee, "Scalable architectural support for trusted software," in HPCA-16 2010 The Sixteenth International Symposium on High-Performance Computer Architecture. IEEE, 2010, pp. 1–12.

[6] D. Kaplan, J. Powell, and T. Woller, "Amd memory encryption," White paper, 2016. [Online]. Available: http://developer.amd.com/wordpress/media/2013/12/AMD_Memory_Encryption_Whitepaper_v7-Public.pdf

[7] D. L. Osisek, K. M. Jackson, and P. H. Gum, "ESA/390 interpretive-execution architecture, foundation for VM/ESA," IBM Systems Journal, vol. 30, no. 1, 1991, pp. 34–51.

[8] M. Mushtaq, J. Bricq, M. K. Bhatti, A. Akram, V. Lapotre, G. Gogniat, and P. Benoit, "Whisper: A tool for run-time detection of side-channel attacks," IEEE Access, vol. 8, 2020, pp. 83 871–83 900.

[9] Z. Allaf, M. Adda, and A. Gegov, "A comparison study on Flush+Reload and Prime+Probe attacks on AES using machine learning approaches," UK Workshop on Computational Intelligence, 2017.

[10] M. Mushtaq, A. Akram, M. K. Bhatti, M. Chaudhry, V. Lapotre, and G. Gogniat, "Nights-watch: A cache-based side-channel intrusion detector using hardware performance counters," in Proceedings of the 7th International Workshop on Hardware and Architectural Support for Security and Privacy, ser. HASP '18. New York, NY, USA: ACM, 2018, pp. 1:1–1:8.

[11] M. Sabbagh, Y. Fei, T. Wahl, and A. A. Ding, "SCADET: a side-channel attack detection tool for tracking Prime+ Probe," in 2018 IEEE/ACM International Conference on Computer-Aided Design (ICCAD), 2018.

[12] M. Mushtaq, A. Akram, M. Bhatti, N. B. R. Rao, V. Lapotre, and G. Gogniat, "Run-time detection of Prime+ Probe side-channel attack on AES encryption algorithm," in Global Information Infrastructure and Networking Symposium, Greece, 2018.

[13] M. Mushtaq, A. Akram, M. K. Bhatti, M. Chaudhry, M. Yousaf, U. Farooq, V. Lapotre, and G. Gogniat, "Machine Learning For Security: The Case of Side-Channel Attack Detection at Run-time," in 25th IEEE International Conference on Electronics Circuits and Systems, Bordeaux, FRANCE, 2018.

[14] S. Briongos, G. Irazoqui, P. Malagón, and T. Eisenbarth, "CacheShield: Detecting cache attacks through self-observation," in Proceedings of the 8th Conference on Data & Application Security & Privacy. ACM, 2018, pp. 224–235.

[15] Y. Kulah, B. Dincer, C. Yilmaz, and E. Savas, "SpyDetector: An approach for detecting side-channel attacks at runtime," IJIS, 2018.

[16] M. Payer, "Hexpads: a platform to detect "stealth" attacks," in International Symposium on Engineering Secure Software and Systems. Springer, 2016, pp. 138–154.

[17] S. Briongos, P. Malagón, J. L. Risco-Martín, and J. M. Moya, "Modeling side-channel cache attacks on aes," in Proc. of the Summer Computer Simulation Conference. Society for Computer Simulation International, 2016, p. 37.

[18] A. Raj and J. Dharanipragada, "Keep the PokerFace on! Thwarting cache side channel attacks by memory bus monitoring and cache obfuscation," Journal of Cloud Computing, vol. 6, no. 1, 2017, p. 28.

[19] M. Seaborn and T. Dullien, "Exploiting the dram rowhammer bug to gain kernel privileges," Black Hat, vol. 15, 2015, p. 71.

[20] A. Barresi, K. Razavi, M. Payer, and T. R. Gross, "{CAIN}: Silently breaking {ASLR} in the cloud," in 9th {USENIX} Workshop on Offensive Technologies ({WOOT} 15), 2015.

[21] M.-M. Bazm, T. Sautereau, M. Lacoste, M. Sudholt, and J.-M. Menaud, "Cache-based side-channel attacks detection through intel cache monitoring technology and hardware performance counters," in Fog and Mobile Edge Computing (FMEC), 2018 Third International Conference on. IEEE, 2018, pp. 7–12.

[22] "Benefits of Intel cache monitoring technology in the Intel Xeon processor E5 v3 family," 2018, https://software.intel.com/en-us/blogs/2014/06/18/benefit-of-cache-monitoring.

[23] "Gaussian anomaly detection," 2018, https://wiseodd.github.io/techblog/2016/01/16/gaussian-anomaly-detection/.

[24] M. Godfrey and M. Zulkernine, "Preventing cache-based side-channel attacks in a cloud environment," IEEE Transactions on Cloud Computing, vol. 2, no. 4, Oct 2014, pp. 395–408.

[25] T. Zhang, Y. Zhang, and R. B. Lee, "CloudRadar: A real-time side-channel attack detection system in clouds," in International Symposium on Research in Attacks, Intrusions, and Defenses. Springer, 2016.

[26] T. Kim, M. Peinado, and G. Mainar-Ruiz, "STEALTHMEM: System-Level Protection Against Cache-Based Side Channel Attacks in the Cloud," in USENIX Security, 2012, pp. 189–204.

[27] F. Liu, H. Wu, K. Mai, and R. B. Lee, "Newcache: secure cache architecture thwarting cache side channel attacks," IEEE Micro Special Issues on Security, vol. 36, 2016.

[28] Z. Wang and R. B. Lee, "New cache designs for thwarting software cache-based side channel attacks," SIGARCH Comput. Archit. News, vol. 35, no. 2, Jun. 2007, pp. 494–505.

[29] W.-M. Hu, "Reducing timing channels with fuzzy time," Journal of computer security, vol. 1, no. 3-4, 1992, pp. 233–254.

[30] Y. Zhang, A. Juels, M. K. Reiter, and T. Ristenpart, "Cross-VM Side Channels and Their Use to Extract Private Keys," in ACM CCS, NY, USA, 2012.

[31] V. Varadarajan, T. Ristenpart, and M. Swift, "Scheduler-based defenses against cross-VM side-channels," in 23rd USENIX Security Symposium, San Diego, CA, 2014.

[32] PerfMon, "$https://knowledge.ni.com/$," 2018.

[33] OProfile, "$http://oprofile.sourceforge.net/$," 2018.

[34] A. C. De Melo, "The new linux perf tools," in Slides from Linux Kongress, vol. 18, 2010.

[35] P. Tool, "$http://lacasa.uah.edu/$," 2018.

[36] I. V-Tune, "$https://software.intel.com/en-us/vtune-amplifier-cookbook$," 2018.

[37] "Performance application programming interface," in $http://icl.cs.utk.edu/papi/$, 2018.

[38] M. S. Inci, B. Gulmezoglu, G. Irazoqui, T. Eisenbarth, and B. Sunar, "Cache attacks enable bulk key recovery on the cloud," in International Conference on Cryptographic Hardware and Embedded Systems (CHES), vol. 9813, 08 2016, pp. 368–388.

[39] V. Weaver and J. Dongarra, "Can hardware performance counters produce expected, deterministic results," in Proc. of the 3rd Workshop on Functionality of Hardware Performance Monitoring, 2010.

[40] J. Dongarra, K. London, S. Moore, P. Mucci, D. Terpstra, H. You, and M. Zhou, "Experiences and lessons learned with a portable interface to hardware performance counters," in Proceedings International Parallel and Distributed Processing Symposium. IEEE, 2003, pp. 6–pp.

[41] S. V. Moore, "A comparison of counting and sampling modes of using performance monitoring hardware," in International Conference on Computational Science. Springer, 2002, pp. 904–912.

[42] M. Maxwell, P. Teller, L. Salayandia, and S. Moore, "Accuracy of performance monitoring hardware," in Proceedings of the Los Alamos Computer Science Institute Symposium (LACSIâ02). Citeseer, 2002.

Side-Channel Attacks on RISC-V Processors: Current Progress, Challenges, and Opportunities

Mahya Morid Ahmadi[1], Faiq Khalid[1], Muhammad Shafique[2]
[1]*Technische Universität Wien (TU Wien), Vienna, Austria*
[2]*Division of Engineering, New York University Abu Dhabi (NYUAD), Abu Dhabi, United Arab Emirates*
Email: {mahya.ahmadi,faiq.khalid}@tuwien.ac.at, muhammad.shafique@nyu.edu

***Abstract*—Side-channel attacks on microprocessors, like the RISC-V, exhibit security vulnerabilities that lead to several design challenges. Hence, it is imperative to study and analyze these security vulnerabilities comprehensively. In this paper, we present a brief yet comprehensive study of the security vulnerabilities in modern microprocessors with respect to side-channel attacks and their respective mitigation techniques. The focus of this paper is to analyze the hardware-exploitable side-channel attack using power consumption and software-exploitable side-channel attacks to manipulate cache. Towards this, we perform an in-depth analysis of the applicability and practical implications of cache attacks on RISC-V microprocessors and their associated challenges. Finally, based on the comparative study and our analysis, we highlight some key research directions to develop robust RISC-V microprocessors that are resilient to side-channel attacks.**

Keywords–RISC-V; Side-channel; Secure ISA; microprocessors; cache; hardware security.

I. INTRODUCTION

The exponential increase in using advanced microprocessors for critical applications (e.g., surveillance systems) makes these systems vulnerable to several security threats, e.g., remote micro-architectural [1] and side-channel attacks [2]. These attacks may lead to system failure, information leakage, and denial-of-service. Therefore, it is imperative to study security as a fundamental parameter along with performance constraints in the early design stages of these microprocessors, especially the emerging microprocessors like in fifth generation of Reduced Instruction Set Computer (RISC-V). To address this critical issue in microprocessors, researchers have developed several defenses against these threats. However, broadly, research in the security of microprocessors has been mostly divided into independent directions of hardware and software threats [3][4]. In hardware security, researchers are focused on chip modification and physical intrusions [5], and at the software level, they are studying software stack attacks like software malware [6]. Therefore, these are not applicable to the advanced attacks, such as the software-exploitable hardware attacks. These attacks combine the software and hardware bugs to exploit the microprocessor at run-time. For example, software-exploitable timing side-channels [2][7] has been exposed only a couple of years ago. As shown in Figure 1, the execution of software leaves side-channel traces at different levels of the system. These traces can be exploited by software-exploitable side-channel attacks to remotely leak confidential information from the trusted hardware with high bandwidth microarchitectural channels. Typically, these attacks target shared resources like last-level cache, which are inevitable in the high performance emerging microprocessors [8]. Recent studies show that these vulnerabilities are not limited to current microprocessors, but the next generation of microprocessors are also vulnerable

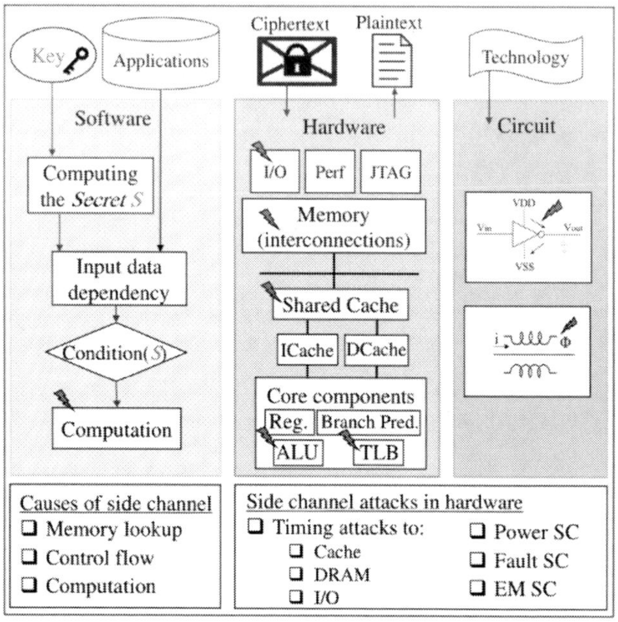

Figure 1. Security vulnerabilities in microprocessors that can be exploited by side-channel data leakage attacks, i.e., timing attack to cache, memory and I/O, and power, fault-based, and electro-magnetic SC attacks.

to these attacks. Hence, it is imperative to study these vulnerabilities in emerging microprocessors, like RISC-V, to make them robust against these powerful attacks.

Therefore, the main focus of this paper is to highlight the security vulnerabilities in one of the most important emerging microprocessors, i.e., RISC-V. The reason behind this is that RISC-V is predicted to be a widely-adopted architecture in the coming days, as its rapid proliferation has already been witnessed in both industrial and academic Research and Development (R&D) projects and product lines [9]. Moreover, RISC-V [10], as an open-source, with extensible Instruction Set Architecture (ISA), is rapidly becoming the mainstream architecture for emerging embedded systems. The flexibility of this ISA made it popular in lightweight embedded systems of edge devices as well as server-side complex multi-core systems. Open hardware designs are essential for security, low-power applications, and fast R&D cycles. Since the RISC-V microprocessors are in the early stage of R&D, therefore, it is the right time to investigate security solutions there, with an eye to the past mistakes to avoid them in the next-generation of processors. To protect emerging embedded systems against security vulnerabilities, first, the applicability of the state-of-the-art software-exploitable attacks on RISC-V processors must be studied. Then, based on the observations of these studies, a new attack surface can be found that can exploit the unique features of RISC-V ISA (e.g., memory model). Although researchers have developed several security solutions for RISC-V, their primary focus is on the software attacks. However, there are a few security solutions for software-exploitable hardware attacks on RISC-V, which leads to a key research question about *how to design a robust RISC-V microprocessor that can tolerate software, hardware, and software-exploitable hardware attacks?*

Towards the above-mentioned research question, in this paper, **we made the following key contributions**:

1) We also provide a brief yet comprehensive overview and categorization (**Section II-A**) of the different side-channel attacks for microprocessors and their respective defenses(**Section II-B**).
2) We first study the side-channel data leakage attack on RISC-V processors running confidential applications like RSA encryption (**Sections III-A and III-B**).
3) Based on the study, we demonstrated the architectural vulnerabilities in a high-performance RISC-V microprocessor by successfully implementing a cross-core timing side-channel attack on the RISC-V microprocessors (**Section IV**). Our results show that RISC-V is vulnerable to timing side-channel attacks; hence, a lightweight yet powerful defense mechanism is required.
4) Towards the end, we briefly discuss the potential defenses for the cross-layer side-channel attacks on the RISC-V microprocessor (**Section V**) and highlighted research challenges and opportunities for cross-layer side-channel attacks on a RISC-V microprocessor (**Section VI**).

II. BACKGROUND

In this section, we provide the necessary background information for side-channel attacks on RISC-V microprocessors. First, we presents the taxonomy for state-of-the-art side-channel attacks with the focus on power side-channel attacks and timing attacks. Then, we discuss the vulnerabilities in the encryption algorithms, and towards the end, we present a brief overview of the RISC-V ISA.

A. Side-Channel Attacks

There is a large body of the work on hardware attack to microprocessors [2]. However, in this paper, we focus on attacks in hardware that are exploiting an unwanted channel to leak confidential data, which are known as side-channels. The principle of a security manipulation starts with forcing the victim to transfer the critical data to the target location, then store it or consume it, which gives the opportunity to attacker to steal the data. If the leaking channel of data is built using physical parameters of the system, which is dependant on the control flow, it is called a side-channel. There are several side-channels reported in hardware, and among the most exploited ones, we can name power, timing, and temperature.

In Figure 2, we are presenting a known taxonomy of side-channel attack and their mitigation techniques in general-purpose microprocessors. Based on the attack model, attacks are divided into two categories: sourced from software and sourced from the hardware. Attacks from hardware exploit physical features, e.g., dynamic power, by implanting sensors in shared resources of the system. While the former category requires physical access to the microprocessor, attacks from software can be exploited remotely. Side-channel attacks from software leak the confidential data through microarchitectural events of shared resources, e.g., timing attack to cache [11]. As the efforts on the side-channel attack to RISC-V processors are focused on power and timing attacks, we are elaborating on these attacks in the following sections.

*1) **Power attacks**:* In cryptographic algorithms, the computation is based on a secret value *S*, which is not necessarily the key to encryption but it is derived from the key. The activity of encryption software causes data dependant signal transitions in the current surges of the hardware, which are visible in internal wires, power, and ground connection. By collecting the dynamic power traces, an adversary can find the secret value correlated to the input data patter while considering measurement errors and enviornmental noise.

Power traces built on the direct current correspondence of the software operation, are analyzed as Simple Power Analysis (SPA). In this analysis it is assumed that a change in each bit of *S* is visible in the leakage power pattern. In attack to applications with complicated relation of input and application flow, Differential Power Analysis (DPA) can reveal the *S* by statistical tests on the differentiation of many power traces. DPA is a very powerful technique that can easily eliminate the random noise sourced from environment or obfuscation mitigation techniques.

*2) **Timing attacks**:* Microarchitectural side-channels are typically timing-based channels, as shown in Figure 3. Due to sharing functional units among different programs, an attacker can, in general, observe the timing of the operation of the individual functional unit and its output. Since the designs of the functional units are knows to the attacker, these timing leakages reveal whether the fast or slow execution path was taken [12]. In the taxonomy presented in Figure 2, Software-to-hardware side-channel attacks are categorized based on the shared unit. In [13], the attacker manipulates

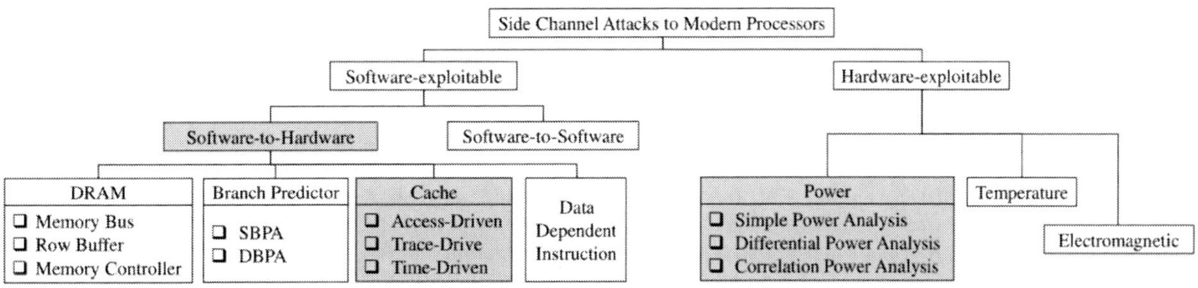

Figure 2. Taxonomy of side-channel attacks to processors. The main focus of this paper is to study software-to-hardware side-channel attacks, that exploited as timing side-channels in cache, and power side-channel attacks, as shown by the highlighted box. In this figure, SBPA and DBPA represent the simple branch prediction analysis and dynamic branch prediction analysis, respectively.

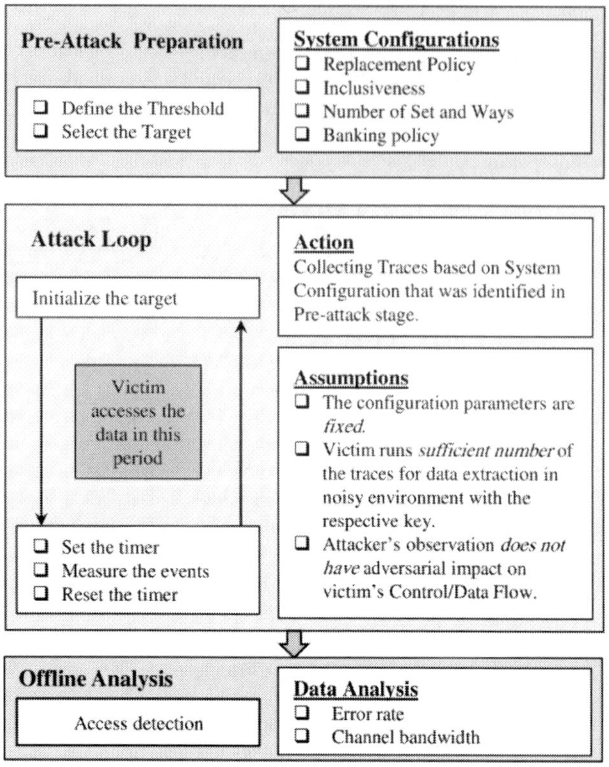

Figure 3. Principles of timing attacks to shared components. Each timing attack, is consist of three stages: **Pre-attack**, **attack loop** and **data analysis**.

a shared branch predictor to infers victim's execution path. Cache, as an inevitable unit of microprocessor, has been the target of side-channel attacks. Cache timing attacks are based on the contention of lines between victim and attacker or data-reuse in the application. They can exploit strong isolation techniques from the core level to threads.

With Osvic [14] proposing several exploitation techniques, the timing attacks can be categorized as Time-Driven and Access-Driven, based on the source of leakage, an attacker's access, and application. Later on, trace-driven attacks were also recognized as a separate category.

- *Access-Driven Attacks:* These attacks are independent of the victim's performance counters, but they measure the effect of spatial and temporal resource sharing between the attacker's application and victim's application. The pieces of evidence in the attacker's workspace about the victim's access are used to reveal the encryption key. Since this attack leaves no trace of access, it is considered more stealthy. *PRIME+PROBE* [15][16] is a cross-core and cross-VM Access-Driven attack, which finds the pattern of victim application memory access without the need to flush the cache or assuming shared addresses in the memory. *FLUSH+RELOAD* [17] is another example where the attacker shares an address in the memory with the victim. The attacker benefits the shared virtual memory such as page deduplication or shared libraries managed by the operating system to make contention with the victim. In this attack, the attacker tries to flush the shared addresses and measure his second access to find the victim's internal execution path. Although this attack has been exploited using several variants, the shared address assumption limits the threat model. Also, there is a need for an atomic instruction for flushing a specific line which is not present in all architectures (e.g., RISC-V). As another example is *FLUSH+FLUSH* [18], where malicious user records the loop time for *clflush* instruction in the attack-loop phase.
- *Time-Driven Attacks:* In this category of attacks, attacker attempts to measure the victim's execution time. The execution time of applications is dependant on several parameters like execution path, data flow, and memory access time. Hence, these attacks require a large and detailed execution profile for key extraction. *EVICT+RELOAD* [19] is a Time-Driven cache attack, whereby evicting specific cache lines, the attacker prepares the system to reveal the victim's control flow. By forcing the victim to run enough times, attacker gains the required number of traces to extract key-dependent memory accesses. This attack is based on the average execution time of a confidential program. Therefore, it needs a large number of sample data to recognize the key.
- *Trace-Driven Attacks:* In this category, the attacker collects the traces of encryption on a shared resource, e.g., cache, based on a known message attack. These traces can form a profile of hit and miss in the cache, which gives information about the key-dependent lookup addresses. This ability gives an adversary the opportunity to make inferences about the secret key. In [20], cache traces are determined by the power consumption in the cache for each hit and miss to break the AES encryption algorithm.

B. Defense Mechanisms

In Figure 4, defense mechanisms are categorized into three subsets, based on the source of leakage channel they are protecting against. Microarchitectural mitigation techniques, e.g., isolation, are implemented both in software and hardware levels that each can address a specific range of attacks [29]. Also, mitigation techniques against power side-channels, are proposed both at circuit level, as resilient processors, and algorithmic level, as resilient application implementation. We will present works in these categories in Section IV.

C. Data Dependant Implementation of Encryption Algorithms

In an attack on cryptographic algorithms, the encryption key is the target of the attacker. Two implementation models are mostly analyzed in the literature for the security of encryption application implementation, conditional control flow, and conditional lookup table, which are respectively used in Rivest–Shamir–Adleman (RSA) and Advanced Encryption Standard (AES) encryption systems.

1) *Conditional Control Flow:* RSA is a cryptosystem for exchanging the key between two parties. To calculate the private key and the public key, modular exponentiation is implemented using a square-and-multiply algorithm that computes $r = b^e \ mod \ m$ dependant to bits of e in a conditional loop. As shown in Figure 5, line 5 will be executed if the condition in line 4 is fulfilled and it causes bit-dependant physical footprints like dynamic power consumption and execution time. In [21], Mushtaq et al. have presented a comprehensive survey in attacks and countermeasures on RSA.
2) *Conditional Table Lookup:* In block cipher cryptosystems, the secret of the system is not directly used for encryption,

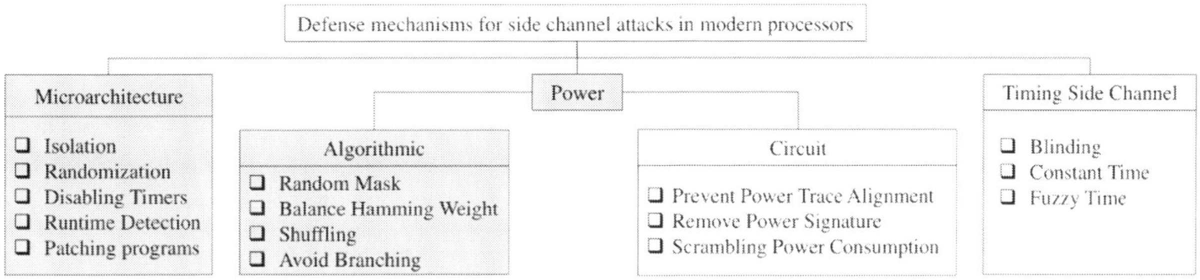

Figure 4. A taxonomy of defense techniques against side-channel attacks in the processors is presented. Based on the defense point of application, mechanisms are divided into 3 categories. In this paper, we give an overview on defense mechanisms in power and microarchitecture categories.

but the key enables an address in the pre-computed tables of data. When the index used to access a Look-Up Table (LUT), depends on the secret data, the access time and dynamic power consumption may vary due to the behavior of memory access. Such data leakages have been exploited in various block ciphers, e.g., AES in [22] that implements S-Boxes using lookup tables to reduce hardware overhead.

```
r ← 1
for i from n − 1 downto 0 do
    r ← r^2 mod m
    if e_i == 1 then
        r ← r·b mod m
    end
end
```

Data-dependent conditional loop

Figure 5. Data-dependent implementation of modular exponentiation which is used in RSA encryption algorithm.

D. RISC-V Architecture

RISC-V [10] with open-source ISA is received as an alternative in academia and also popular in the IoT industry. Since it is a flexible, upgradeable, and optimizable architecture, it is predicted to be adopted widely in emerging embedded systems. RISC-V ISA is not limited to a specific hardware implementation of a processor core. The modular architecture implementation with variants of address space sizes makes it suitable for lightweight edge devices to the high-performance servers. The base integer instruction set is flexible to adopt the required software stack and to add additional requirements. Moreover, the simplicity of the design enables the RISC-V to be an ideal base for the application-specific design. Accelerators and co-processors can share the compiler tool-chain, operating system binaries, and control processor implementations. It speeds up the process of agile hardware processor design by the support of an active and diverse community for open-source contributions. Figure 6 shows an overview of the RISC-V ecosystem and respective tools.

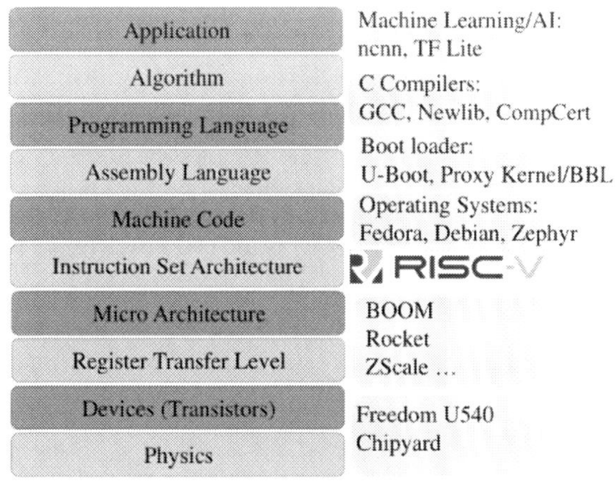

Figure 6. RISC-V ecosystem is shown. RISC-V implements the ISA and connects software stack to hardware. In each layer some examples, of the current available implementations are noted. It should be mentioned that there are other products in the market and academia which are not named here.

III. Side-channel Attacks on RISC-V Microprocessors

In this section, we discuss state-of-the side-channel attacks on RISC-V microprocessors.

A. Power Side-Channel Attacks

Mulder et al. in [23] discuss power side-channel vulnerabilities of RISC-V microprocessor. In this work, they distinguish between different types of data leakage by categorizing them into direct-value leaks, data-overwrites and circuit-level leaks. Since direct-value leakage can be protected using masking techniques, they show software masking is not sufficient for mitigating power side-channel. On the other hand, since side-channel analysis is usually postponed to post-fabrication stages of hardware production, the state-of-the-art is focused on studying the software implementation of cryptographic algorithm. Therefore, a promising research direction is to apply the mitigation technique in the architectural level to prevent exceeding complexity of the microprocessor-based systems. In this work, they exploit memory access patterns of an AES encryption algorithm through a data overwrite leakage. This leakage happens when the data and the mask are accessed repetitively through memory connections. The replaced data in intermediate registers causes a peak in consumed power, which is leaked by power side-channel attack.

B. Timing Side-Channel Attacks

Recent attacks on modern processors have shown that special features of emerging architectures can be a source of the attack in lower hardware levels, as well as in the previous generation. In [24], Gonzalez et al. replicated Spectre [25] attack on BOOM (Berkeley out-of-order-machine) core and exploits in-core data cache for leaking the confidential data. Since the *clflush* instruction is not implemented in the RISC-V ISA, the authors implement an atomic instruction to replace the targeted lines with dummy data and evict the victim's shared page. More recently, Le et al. in [27], showed a side-channel attack to physically-implemented BOOM. In this attack, they target the conditional branch, which is trained to execute an instruction that assesses the confidential data.

IV. *PRIME+PROBE* ATTACK ON RISC-V

To identify the vulnerabilities of RISC-V against timing side-channel attacks, we implemented a state-of-the-art cache timing attack (*PRIME+PROBE*) to RSA encryption algorithm running on different RISC-V hardware platforms, i.e., an out-of-order speculative RISC-V core (BOOM, implemented as SoC on the FPGA) and a commercial in-order RISC-V CPU (HiFive Unleashed).

A. *Design Challenges*

Most of the timing side-channel attacks are applicable to traditional microprocessors' architecture. However, the implementation of these attacks on the RISC-V microprocessors exhibits the following design challenges:

1) The cache addressing is not determined by RISC-V ISA, and it differs with implementation. For instance, the last-level cache addressing for Rocket SoC is designed to be virtually-indexed, which is the one that helps to build a shared set between the victim and the attacker.
2) In this work, we replicate the attack on a high-performance commercial processor to find out the impact of branch prediction and out-of-order units on the timing of application execution. For instance, if the attacker accesses to one set in the cache, the prefetch unit can learn the access pattern and predict the execution in pause times, while shuffling the lines in this attack prevents this.
3) The RISC-V ISA does not support the *clflush* instruction that is exploited by cache timing attacks in Intel microprocessors (*FLUSH+RELOAD*). Therefore, we choose another attack that is independent of special instruction or shared addresses in the victim's software space. We observe that RISC-V microprocessors reveal secrets of the system with the same trend in bandwidth as commercial microprocessors.

B. *Experimental analysis on hardware platforms*

We performed the *PRIME+PROBE* attack on a Rocket SoC with BOOM RISC-V multi-core implemented on the Zedboard, Xilinx Zynq-7000 FPGA board, and we show the successful implementation of the cache timing attack (*PRIME+PROBE*) to the RSA encryption Algorithm on RISC-V ISA in Figure 7(a). For the comprehensive analysis, we also performed the *PRIME+PROBE* attack on HiFive Unleashed, i.e., a commercial RISC-V multi-core CPU (see Figure 7(b)). Since, in the *PRIME+PROBE* attack, the attacker makes consecutive accesses to targeted cache lines in each determined time slot. By measuring the access time, the attacker can decide whether the content of the requested address is present in the cache or it has been replaced by the victim's access. By analyzing the results in Figures 7(a) and (b), we made the following key observations:

1) The difference between cache access time for key-bit 0 (see labels A0 and B0 in Figure 7) and key-bit 1 (see labels A1 and B1 in Figure 7) is distinguishable even when other processes are running on the shared platform. In our attack implementation, we have exploited this timing differences to extract the key.
2) The identified timing vulnerabilities exist in the both FPGA implementation and HiFive Unleashed board that can be exploited by the *PRIME+PROBE* attack. Hence, these vulnerabilities are independent of the hardware platform. This observation leads us to a conclusion that mitigation technique for FPGA implementations can also be deployed ASIC implementation of RISV-V microprocessors.
3) These timing vulnerabilities can be exploited to perform other software-exploitable attacks on the RISC-V hardware, for example, Spectre [25] and Meltdown [26].

V. DEFENSE MECHANISMS FOR SIDE-CHANNEL ATTACKS ON RISC-V MICROPROCESSORS

The usage of high-performance processors, e.g., commercial RISC-V CPUs [24], in Internet-of-Things (IoT) devices, have already been shown to be vulnerable to microarchitectural attacks like Spectre [25] and Meltdown [26]. Efforts in defense techniques are focused on protecting sensitive data in memory locations [30][31], and protecting the software by providing an isolated execution environment [32][33]. Yu et al in [34] discuss a compiler-based solution for securing data oblivious code generation for preventing the side-channel attack, which is not applicable at software level. To protect the RISC-V CPU against power side-channel attacks, Mulder et al. [23] have proposed a masking solution at the architecture level.

(a) FPGA implementation of RISC-V multicore and map of cache in PRIME+PROBE attack (b) HiFive Unleashed and map of cache in PRIME+PROBE attack

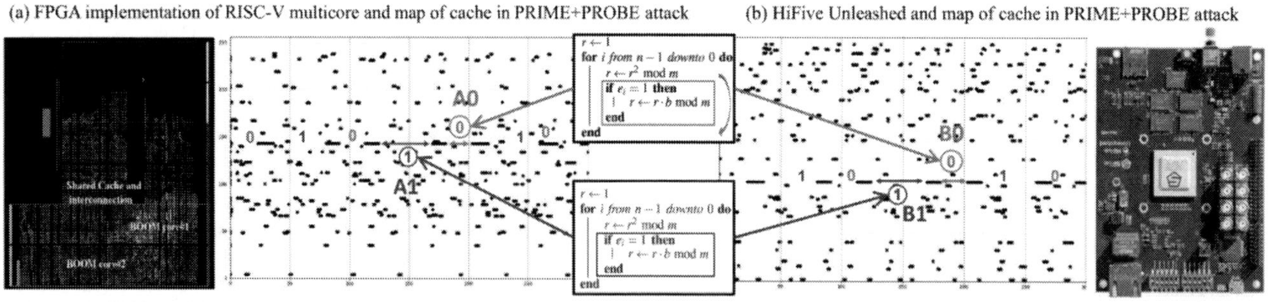

Figure 7. *PRIME+PROBE* cache timing attack on RISC-V hardware platforms which presents the content map of the cache for **300** time slots, when our attack is priming **256** sets. The access pattern reveals the keys of RSA algorithm. The long empty interval means victim's data was processing and it was present in the cache, while short empty interval indicates that the loop was not executed and victim releases the target set. Note, in this figure, Where the key bits are 1, the cache intervals are longer than key bits that are 0 because of the data dependant conditional flow in the RSA Algorithm.

VI. Open Research Challenges and Road Ahead

Currently, the focus of research in the security of RISC-V is on the security of the software. While it is crucial to protect software integrity, hardware security is a significant threat that needs to be addressed accordingly. In the following, we mention two main challenges in this research direction.

1) *New features in ISA and lack of stable toolchain:* Earlier studies assume that ISA is independent of hardware implementation, but the data leakage analysis shows that ISA can be exploited as side-channels. The first step is to examine the applicability of current attack vectors in RISC-V processors and then study the new features of RISC-V ISA, which introduces new variables to SCAs. To this aim, a reliable and stable toolchain is required.
2) *Need for generic defense mechanisms:* RISC-V, as a new open-source ISA, has a high potential to be the platform for state-of-the-art defense mechanisms. However, our observations show that most of the proposed techniques utilize special features of processors, such as Intel's x86 and ARM, which are not available in RISC-V processors. It will be worthy of proposing generic methodologies for addressing the gap of security studies between software and hardware by utilizing RISC-V capabilities. These defense mechanisms in the early stages of design can be adopted even for lightweight processors and are not limited to complicated high-performance multi-cores.

Acknowledgment

This work was partially supported by Doctoral College Resilient Embedded Systems which is run jointly by TU Wien's Faculty of Informatics and FH-Technikum Wien.

References

[1] K. Shafique, B. A. Khawaja, F. Sabir, S. Qazi, M. Mustaqim, "Internet of things (IoT) for next-generation smart systems: A review of current challenges, future trends and prospects for emerging 5G-IoT scenarios," IEEE Access 8, 2020, pp. 23022-23040.

[2] Q. Ge, Y. Yarom, D. Cock, G. Heiser, "A survey of microarchitectural timing attacks and countermeasures on contemporary hardware," Journal of Cryptographic Engineering 8.1, 2018, pp. 1-27.

[3] D. Ratasich, F. Khalid, F. Geissler, R. Grosu, M. Shafique, E. Bartocci, "A roadmap toward the resilient internet of things for cyber-physical systems," IEEE Access 7 (2019): 13260-13283.

[4] F. Khalid, S. Rehman, M. Shafique, "Overview of security for smart cyber-physical systems." Security of Cyber-Physical Systems. Springer, Cham, 2020. 5-24.

[5] M. M. Kermani, M. Zhang, A. Raghunathan, N. K. Jha, "Emerging frontiers in embedded security," International Conference on Embedded Systems, 2013, pp. 203-208.

[6] Y. Ye, T. Li, D. Adjeroh, S. Sitharama Iyengar, "A survey on malware detection using data mining techniques." ACM Computing Surveys (CSUR) 50.3 (2017): 1-40.

[7] Y. Lyu, Yangdi, and P. Mishra, "A survey of side-channel attacks on caches and countermeasures." Journal of Hardware and Systems Security 2.1, 2018, pp. 33-50.

[8] A. Akram, M. Mushtaq, M. K. Bhatti, V. Lapotre, G. Gogniat, "Meet the Sherlock Holmes' of Side Channel Leakage: A Survey of Cache SCA Detection Techniques," in IEEE Access 8, 2020, pp. 70836-70860.

[9] M. Gautschi et al., "Near-threshold RISC-V core with DSP extensions for scalable IoT endpoint devices." IEEE Transactions on Very Large Scale Integration (VLSI) Systems 25.10 (2017): 2700-2713.

[10] "The RISC-V Instruction Set Manual, Volume I: User-Level ISA, Document Version 2.2," Editors Andrew Waterman and Krste Asanovic, RISC-V Foundation, May 2017.

[11] M. Mushtaq, A. Akram, M. K. Bhatti, V. Lapotre, G. Gogniat, "Cache-Based Side-Channel Intrusion Detection using Hardware Performance Counters," CryptArchi 2018.

[12] J. Szefer, "Survey of microarchitectural side and covert channels, attacks,and defenses," Journal of Hardware and Systems Security 3.3, 2019, pp. 219-234.

[13] D. Evtyushkin, R. Riley, N. Abu-Ghazaleh, D. Ponomarev, "Branchscope: A new side channel attack on directional branch predictor," ACM SIGPLAN Notices 53.2, 2018, pp. 693-707.

[14] D. A. Osvik, A. Shamir, E. Tromer, "Cache Attacks and Countermeasures: The Case of AES," Cryptographers' track at the RSA conference, 2006, pp. 1-20.

[15] F. Liu, Y. Yarom, Q. Ge, G. Heiser, R. B. Lee, "Last-level cache side-channel attacks are practical," IEEE symposium on Security and Privacy. IEEE, 2015, pp. 605-622.

[16] M. Kayaalp, N. Abu-Ghazaleh, D. Ponomarev, A. Jaleel, "A high-resolution side-channel attack on last-level cache," IEEE/ACM DAC, 2016, pp. 1-6.

[17] Y. Yarom, K. Falkner, "FLUSH + RELOAD: A High Resolution Low Noise L3 Cache Side-Channel Attack," USENIX Security, 2014, pp. 719-732.

[18] D. Gruss, C. Maurice, K. Wagner, S. Mangard, "Flush+ Flush: a fast and stealthy cache attack." International Conference on Detection of Intrusions and Malware, and Vulnerability Assessment. Springer, Cham, 2016, pp. 279-299.

[19] M. Lipp, D. Gruss, R. Spreitzer, C. Maurice, S. Mangard, "ARMageddon: cache attacks on mobile devices" USENIX Security, 2016, pp. 549-564.

[20] O. Acıiçmez, and Ç. Kaya Koç, "Trace-driven cache attacks on AES," International Conference on Information and Communications Security. Springer, 2006, pp. 112-121.

[21] M. Mushtaq, M. A. Mukhtar, V. Lapotre, M. K. Bhatti, G. Gogniat, "Winter is here A decade of cache-based side-channel attacks, detection & mitigation for RSA," Information Systems, 2020, p. 101524.

[22] M. Renauld, F. X. Standaert, N. Veyrat-Charvillon, "Algebraic side-channel attacks on the AES: Why time also matters in DPA," International Workshop on Cryptographic Hardware and Embedded Systems, 2009, pp. 97-111.

[23] E. D. Mulder, S. Gummall, M. Hutter, "Protecting RISC-V against Side-Channel Attacks," IEEE/ACM DAC, 2019, pp. 1-4.

[24] A. Gonzalez, B. Korpan, J. Zhao, E. Younis, K. Asanović, "Replicating and Mitigating Spectre Attacks on a Open Source RISC-V Microarchitecture," CARRV, 2019.

[25] P. Kocher et al., "Spectre attacks: Exploiting speculative execution," IEEE symposium on Security and Privacy. IEEE, 2019, pp. 1-19.

[26] M. Lipp et al., "Meltdown: Reading Kernel Memory from User Space," USENIX Security, 2018, pp. 973-990.

[27] A. T. Le, B. A. Dao, K. Suzaki, C. K. Pham, "Experiment on Replication of Side Channel Attack via Cache of RISC-V Berkeley Out-of-Order Machine (BOOM) Implemented on FPGA," CARRV, 2020.

[28] SiFive Co. 'HiFIve Unleashed', 2014. [Online]. Available: https://www.sifive.com/boards/hifive-unleashed. [Accessed: 01- Aug-2020].

[29] Z. He and R. B. Lee, "How secure is your cache against side-channel attacks?," IEEE/ACM International Symposium on Microarchitecture, 2017, pp. 341-353.

[30] I. Lebedev et al., "Sanctorum: A lightweight security monitor for secure enclaves," IEEE DATE, 2019, pp. 1142-1147.

[31] A. Menon, S. Murugan, C. Rebeiro, N. Gala, K. Veezhinathan, "Shakti-T: A RISC-V processor with light weight security extensions," Proceedings of the Hardware and Architectural Support for Security and Privacy, 2017, pp. 1-8.

[32] S. Weiser, M. Werner, Mario, F. Brasser, M. Malenko, S. Mangard, A. R. Sadeghi, "TIMBER-V: Tag-Isolated Memory Bringing Fine-grained Enclaves to RISC-V," NDSS, 2019.

[33] D. Lee, D. Kohlbrenner, S. Shinde, D. Song, K. Asanović, "Keystone: A Framework for Architecting TEEs,"arXiv:1907.10119, 2019.

[34] J. Yu, L. Hsiung, M. El'Hajj, C. W. Fletcher, "Data Oblivious ISA Extensions for Side Channel-Resistant and High Performance Computing," NDSS, 2019.

Exploiting Vulnerabilities in Deep Neural Networks: Adversarial and Fault-Injection Attacks

Faiq Khalid[1], Muhammad Abdullah Hanif[1], Muhammad Shafique[2]
[1]*Technische Universität Wien (TU Wien), Vienna, Austria*
[2]*Division of Engineering, New York University Abu Dhabi (NYUAD), Abu Dhabi, United Arab Emirates*
Email: {faiq.khalid,muhammad.hanif}@tuwien.ac.at, muhammad.shafique@nyu.edu

***Abstract*—From tiny pacemaker chips to aircraft collision avoidance systems, the state-of-the-art Cyber-Physical Systems (CPS) have increasingly started to rely on Deep Neural Networks (DNNs). However, as concluded in various studies, DNNs are highly susceptible to security threats, including adversarial attacks. In this paper, we first discuss different vulnerabilities that can be exploited for generating security attacks for neural network-based systems. We then provide an overview of existing adversarial and fault-injection-based attacks on DNNs. We also present a brief analysis to highlight different challenges in the practical implementation of the adversarial attacks. Finally, we also discuss various prospective ways to develop robust DNN-based systems that are resilient to adversarial and fault-injection attacks.**

Keywords–Deep Neural Networks; Adversarial Attacks; Machine Learning Security; Fault-injection Attacks.

I. Introduction

Machine Learning (ML) algorithms have become popular in many applications, especially smart Cyber-Physical Systems (CPS), because of their ability to process and classify the enormous data [1]–[3], e.g., image recognition, object detection. The state-of-the-art ML systems are mostly based on Deep Neural Networks (DNNs), which consists of many layers of neurons connected into a mesh. The input follows this mesh from the input layer, through the hidden layers, to reach the output layer. The output node/neuron with the highest value indicates the decision of the DNN. However, due to several uncertainties in feature selection, ML algorithms inherently posses several security vulnerabilities, e.g., sensitivity for small input noise. Several attacks have been proposed to exploit these security vulnerabilities, for example, adversarial attacks [4]–[6] (see Figure 1). Depending upon the extent of the access to the training process, the DNN model, or the inference, the adversarial attacks can either exploit the input sensitivity of the trained DNN during the inference or manipulate the training process, DNN model or training dataset.

Since the discovery of adversarial attacks, several studies have been performed but are mainly focused on the optimization and effectiveness of input data perturbation. In most of the practical cases, it is very challenging to manipulate the input of the DNN or corrupt the input data because of the limited access of DNN-based system or training process. However, the advancements in the communication network and computational elements of the CPS make us capable of putting the computing elements and sensors anywhere. This enables easy access to the computing elements and sensor, thereby opening a broader attack surface. Recently, this easy-to-get physical access is exploited to generate fault-injection attacks (see Figure 1). In these attacks, attackers can externally inject the faults in data stored in the memory, the control path of a DNN-based system, or the computational blocks to manipulate the DNN output. These faults can be injected using well-known techniques, e.g., variations in voltage, Electromagnetic (EM) interference, and heavy-ion radiation.

A. Novel Contributions

To encompass the complete attack surface in the DNN-based system, in this paper, we study the security vulnerabilities with respect to adversarial attack and the emerging fault-injection attacks. **In summary, the contributions of this paper are:**

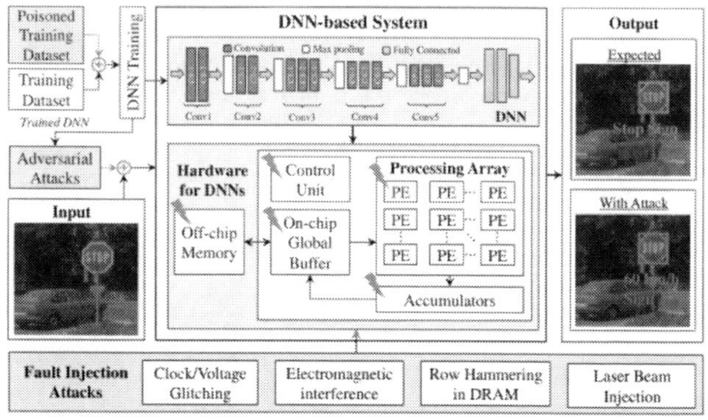

Figure 1. Security threats (i.e., adversarial and fault-injection attacks) to a DNN-based system. Fault-injection attacks can be performed by physically injecting faults in the off-chip and on-chip memories, and in the Processing Elements (PEs). The "Stop" sign image is take from the German Traffic Sign Detection dataset [7].

1) We first study and discuss the different sets of assumptions and parameters of the threat model that can be used to show the effectiveness and practicability of an attack (**Section II**).
2) We discuss the different aspects, with respect to threat model, optimization algorithms, and computational cost, of the adversarial attacks (**Section III**) and fault-injection attacks (**Section V**).
3) Most of the adversarial attacks do not consider the overall pipeline in the DNN-based system and ignore the pre-processing stages. Therefore, in this paper, we provide a brief analysis to highlight the challenges in the practical implementation of the adversarial attacks (**Section IV**). Based on this analysis, we conclude that the adversarial attack must be strong enough not to be nullified by the input pre-processing (which is low-pass filtering in our analysis).
4) Towards the end, we highlight different research directions on the road ahead towards developing a robust DNN-based system with stronger defenses against these attacks (**Section VI**).

II. Threat Model

The effectiveness of an attack depend upon different assumptions and parameters. Different configurations of these assumptions and parameters generate several scenarios that are known as threat models. Therefore, in the context of DNN security, the threat model is based on the following set of parameters (see Figure 2):

- **Attacker's Knowledge:** Depending upon the information about the targeted ML system and attacker's access, the attack can either be black-box or white-box (see Figure 3). In *white-box attacks*, the attacker has full access to the trained DNNs; thereby, allowing him to exploit DNN parameters to generate adversarial noise. In *black-box attacks*, attacker has access only to the input and output of the DNN.
- **Attacker's Goal:** Depending upon the targeted payload, the attack can either be targeted or un-targeted. In the *targeted attack*, the attacker modifies the DNN, input, or other parameters to achieve a particular misclassification. On the other hand, in the *un-targeted attack*, the attacker's aim is only to maximize the prediction error.

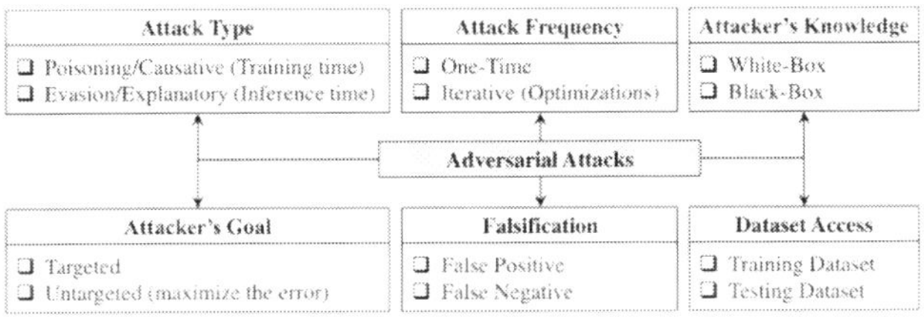

Figure 2. Threat model for adversarial attacks on DNNs. This model shows different assumptions and parameters that are required to generate an adversarial attack.

- **Attack Frequency:** To exploit a trade-off between resources, timing, and effectiveness, the attack can be wither one-shot or iterative. In *one-shot*, the attack is optimized only once, but *iterative* attack optimizes the payload of the attack over multiple iterations.
- **Attack Falsification:** Depending upon the payload of the attack, these attacks can either be false positive or false negative attacks. In *false-positive* attacks, a negative sample is misclassified as a positive sample. In *false-negative* attacks, a positive sample is misclassified as a negative sample.
- **Attack Type:** This parameter is related to the targeted phase of the ML design cycle. For example, depending upon the access, the attacker can target training, inference, or hardware of the DNN.
- **Dataset Access:** The attack effectiveness and strength also depends upon the attacker's access to the different datasets. For example, the strength of the evasion attacks can significantly increase if the attacker has access to training and testing datasets.

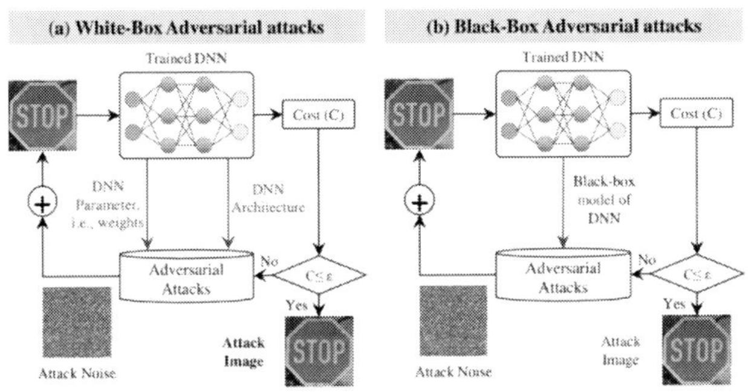

Figure 3. An overview of the adversarial attack on machine learning. (a) In a white-box setting, the attacker has access to the network architecture and network parameters, i.e., weight, number of neurons, number of layers, activation functions, and convolution filters. (b) In a black-box setting, the attacker has access to the input and output of the network.

III. Adversarial Attacks

The addition of imperceptible noise to the input can change the output of the DNN, and this phenomenon is known as the adversarial attack. It can also reduce the confidence classification that cause un-targeted misclassification, or it can also induce targeted misclassification. Several adversarial attacks have been proposed that manipulate the system to behave erroneously. Broadly, these attacks are categorized as causative and exploratory attacks.

A. Evasion (Exploratory) Attacks

In these attacks, an attacker introduces an imperceptible noise at the input of the trained DNN during the inference. This imperceptible noise (known as adversarial noise) can either perform targeted misclassification or maximize the prediction error. Since these attacks explore vulnerabilities of the trained DNN during inference, therefore, these attacks are also known as exploratory attacks. On the basis of how the attacker implements the adversarial attack, the attacks can be divided into three categories: *gradient-based*, *score-based* and *decision-based* attacks, as shown in Table I.

1) Gradient-based Attacks: The gradient-based attacks make use of the network gradients to craft the attack noise. There are several gradient-based attacks that utilize different optimization algorithms and imperceptibility parameters to improve the effectiveness of these attacks (see the summary of gradient-based attacks in Table I). However, most of them are based basic gradient-based attacks, i.e., Fast Gradient Sign Method (FGSM) [8], iterative-FGSM (iFGSM) [9], Jacobian Saliency Map Attack (JSMA) [12], Carlini and Wagner (C&W) [14] attack and training dataset unaware attack (TrISec) [26]. In this section, we only discuss these basic gradient-based attacks.

- *Fast Gradient Sign Method (FGSM)* [8] is a gradient-based attack that utilizes use of the cost function $J(p, x, y_{True})$ for the network with parameters p, input x and the correct output class y_{True} to determine the direction in which the adversarial noise will have the greatest impact. Afterwards, a small noise ϵ is added in a single iteration to the input, in the direction of the obtained gradient.
- The *Iterative Fast Sign Method (iFGSM)* [9] is a variant of FGSM that is preferred for targeted misclassification. Here, the cost function chosen corresponds to a specific target (misclassification) class. Instead of perturbing the input in one step, the input is perturbed by α in each step.
- In *Jacobian Saliency Map Attack (JSMA)* [12], initially the forward derivative, i.e., the Jacobian, of the network F with respect to all input nodes is determined. Accordingly, saliency map is constructed, which highlights the inputs that are the most vulnerable to noise. This map can be used to perturb the minimum number of inputs to implement a successful attack. A vulnerable input node is then perturbed towards the target class. If the perturbation is found to be insufficient, then the whole process of finding Jacobian and constructing the saliency map is repeated until a successful attack is implemented or the perturbation added to the input exceeds a given threshold γ.
- The *Carlini and Wagner (C&W) attack* [14] is a white-box approach to adversarial attack. The main idea is to consider finding the appropriate perturbation for the adversarial attack as a dual optimization problem. The first objective is to minimize the noise with respect to l_p norm, added to an image with the objective of obtaining a specific target label at output. The second objective is to minimize $f(x + \epsilon)$ to a non-positive value, where the output label of the input changes to the targeted misclassification label.
- *TrISec* [26] proposes a training data "unaware" adversarial attack. The attack is again modeled as an optimization problem. Backpropagation is used to obtain the noise that causes targeted misclassification while minimizing the cost function associated with the network. The probability $P(F(x + \epsilon) = y_{Target})$ of the target class is simultaneously maximized to ensure a minimal and scattered perturbation based on two parameters, i.e., Cross-correlation Coefficient (CC) and Structural Similarity Index (SSI). CC ensures that the noise added to the input is imperceptible (to humans), while SSI ensures that noise is spread across the whole input instead of being focused in a small region, hence, improving the imperceptibility withe respect to subjective analysis.

Note, these attacks require the attacker to have access to the network's internal parameters to calculate the gradients and hence are generally carried out in a white-box environment. Note, all the white-box attacks can be implemented in the black-box environment when they are combined with model stealing attacks. These attacks are known as substitute model attacks. However, it is not always possible to have the white-box access to the trained DNN.

TABLE I. A BRIEF OVERVIEW OF THE CATEGORIZATION OF THE STATE-OF-THE-ART ADVERSARIAL ATTACKS ON MACHINE LEARNING SYSTEMS. (SVM: SUPPORT VECTOR MACHINES, SSI: STRUCTURAL SIMILARITY INDEX, AND CC: CROSS-CORRELATION COEFFICIENT

Adversarial Attacks		Type	Knowledge	Frequency	Goal	Imperceptibility
Gradient-based Attacks	Fast Gradient Sign Method (FGSM)[8]	Evasion	White-Box	One-shot	Targeted/Un-targeted	l_1, l_2, l_{inf} norms
	Basic Iterative Method (BIM) or Iterative FGSM[9]	Evasion	White-Box	Iterative	Targeted/Un-targeted	l_1, l_2, l_{inf} norms
	Projected Gradient Descent (PGD)[10]	Evasion	White-Box	Iterative	Targeted/Un-targeted	ϵ norm
	Auto-PGD[11]	Evasion	White-Box	Iterative	Targeted/Un-targeted	l_{inf} norm
	Jacobian-based Saliency Map Attack (JSMA)[12]	Evasion	White-Box	Iterative	Targeted/Un-targeted	l_0 norm
	Iterative Frame Saliency[13]	Evasion	White-Box	Iterative/One-shot	Un-targeted	l_0 norm
	Carlini & Wagner l_2 attack[14]	Evasion	White-Box	Iterative	Targeted/Un-targeted	l_2 norm
	Carlini & Wagner l_{inf} attack[14]	Evasion	White-Box	Iterative	Targeted/Un-targeted	l_{inf} norm
	DeepFool[15]	Evasion	White-Box	Iterative	Un-targeted	l_2 norm
	Universal Perturbations[16]	Evasion	White-Box	Iterative	Un-targeted	l_p norm
	Newton Fool[17]	Evasion	White-Box	Iterative	Un-targeted	Tuning parameter
	Feature Adversaries[18]	Evasion	White-Box	Iterative	Targeted	l_{inf} norm
	Adversarial Patch[19][20]	Evasion	White-Box	Iterative	Targeted/Un-targeted	-
	Elastic-Net (EAD)[21]	Evasion	White-Box	Iterative	Targeted/Un-targeted	l_1, l_2, l_{inf} norms
	Dpatch[22]	Evasion	White-Box	Iterative	Targeted/Un-targeted	-
	High Confidence Low Uncertainty[23]	Evasion	White-Box	Iterative	Targeted	l_2 norm
	Waaserstein Attack[24]	Evasion	White-Box	Iterative	Targeted/Un-targeted	l_p norm
	Shadow Attack[25]	Evasion	White-Box	Iterative	Targeted/Un-targeted	l_2, l_{inf} norms
	TrISec[26]	Evasion	White-Box	Iterative	Targeted/Un-targeted	SSI, CR
Score-based Attacks	Zeroth Order Optimization (ZOO)[27]	Evasion	Black-Box	Iterative	Targeted	l_2 norm
	Local Search[28]	Evasion	Black-Box	Iterative	Un-targeted	-
	Copy and Paste[29]	Evasion	Black-Box	Iterative	Targeted/Un-targeted	l_2 norm
Decision-based Attacks	HopskipJump[30]	Evasion	Black-Box	Iterative	Targeted/Un-targeted	l_2 norm
	Query Efficient Attack [31]	Evasion	Black-Box	Iterative	Targeted/Un-targeted	l_2 norm
	Decision-based Attack [32]	Evasion	Black-Box	Iterative	Targeted/Un-targeted	l_2 norm
	Query Efficient Boundary Attack (QEBA)[33]	Evasion	Black-Box	Iterative	Targeted/Un-targeted	l_2 norm
	Geometry-Inspired Decision-based (qFool)[34]	Evasion	Black-Box	Iterative	Targeted/Un-targeted	l_2 norm
	Threshold Attack[35]	Evasion	Black-Box	Iterative	Targeted/Un-targeted	l_p norm
	Square Attack[36]	Evasion	Black-Box	Iterative	Targeted/Un-targeted	l_p norm
	Pixel Attacks[37][35]	Evasion	Black-Box	Iterative	Targeted/Un-targeted	l_p norm
	FaDec[38]	Evasion	Black-Box	Iterative	Targeted/Un-targted	l_2 norm, SSI, CR
Dataset Poisoning	Poisoning Attack on SVM [39][40]	Poisoning	White-Box	Iterative	Targeted	-
	Targeted Clean-Label Poisoning [41]	Poisoning	White-Box	One-shot	Targeted	-
	Watermarking [42]	Poisoning	White-Box	One-shot	Targeted	-
	Efficient Dataset Poisoning [42]	Poisoning	White-Box	Iterative	Targeted/Un-targeted	-
	BadNets [43]	Poisoning	White-Box	Iterative	Targeted	-
	Targeted Backdoor [44]	Poisoning	White-Box	Iterative	Targeted	-
	Dynamic Backdoor Attacks [45]	Poisoning	White-Box	Iterative	Targeted	-
	Feature Collision Attack [42]	Poisoning	White-Box	Iterative	Targeted/Un-targeted	-
Model Poisoning	Weight poisoning [46]	Poisoning	White-Box	One-shot	Targeted/Un-targeted	-
	Local Model Poisoning [47]	Poisoning	White-Box	One-shot	Targeted/Un-targeted	-

2) Score-based Evasion Attacks: In these attacks, the attacker has access to output scores/probabilities [27][28]. The generation of attack is formulated as an optimization problem where the change in output scores due to the input manipulation is used to predict the direction and strength of the next input manipulation.

3) Decision-based Evasion Attacks: These attacks make input alterations in a reverse direction - the procedure starts with a larger input noise that causes output misclassification. The manipulations are then iteratively reduced until they are imperceptible, while still triggering the adversarial attack [30]–[37]. Since these attack aims to estimate the adversarial example at the classification boundary, therefore, these attacks are also known as boundary attacks. In these attacks, the attack starts from a seed input from the target class (in case of a targeted attack) or any other incorrect output class (for random misclassification). The algorithm progresses iteratively towards the decision boundary of the true output class for input under attack. The objective is not only to reach the decision boundary, but also to explore the different parts of the boundary to ensure that a minimum amount of noise is being added to the input. Hence, no knowledge of the DNN's gradients, parameters, or output scores is required for a successful attack. However, the cost of these attacks in terms of the number of queries is very large.

To reduce the number of queries, a *Resource Efficient Decision-based attack (FaDec-attack)* [38] finds targeted and un-targeted adversarial perturbations at a reduced computational cost. Like the boundary attack, a seed input from an incorrect class is chosen. The seed is iteratively modified to minimize its distance to the classification boundary of the original input. To reduce the computational cost of these attacks, adaptive step sizes are used to reach the smallest perturbation in the least number of iterations.

B. Poisoning (Causative) Attacks

In these attacks, the attacker manipulates the training algorithm, un-trained model, training dataset to influence, or corrupt the ML model itself. Based on the targeted components of the training process, these attacks can be categorized as dataset poisoning and model poisoning attacks (see Table I).

- *Dataset Poisoning:* In these attacks, attacker manipulate the training dataset by adding patches (tailored noise) or randomly distributed noise [39]–[44], [48]. These poisoned images influence different parameters of the DNN model such that it performs either target misclassification or maximizes the classification error. Since these attacks introduce the backdoors in the trained network that can be exploited during inference, therefore, these attacks are also known as backdoor attacks.
- *Model Poisoning:* Another type of causative attack is to slightly modify the DNN architecture such that for a particular trigger, it performs either target misclassification or maximizes the classification error [46][47].

IV. PRACTICAL IMPLICATION OF EVASION ATTACKS

In adversarial attacks, the attack noise must be large enough to be captured by the acquisition device (for instance, camera) but

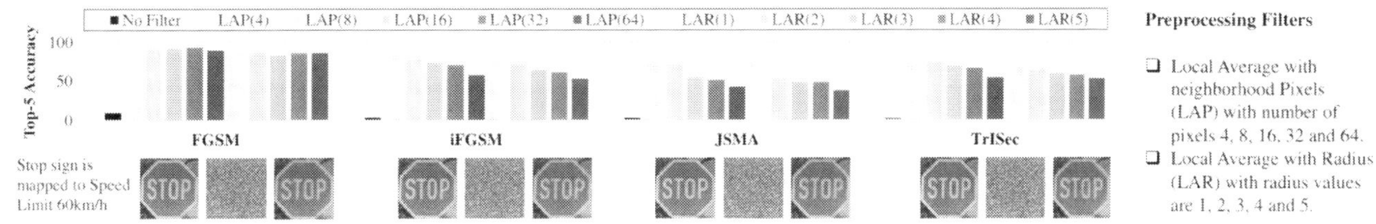

Figure 4. Effects of the preprocessing filters on some white-box adversarial attacks. It can be observed that introducing a simple low-pass filter can significantly impact the robustness of the adversarial attack. For example, in all attacks, the top-5 accuracy increases significantly, i.e., 10% to 89% with the addition of input preprocessing. However, as the smoothing factor of the filters surpasses a certain threshold, the top-5 accuracy started to decrease. The reason behind this behavior is that after this threshold, the filters started to affect the important features.

imperceptible to the subjective analysis (by a human observer). A complete pipeline of the DNN-based classifier consists of an input sensor (for instance, a camera), a preprocessing module (e.g., filters), and a classifier. The robustness of the adversarial attacks depends upon the attacker's access to the different parts of the pipeline stages.

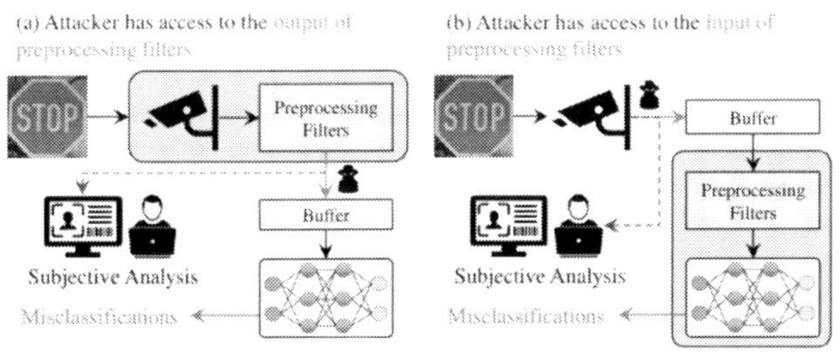

Figure 5. Practical implications of the adversarial attacks with respect to the attacker access. (a) Attack Model I: the attacker has access to the output of preprocessing filters. (b) Attack Model II: the attacker has access to the input of preprocessing filters. Note, for a successful attack, the adversarial noise should be robust to environmental changes.

Traditionally, the adversarial attacks assumed that the attacker has access to the pre-processed input, as shown in Figure 5(a). However, in real-world scenarios, it is very difficult to get access to the output of the preprocessing. The more realistic attack model considers the attacker to have access to the input of the preprocessing module (see Figure 5(b)), for example, the camera is compromised, and it is generating and adding the adversarial noise. To analyze the impact of attack model II, we perform an analysis with low pass filters as a preprocessing module for basic white-box adversarial attacks, i.e., FGSM, JSMA, iFGSM, and TrISec. In this analysis, we choose the two commonly used noise filters: *Local Average with neighborhood Pixels* (LAP) and *Local Average with Radius* (LAR). Figure 4 shows the impact of preprocessing filters on the adversarial attack and the key observations from the analysis are as follows:

1) In the case of attack model II, the filters significantly reduces the effectiveness of all the implemented adversarial attacks.
2) The increase in the number of neighboring pixels in the LAP filter worsens the performance of the DNN because it affects the key features of the input. Similarly, an increase in the LAR filter radius debilitates the performance of the DNN.

Based on the above-mentioned observations, in the context of adversarial attacks, we identify the following research directions:

1) To increase the robustness of adversarial attacks, it is imperative to incorporate the effects of preprocessing modules. For example, recently, researchers have presented that by incorporating the effects of preprocessing filters in optimization algorithms of existing adversarial attacks, the robustness of these attacks can be increased [49]. Although this analysis considers only white-box attacks, it can effectively be extended to black-box attacks.
2) On the other hand, under a particular attack setting, preprocessing modules can also be used to nullify the adversarial attacks. For example, quantization [50], Sobel filters [51] and transformations [52] are used to defend against adversarial attacks. However, the scope of these defenses is very limited, and most of them are breakable using black-box attacks. Therefore, it is a dire need to explore the practical implications of the adversarial attack to develop more powerful defenses.

V. Fault-Injection Attacks

Similar to adversarial attacks where the input to a DNN is modified to achieve misclassification, network parameters or computations can also be modified to achieve the same goal. Fault-injection attacks on DNNs refer to the attacks where an attacker tries to manipulate the output of a DNN by injecting faults in its parameters or in the data or control path of the hardware. There are several techniques that can be used for injecting faults, e.g., variations in voltage/clock signal, EM interference and heavy-ion radiation.

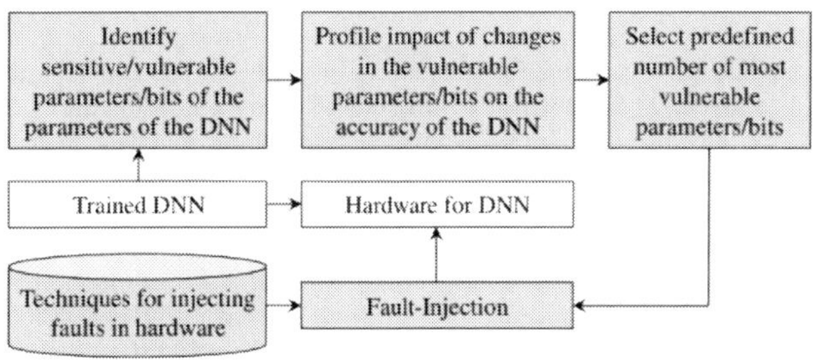

Figure 6. An overview of the design methodology for fault-injection attacks on ML-based systems.

Several studies have been conducted towards modifying the network parameters to attack DNNs. Liu et al. in [53] proposed two fault injection attacks, i.e., Single Bias Attack (SBA) and Gradient Descent Attack (GDA). Since the output of the DNNs is highly dependent on the biases in the output layer, SBA is realized by increasing only a single bias value corresponding to the neuron designated for the adversarial class. SBA is designed for the cases where the stealthiness of the attack is not necessary. For cases where stealthiness is important, GDA has been proposed that uses gradient descent to find the set of parameters to be modified and applies modifications to only some selected ones to minimize the impact of the injected faults on input patterns other than the specified one. Along the same direction, Zhao et al. in [54] proposed fault sneaking attack where they apply Alternating Direction Method of Multipliers (ADMM) [55] to optimize the attack while ensuring that the classification of images other than the ones specified is unaffected and the modification in the parameters is minimum. A generic flow of the fault-injection attacks on DNNs is shown in Figure 6.

To increase the stealthiness of the attack, Rakin et al. in [56] proposed a methodology, Bit-Flip Attack (BFA), for attacking DNNs by flipping a small number of bits in the weights of the DNN. The bit-flips can be performed through Row-Hammer attack [57][58] or laser injection [59][60] when the weights are in the DRAM or the SRAM of the system, respectively. BFA focuses on identifying the most vulnerable bits in a given DNN that can maximize the accuracy degradation while requiring a very small number of bit-flips in the binary representation of the parameters of the DNN. It employs gradient ranking and progressive search to locate the most vulnerable bits. It is designed for quantized neural networks, i.e., where the weight magnitude is constrained based on the fixed-point representation. For floating-point representation, even a single bit-flip at the most significant location of the exponent of one of the weights of the DNN can result in the network generating completely random output [5] (see Figure 7). The results showed that BFA causes the ResNet-18 network to generate completely random output with only 13 bit-flips on the ImageNet dataset. Figure 9 presents the results for the AlexNet and the ResNet-50 networks under BFA.

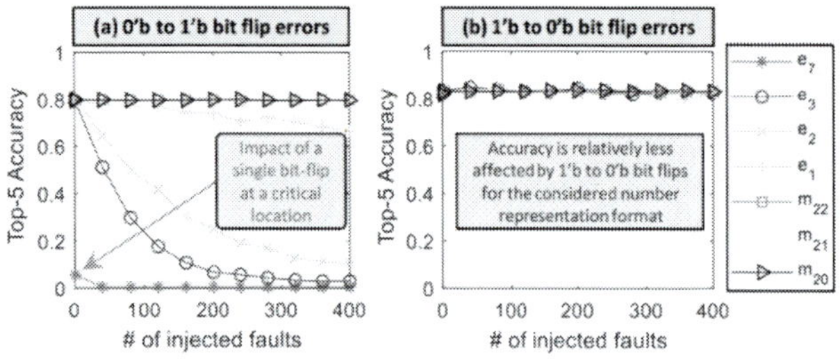

Figure 7. Impact of bit-flips in the weights of the VGG-f network on its classification accuracy on ImageNet dataset [5]. Figure 8 shows the number representation format used for weights and activations for the analysis.

Studies have also been conducted for injecting faults in the computations during the execution of the DNNs. Towards this, Breier et al. in [61] performed an analysis of using a laser to inject faults during the execution of activation functions in a DNN to achieve misclassification. They focused on the instruction skip/change attack model, as it is one of the most basic (and repeatable) attacks for microcontrollers [62], to target four different activation functions, i.e., ReLU, sigmoid, Tanh and softmax. Batina et al. in [63] showed that it is possible to reverse engineer a neural network using a side-channel analysis, e.g., by measuring the power consumption of the device during the execution of a DNN. Therefore, the attack proposed by Breier et al. can be employed even when the DNN is unknown.

VI. Research Directions

Although DNNs are rapidly evolving and becoming an integral part of the decision-making process in CPS. However, the security vulnerabilities of DNNs, e.g., adversarial and fault-injection attacks, raises several concerns regarding their use in CPS. Therefore, stronger defenses against these attacks are required. Towards this, we identify some of the critical research directions:

1) Several defenses have been proposed to counter the adversarial attacks [49]–[51]. However, all the available countermeasures are effective only against a particular type of adversarial attacks. This calls for a deeper understanding of the existing attacks, to enable the design of an optimal defense.
2) The security measures proposed for adversarial attacks are mainly effective against only a subclass of these attacks. Therefore, formal verification of DNNs is emerging as a promising approach to ensure adversarial robustness of DNNs [6][64], which can also help in developing verifiable security measures. The sound mathematical reasoning of formal verification techniques can provide complete and reliable security guarantees to protect DNNs against adversarial attacks.
3) To improve the resilience of DNNs against hardware-induced reliability threats, several low-cost fault-mitigation techniques have been proposed, e.g., range restriction-based fault mitigation [65][66]. These techniques have the potential of acting as a strong countermeasure against fault-injection attacks. However, their effectiveness as a countermeasure has not been studied so far. Alongside security, such studies can also help in further improving the reliability of DNN-based systems.

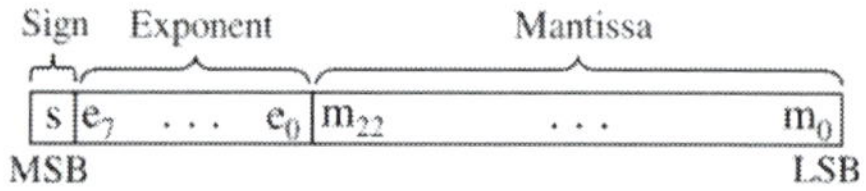

Figure 8. Single-precision floating-point representation

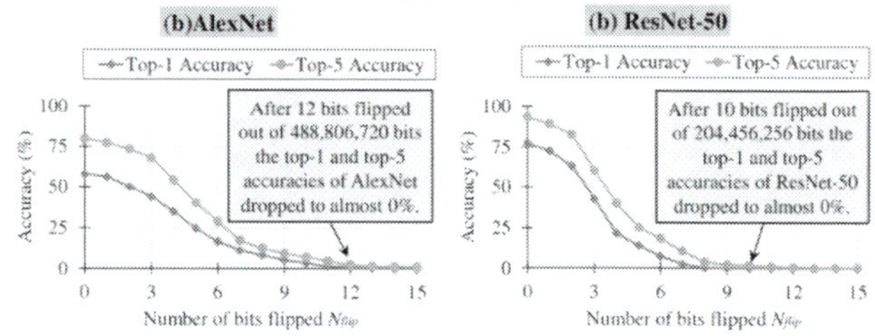

Figure 9. Accuracy vs. the number of bit-flips (N_{flip}) under BFA, for the AlexNet and the ResNet-50 on the ImageNet dataset (data source: [56]).

Acknowledgment

This work is supported in parts by the Austrian Research Promotion Agency (FFG) and the Austrian Federal Ministry for Transport, Innovation, and Technology (BMVIT) under the "ICT of the Future" project, IoT4CPS: Trustworthy IoT for Cyber-Physical Systems.

References

[1] M. Shafique et al., "An overview of next-generation architectures for machine learning: Roadmap, opportunities and challenges in the IoT era," in IEEE DATE, 2018, pp. 827–832.
[2] F. Kriebel, S. Rehman, M. A. Hanif, F. Khalid, and M. Shafique, "Robustness for smart cyber physical systems and internet-of-things: From adaptive robustness methods to reliability and security for machine learning," in IEEE ISVLSI, 2018, pp. 581–586.
[3] A. Marchisio et al., "Deep learning for edge computing: Current trends, cross-layer optimizations, and open research challenges," in IEEE ISVLSI, 2019, pp. 553–559.
[4] J. J. Zhang et al., "Building robust machine learning systems: Current progress, research challenges, and opportunities," in IEEE/ACM DAC, 2019, pp. 1–4.
[5] M. A. Hanif, F. Khalid, R. V. W. Putra, S. Rehman, and M. Shafique, "Robust machine learning systems: Reliability and security for deep neural networks," in IEEE IOLTS, 2018, pp. 257–260.
[6] M. Shafique et al., "Robust machine learning systems: Challenges, current trends, perspectives, and the road ahead," IEEE Design & Test, vol. 37, no. 2, 2020, pp. 30–57.
[7] S. Houben, J. Stallkamp, J. Salmen, M. Schlipsing, and C. Igel, "Detection of Traffic Signs in Real-World Images: The German Traffic Sign Detection Benchmark," in IEEE IJCNN, no. 1288, 2013.
[8] A. Kurakin, I. Goodfellow, and S. Bengio, "Explaining and harnessing adversarial examples," arXiv:1412.6572, 2014.
[9] ——, "Adversarial examples in the physical world," arXiv:1607.02533, 2016.

[10] A. Madry, A. Makelov, L. Schmidt, D. Tsipras, and A. Vladu, "Towards deep learning models resistant to adversarial attacks," arXiv:1706.06083, 2017.
[11] F. Croce and M. Hein, "Reliable evaluation of adversarial robustness with an ensemble of diverse parameter-free attacks," arXiv:2003.01690, 2020.
[12] N. Papernot, P. McDaniel, S. Jha, M. Fredrikson, Z. B. Celik, and A. Swami, "The limitations of deep learning in adversarial settings," in IEEE Euro S&P, 2016, pp. 372–387.
[13] N. Inkawhich, M. Inkawhich, Y. Chen, and H. Li, "Adversarial attacks for optical flow-based action recognition classifiers," arXiv:1811.11875, 2018.
[14] N. Carlini and D. Wagner, "Towards evaluating the robustness of neural networks," in IEEE S&P, 2017, pp. 39–57.
[15] S.-M. Moosavi-Dezfooli, A. Fawzi, and P. Frossard, "Deepfool: a simple and accurate method to fool deep neural networks," in IEEE/CVF CVPR, 2016, pp. 2574–2582.
[16] S.-M. Moosavi-Dezfooli et al., "Universal adversarial perturbations," in IEEE/CVF CVPR, 2017, pp. 1765–1773.
[17] U. Jang, X. Wu, and S. Jha, "Objective metrics and gradient descent algorithms for adversarial examples in machine learning," in ACM ACSAC, 2017, pp. 262–277.
[18] S. Sabour, Y. Cao, F. Faghri, and D. J. Fleet, "Adversarial manipulation of deep representations," arXiv preprint arXiv:1511.05122, 2015.
[19] T. B. Brown, D. Mané, A. Roy, M. Abadi, and J. Gilmer, "Adversarial patch," arXiv:1712.09665, 2017.
[20] A. Liu et al., "Perceptual-sensitive gan for generating adversarial patches," in AAAI, vol. 33, 2019, pp. 1028–1035.
[21] P.-Y. Chen, Y. Sharma, H. Zhang, J. Yi, and C.-J. Hsieh, "Ead: elastic-net attacks to deep neural networks via adversarial examples," in AAAI, 2018.
[22] X. Liu, H. Yang, Z. Liu, L. Song, H. Li, and Y. Chen, "Dpatch: An adversarial patch attack on object detectors," arXiv:1806.02299, 2018.
[23] K. Grosse, D. Pfaff, M. T. Smith, and M. Backes, "The limitations of model uncertainty in adversarial settings," arXiv:1812.02606, 2018.
[24] E. Wong, F. R. Schmidt, and J. Z. Kolter, "Wasserstein adversarial examples via projected sinkhorn iterations," arXiv:1902.07906, 2019.
[25] A. Ghiasi, A. Shafahi, and T. Goldstein, "Breaking certified defenses: Semantic adversarial examples with spoofed robustness certificates," arXiv:2003.08937, 2020.
[26] F. Khalid, M. A. Hanif, S. Rehman, R. Ahmed, and M. Shafique, "Trisec: training data-unaware imperceptible security attacks on deep neural networks," in IEEE IOLTS, 2019, pp. 188–193.
[27] P.-Y. Chen, H. Zhang, Y. Sharma, J. Yi, and C.-J. Hsieh, "Zoo: Zeroth order optimization based black-box attacks to deep neural networks without training substitute models," in ACM WAIS, 2017, pp. 15–26.
[28] N. Narodytska and S. P. Kasiviswanathan, "Simple black-box adversarial perturbations for deep networks," arXiv:1612.06299, 2016.
[29] T. Brunner, F. Diehl, and A. Knoll, "Copy and paste: A simple but effective initialization method for black-box adversarial attacks," arXiv:1906.06086, 2019.
[30] J. Chen, M. I. Jordan, and M. J. Wainwright, "Hopskipjumpattack: A query-efficient decision-based attack," in IEEE S&P, 2020, pp. 1277–1294.
[31] M. Cheng, T. Le, P.-Y. Chen, J. Yi, H. Zhang, and C.-J. Hsieh, "Query-efficient hard-label black-box attack: An optimization-based approach," arXiv:1807.04457, 2018.
[32] W. Brendel, J. Rauber, and M. Bethge, "Decision-based adversarial attacks: Reliable attacks against black-box machine learning models," arXiv:1712.04248, 2017.
[33] H. Li, X. Xu, X. Zhang, S. Yang, and B. Li, "Qeba: Query-efficient boundary-based blackbox attack," in IEEE/CVF CVPR, 2020, pp. 1221–1230.
[34] Y. Liu, S.-M. Moosavi-Dezfooli, and P. Frossard, "A geometry-inspired decision-based attack," in IEEE/CVF CVPR, 2019, pp. 4890–4898.
[35] D. V. Vargas and S. Kotyan, "Robustness assessment for adversarial machine learning: Problems, solutions and a survey of current neural networks and defenses," arXiv:1906.06026, 2019.
[36] M. Andriushchenko, F. Croce, N. Flammarion, and M. Hein, "Square attack: a query-efficient black-box adversarial attack via random search," arXiv:1912.00049, 2019.
[37] J. Su, D. V. Vargas, and K. Sakurai, "One pixel attack for fooling deep neural networks," IEEE TEC, vol. 23, no. 5, 2019, pp. 828–841.
[38] F. Khalid, H. Ali, M. A. Hanif, S. Rehman, R. Ahmed, and M. Shafique, "Fadec: A fast decision-based attack for adversarial machine learning," 2020, pp. 1–8.
[39] H. Xiao, B. Biggio, B. Nelson, H. Xiao, C. Eckert, and F. Roli, "Support vector machines under adversarial label contamination," Neurocomputing, vol. 160, 2015, pp. 53–62.
[40] B. Biggio, B. Nelson, and P. Laskov, "Poisoning attacks against support vector machines," arXiv:1206.6389, 2012.
[41] C. Zhu et al., "Transferable clean-label poisoning attacks on deep neural nets," arXiv:1905.05897, 2019.
[42] A. Shafahi et al., "Poison frogs! targeted clean-label poisoning attacks on neural networks," in NIPS, 2018, pp. 6103–6113.
[43] T. Gu, K. Liu, B. Dolan-Gavitt, and S. Garg, "Badnets: Evaluating backdooring attacks on deep neural networks," IEEE Access, vol. 7, 2019, pp. 47 230–47 244.
[44] X. Chen, C. Liu, B. Li, K. Lu, and D. Song, "Targeted backdoor attacks on deep learning systems using data poisoning," arXiv:1712.05526, 2017.
[45] A. Salem, R. Wen, M. Backes, S. Ma, and Y. Zhang, "Dynamic backdoor attacks against machine learning models," arXiv:2003.03675, 2020.
[46] K. Kurita, P. Michel, and G. Neubig, "Weight poisoning attacks on pre-trained models," arXiv:2004.06660, 2020.
[47] M. Fang, X. Cao, J. Jia, and N. Gong, "Local model poisoning attacks to byzantine-robust federated learning," arXiv:1911.11815, 2019.
[48] M. Jagielski, A. Oprea, B. Biggio, C. Liu, C. Nita-Rotaru, and B. Li, "Manipulating machine learning: Poisoning attacks and countermeasures for regression learning," in IEEE S&P, 2018, pp. 19–35.
[49] F. Khalid, M. A. Hanif, S. Rehman, J. Qadir, and M. Shafique, "Fademl: understanding the impact of pre-processing noise filtering on adversarial machine learning," in IEEE DATE, 2019, pp. 902–907.
[50] F. Khalid et al., "Qusecnets: Quantization-based defense mechanism for securing deep neural network against adversarial attacks," in IEEE IOLTS, 2019, pp. 182–187.
[51] H. Ali et al., "Sscnets: Robustifying dnns using secure selective convolutional filters," IEEE Design & Test, vol. 37, no. 2, 2019, pp. 58–65.
[52] E. Raff, J. Sylvester, S. Forsyth, and M. McLean, "Barrage of random transforms for adversarially robust defense," in IEEE CVPR, 2019.
[53] Y. Liu, L. Wei, B. Luo, and Q. Xu, "Fault injection attack on deep neural network," in 2017 IEEE/ACM ICCAD, 2017, pp. 131–138.
[54] P. Zhao, S. Wang, C. Gongye, Y. Wang, Y. Fei, and X. Lin, "Fault sneaking attack: A stealthy framework for misleading deep neural networks," in ACM/IEEE DAC, 2019, pp. 1–6.
[55] Q. Liu, X. Shen, and Y. Gu, "Linearized admm for nonconvex nonsmooth optimization with convergence analysis," IEEE Access, vol. 7, 2019, pp. 76 131–76 144.
[56] A. S. Rakin, Z. He, and D. Fan, "Bit-flip attack: Crushing neural network with progressive bit search," in IEEE ICCV, 2019, pp. 1211–1220.
[57] Y. Kim et al., "Flipping bits in memory without accessing them: An experimental study of dram disturbance errors," ACM SIGARCH Computer Architecture News, vol. 42, no. 3, 2014, pp. 361–372.
[58] K. Razavi, B. Gras, E. Bosman, B. Preneel, C. Giuffrida, and H. Bos, "Flip feng shui: Hammering a needle in the software stack," in USENIX security, 2016, pp. 1–18.
[59] B. Selmke, S. Brummer, J. Heyszl, and G. Sigl, "Precise laser fault injections into 90 nm and 45 nm sram-cells," in Springer ICSCRA, 2015, pp. 193–205.
[60] M. Agoyan, J.-M. Dutertre, A.-P. Mirbaha, D. Naccache, A.-L. Ribotta, and A. Tria, "How to flip a bit?" in IEEE IOLTS, 2010, pp. 235–239.
[61] J. Breier, X. Hou, D. Jap, L. Ma, S. Bhasin, and Y. Liu, "Practical fault attack on deep neural networks," in ACM CCS, 2018, pp. 2204–2206.
[62] J. Breier et al., D. Jap, and C.-N. Chen, "Laser profiling for the back-side fault attacks: with a practical laser skip instruction attack on aes," in ACM WCPS, 2015, pp. 99–103.
[63] L. Batina, S. Bhasin, D. Jap, and S. Picek, "Csi neural network: Using side-channels to recover your artificial neural network information," arXiv:1810.09076, 2018.
[64] M. Naseer, M. F. Minhas, F. Khalid, M. A. Hanif, O. Hasan, and M. Shafique, "Fannet: formal analysis of noise tolerance, training bias and input sensitivity in neural networks," in IEEE DATE, 2020, pp. 666–669.
[65] Z. Chen, G. Li, and K. Pattabiraman, "Ranger: Boosting error resilience of deep neural networks through range restriction," arXiv:2003.13874, 2020.
[66] L.-H. Hoang, M. A. Hanif, and M. Shafique, "Ft-clipact: Resilience analysis of deep neural networks and improving their fault tolerance using clipped activation," in IEEE DATE, 2020, pp. 1241–1246.

Cyber and Emergent Technologies

Current and Future Ramifications

Joshua A. Sipper
Air Force Cyber College
Air University
Maxwell AFB, AL, United States
Email: joshua.sipper.1@us.af.mil

Abstract— **We as a cyber community are now living in a cyber meta-reality (a reality about realities) where scientific and technological advances such as microscopic machines, subatomic energy manipulation, and autonomous technologies, heretofore only imagined in science fiction tales are on the verge of practical use. As the need for new, better, and more secure methods of implementing cyber increases, the unfettered desire for greater bandwidth, stronger encryption, and more rapid processing naturally follows. If the cyber community is to capitalize on new technologies, however, we need to stay acquainted with these emergent technologies and understand their ramifications. Otherwise, we stand the chance of either missing opportunities to advance or being trampled by those who do. Today scientists and technologists are buzzing about quantum entanglement, non-linear wave propagation, and Metal Organic Frameworks (MOF). The United States is in a race to the finish to make the potentialities of these amazing ideas, realities. This paper examines four very specialized technological areas and draws on these technologies to construct a cohesive narrative regarding their interoperability in order to highlight the necessity and ramifications of each area's contribution to a holistic technological scaffold. Artificial Intelligence (AI) and Machine Learning (ML) are of course, an increasingly conjoined capability with great promise, yet not fully realized. Emergent technologies related to security such as quantum encryption and multi-factor authentication are rapidly finding their place in the cyber meta-reality. Quantum computing, related to the theory of quantum entanglement and quantum encryption, will likely deliver processing and bandwidth options far beyond current possibilities. Finally, nanotechnologies such as graphene and membrane technology are already in production in some applications and will no doubt become a critical enabler of the entirety of the aforementioned technologies. Additionally, the concept of the cyber microbiome is introduced for consideration.**

Keywords- ***quantum, nanotechnology, meta-reality, microbiome, artificial, machine.***

I. INTRODUCTION

In the cyber community, emergent technologies are a huge factor to be considered as the pace of technological development not only advances cyber capabilities, but also rapidly adds layers of complexity to the already wicked cyber puzzle. Abounding studies, experiments, and research in fields like particle physics (quanta) continuing under the auspices of Conseil Européen pour la Recherche Nucléaire (CERN), coupled with emergent nanotechnologies such as graphene and MOF, point to a near future where processing speed, bandwidth, and the full spectrum implementation of ML and AI can become realities. These possibilities are currently being expressed mostly within their own frameworks as researchers continue to nail down their mechanics, interoperability, and necessary requirements. However, these once embryonic hypotheses are now being demonstrated as realities through scientific theory development within the traditional construct of reproducible laboratory experimentation.

So, what does this mean for us in the cyber community and how can we as a community of practitioners, policy makers, and researchers benefit from these new technologies? How will these new technologies increase the power of cyber now and into the future? How will the cyber meta-reality (Figure 1) change and grow as a result of this technical dynamism? Perhaps most importantly, how will adversaries and threats to peace use the same technologies and how will we defeat them? We cannot pretend to have all of the answers, but we can begin the conversation and explore the possibilities.

Figure 1. Cyber Meta-Reality.

Of course, before we can begin to probe these questions, we must first have a basis of comprehension concerning the technologies that generated said questions. The theories, technologies, and capabilities are beyond doubt complex, still forming, and even dangerous. There are numerous technologies two or more decades old that are no longer emergent, but well established such as stealth, precision and machine automation, drone technology, and others. All of these have upended how warfare and other technologies are used and continue to develop. Developing technologies such as AI and ML are especially cogent contributors as they have been proven to increase efficiency and speed up decision cycles significantly [1]. The necessity and desire that accompanies human intellect drives them onward, moment by moment. Why would anyone want to understand the fundamental building blocks of matter? Because it answers important questions about the creation and inner workings of our cosmos. Because the power generated by separating these basic building blocks has led us into a resplendently wonderful and terrifyingly awful nuclear age. Because, we are curious.

For the cyber community, it comes down to power; the power to continue the creation and expansion of and capabilities within the meta-reality we call cyberspace. The same can be said concerning the nanoparticle constructs of graphene and MOFs. The ability to use these types of nano-constructs as waveguides, conductors, transistors, circuits, and many more applications can provide cool, fast processing and bandwidth operation impossible with the use of legacy electronics. Then, there is the consideration of how both quantum and physical nanotech affect the growth and application of AI and ML. What space will these potentialities grow to inhabit once they are enabled through a seemingly infinite power, processing, and dissemination stream? One might see visions of life, death, or something altogether unimaginable to us right now. But, either way the power offered through these capabilities will likely shape the future of cyber and global communications, politics, commerce, and conflict.

In the following sections, we will first discuss AI and ML and their marked effects on technology no and into the future. Emergent security will be framed in the second section, relating how various technologies are leading to increased security across the cyber meta-reality. In the third section, the amazing rise and potential of quantum computing will be presented. Finally, nanotechnology will be explored in the fourth section, giving insight into how this field affects all of the other areas and has led in concert with these areas to another type of cyber meta-reality that includes a symbiotic, technological multiverse characterized as the cyber microbiome.

II. Artificial Intelligence and Machine Learning

AI and ML are a developing construct still not fully realized within the greater cyber framework. Undoubtedly, even when the cyber meta-reality does finally capitalize on these capabilities, there will be another mountain to climb. However, we must for now consider the mountains before us in that AI and ML are certainly developing and growing in strength and power, capability and usability. With this growth comes several positive and negative ramifications. While AI increases the intelligence level of programs at an individual and collective level, it also adds layers of complexity that must be managed and mitigated (Kott, 2018). AI and ML have been demonstrated on numerous occasions as tools useful in the areas of parsing and grouping data (ML) and actual decision-making (AI). "We have a variety of learning mechanisms for both symbolic and non-symbolic AI that allow autonomous agents to improve their performance and adapt to changing environmental conditions" [2]. AI and ML have found some applicability in the field of intelligent autonomous agents such as the self-driving car experiments conducted by Google and Tesla. Agencies such as DARPA are doubling-down on these studies by going forward with the application of AI and ML on the battlefield in the form of autonomous air, land, sea, space, and cyber capabilities such as drones and in the case of cyber, code. ML and AI are similar, but distinct concepts covering multiple capabilities and constructs. Therefore, it is important to understand their subtleties.

In general, AI is divided into two varied approaches: symbolic and non-symbolic; each represents knowledge in fundamentally different ways, leading to outcomes specific to the respective approach [2]. It is important to understand these two categories in order to properly arrange AI and ML in a construct that supports co-functionality. "The systems developed as part of the DARPA Cyber Grand Challenge are primarily symbolic AI systems. These automated reasoners can identify vulnerabilities in software services, develop a patch, and deploy the patch at machine speed" [2]. The use of symbolic AI is labor intensive and includes the creation of a large matrix of interrelated information to get the AI started. However, as the AI begins to make connections and form heuristic bonds, the system can grow and adapt on its own. The same is true to a great extent for non-symbolic systems which focus instead on the patterns of learning in data for classifying objects, predicting future results, or clustering similar sets of data [2]. However, the true power of AI and ML is not their individual components, but what they can accomplish together. Such is the case in the world of intelligent autonomous agents.

Intelligent autonomous agents have been in development for some time, but are only now coming to fruition as mechanisms capable of the complex decision-making processes necessary for optimal, real-world performance. "The proliferation of intelligent agents is the emerging reality of warfare, and they will form an ever-growing fraction of total military assets. The sheer quantity of targetable friendly agents… make intelligent, autonomous cyber defense agent a necessity on the battlefield of the future" [3]. With the overlap of AI, ML, and Deep Learning (DL) capabilities across the globe, U.S. and NATO capabilities must not only keep pace with this trend, but outstrip it in order to maintain a leading edge against adversaries. This overlap is represented in Figure 2 Artificial Intelligence, Machine Learning, Deep Learning Overlap for Autonomous Agents. Another way to accomplish this goal is through human-machine partnering through cyber interfaces interleaved with AI and ML capable technologies. Human-machine teaming has become a huge topic of research and practice recently, especially as it relates to Defensive Cyberspace Operations (DCO). This teaming aspect has led to a marked need for autonomous, synthetic agents that can assist in processing, targeting, and gap-filling [2]. Through these human-cyber interactions, filtering, parsing, and decision-making can be funneled in such a way to speed up processes such as targeting and battle damage assessment, a vital feedback stream in today's joint all-domain military environments. Of course, as with all emergent capabilities, a note of caution and reflection must be considered. Questions concerning whether autonomous agents might eventually be candidates for "personhood" and held liable for accidents or purposeful destruction have arisen in light of the trend toward cyber autonomy. The European Parliament has even gone so far as to publish a report with "recommendations to the Commission on Civil Law Rules on Robotics" asking questions regarding how to categorize AI and ML enabled autonomous agents [4]. Regardless of these questions, however, the journey toward AI and ML in myriad applications is underway and there is no turning back.

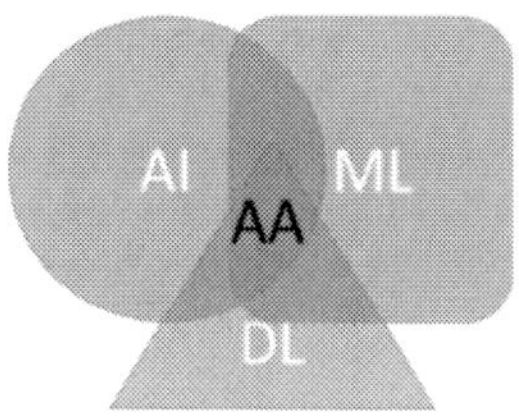

Figure 2. Artificial Intelligence, Machine Learning, Deep Learning Overlap for Autonomous Agents.

III. Emergent Security

Security issues will obviously continue to be paramount in importance as the cyber community goes forward. Protecting information from integrity attacks like man-in-the-middle and infiltrations by using existing encryption standards will only work for so long as adversaries continue to develop more advanced cracking technologies, some of which will undoubtedly include quantum computing capabilities (to be discussed in the following section). Emergent capabilities such as quantum encryption and multi-factor authentication offer the best options currently understood for defense against imminent cracking attempts.

Quantum encryption is a tool still in development that has spurred from the underlying mathematical and physics modeling and applications of particle physics and quantum theory. "A quantum procedure known as quantum cryptography or quantum key distribution can do key distribution so that the communication security cannot be compromised. The idea is based on the quantum principle that observing a quantum system will disturb the system being observed" [5]. In quantum key distribution, the disturbance of the system occurs as a result of a relationship called quantum entanglement. Quantum computers implement superposition states and quantum entanglements to perform simultaneous calculations and produce consequential calculated results. The highly efficient character of quantum entanglement and superposition are the characteristics that enable quantum computers to be exponentially faster, consistently outperforming classical computers in several areas [5]. The idea is that when two particles of matter, in this case most probably subatomic particles called fermions, become related or entangled in a relationship-dependent state, if one particle changes in state, the other one does as well; this is true no matter how far apart the particles are in physical distance which makes the application of state changes between the particles especially useful for quantum encryption and computing.

Multi-factor authentication is another area important to integrity within the cyber meta-reality. While the concept of two-factor authentication is presently in use across a wide array of devices and systems, multi-factor authentication is still a growing area. "Two-factor authentication has reduced incidences of fraud, including identity theft, in e-commerce. Consumers are no longer at high risk from thieves due to the compromise at a single point of failure in a transaction" [6]. However, as thieves and adversaries find ways to exploit weaknesses and circumvent two-factor authentication, the opportunity for deeper layering of authentication is growing. Several areas of authentication are possible according to Waters: location, possession, access, proximity, behavioral, confirmation, witnessed, and radio. By using these techniques together, multiple factors can add strength, thereby denying access to and possible manipulation of data.

IV. Quantum Computing

Probably the most difficult expanse of emergent technology to comprehend and implement is quantum computing. This is due mostly to the profound and sometimes murky depths one must take into the areas of particle physics and applied mathematics, but also because the technologies that enable the manipulation of subatomic particles that make quantum computing possible are still developing and being modeled both mathematically and through actual laboratory experimentation. Information theory and quantum mechanics have historically been separate fields, unrelated in most research. However, it has been recognized as increasingly important and vital to bring these two scientific fields of study together in order to advance both. Only through the study of quantum information science can quantum states be understood and manipulated sufficiently and appropriately to perform information transmission and manipulation at the quantum level [7]. Five important concepts of quantum computing must be considered in order to understand how the capability is possible and why it is so powerful and applicable to the meta-reality of cyber. First, we must comprehend the basic fundamentals of a quantum system: "Quantum mechanics depicts phenomena at microscopic level such as position and momentum of an individual particle like an atom or electron, spin of an electron, detection of light photons, and the emission and absorption of light by atoms" [7]. These characteristics and the ability to manipulate the states of subatomic particles by molding these characteristics is what makes quantum computing possible. This leads to the second component of quantum computing, superposition quantum states. In quantum computing, the primary characteristic of superposition is in the computer's ability to process information. In classical computing, the computer must handle ones and zeroes separately and sequentially. However, in quantum computing, the processor handles ones and zeros at the same time, handling matter in a state that sees it as a one and a zero simultaneously [7]. This interlacing of states between subatomic particles is what forms quantum entanglement (mentioned in the previous section). This ability to relate two particles together and make changes at a distance lead to the third area of quantum computing concepts, quantum circuitry: "A quantum computer can be created from a quantum circuit with quantum gates to perform quantum computation and manipulate quantum information" [7]. This capability can only be accomplished through the relationships formed between the particles in order to make necessary changes and distribute those changes throughout the quantum system (see Figure 3 *Quantum Computing Model*). This leads to the central and fourth concept of quantum entanglement: When two particles are entangled, they actually take on each other's properties and behaviors, allowing them to not only change in close proximity, but at a distance by way of an invisible wave function that connects them [7]. This invisible interlinkage is what makes the changes in states over distances possible. This is a very sophisticated and difficult concept to grasp, only further complicated by the fifth and final concept of quantum teleportation: "Quantum teleportation is a process by which we can transfer the state of a qubit from one location to another, without transmitting it through the intervening space" [7]. It is important to understand that although information concerning the change of the state of one particle to another only transfers the change in state and not the particle itself, resulting in a pure information transfer without actually expending the energy and time it would take to transfer the particle as is currently performed in traditional electron transfer computing.

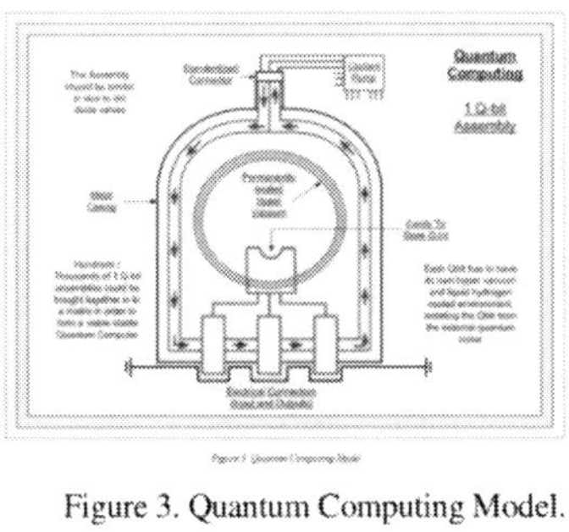

Figure 3. Quantum Computing Model.

Armed with this basic understanding of quantum computing, we can now explore a few of the possibilities conceived through the use of this emergent technology. One of the most valuable capabilities available through the use of quantum computing is termed "quantum speedup". 'Quantum speedup' is simply the phenomenon that is characteristic of quantum computing speeds that allow them to perform certain calculations much faster than traditional computers [8]. This concept evolves from the fact that operations can be accomplished through the use of instantaneous and efficient data state transfer, making the speed potential of quantum computing virtually incalculable. Another area in which quantum computing has been theorized to make an enormous impact is that of collaborative scientific scaffolding to create mechanisms heretofore unheard of: "in theory it would be possible to combine advances in biotechnology, nanotechnology, and quantum computer technology to 'print' new life" [9]. While this might smack of science fiction, this kind of capability may be closer to reality than most understand, as we will see in the following section on nanotechnologies. In fact, Google recently produced a paper about its 53 qubit quantum computer *Sycamore*, titled "Quantum supremacy using a programmable superconducting processor" subsequently reported by *The Verge*, in which was printed, "Google's quantum computer was reportedly able to solve a calculation — proving the randomness of numbers produced by a random number generator — in 3 minutes and 20 seconds that would take the world's fastest traditional supercomputer, Summit, around 10,000 years. This effectively means that the calculation cannot be performed by a traditional computer, making Google the first to demonstrate quantum supremacy" [10]. Add to these advances the impending wave of 5G technologies and the wireless and electromagnetic spectrum (EMS) concerns attached to this ethereal superstructure. Quantum computing offers options for quickly transmitting data at a distance that very well may lead to a quantum 6G capability that far outstrips or possibly supports the 5G instantiation. Quantum properties can likewise support bandwidth traversal between satellites to broaden global data transmission such that hard solutions like undersea cables and hard wired national communications infrastructures could become redundant if not obsolete. Suffice it to say, quantum computing is an area of deep and broad interest in basically every area of life, especially for those of us in the cyber community.

V. NANOTECHNOLOGY

With microcomputers shrinking to smaller and smaller sizes yet offering faster processing, larger storage, wider bandwidth, and greater power, Moore's law is quickly approaching a breaking point. With this reality encroaching on manufacturers and consumers alike, numerous organizations are leveraging new scientific breakthroughs in nanotechnology to deliver the promise of continued lower cost and precipitous technological progress. Of course, the area that is seen to most probabilistically deliver is nanotechnology. Through the discovery and manipulation of such products as graphene and MOFs, materials capable of making the leap downward in size to a level capable of accommodating the attributes necessary for non-linear waveform manipulation, microscopic circuitry, and subatomic particle transmissions necessary for quantum computing are not only possible, but available for experimentation and eventual use. These advances also have direct applicability to advances in AI and ML as the processing, bandwidth, and other system requirements necessary to allow for the rapid acquisition, sorting, filtering, and decision making processes to continue AI and ML potentialities are vital to progression. Similarly, as quantum computing and AI/ML continue to grow, so too will quantum encryption capabilities.

As with quantum computing, it is important to understand some of the mathematical and particle physics concepts undergirding the inner workings of nanotechnology. A great deal of workability is wrapped up in the graphene honeycomb structure (see Figure 4 Graphene Honeycomb Lattice) capable of providing waveform packet containment and direction for subatomic particle manipulation that makes quantum computing viable. "There has been intense interest within the fundamental and applied physics communities in [honeycomb] structures... Graphene, a single atomic layer of carbon atoms, is a two-dimensional structure with carbon atoms located at the sites of honeycomb structures" [11]. To further explain this concept, one must grasp a sometimes comical anecdotal example based on the "nonlinear Schrödinger (NLS) equation" [12]. The story goes that Austrian physicist Erwin Schrödinger's concept of superposition (matter occupying two states simultaneously) can be described through the example of a cat in an enclosure such as a box and with it a device that has a 50% chance of killing the cat. The idea is that until we open the box, we can't state with any degree of certainty whether the cat is alive or dead. So, the cat basically occupies two states (alive and dead) simultaneously. This is a very elementary description of the concept, but it serves as a basic principle of the same issue attached to the ability of a subatomic particle to occupy two states simultaneously which makes quantum entanglement, quantum states, etc. possible. This has been demonstrated in laboratory experiments and through mathematical models such as the ones posited by Fefferman and Weinstein, Ablowitz and Zhu, and Hirokawa and Kosaka. The third team states in their research, "We gave concrete formulae explicitly showing the one-to-one correspondence between every self adjoint extension of the minimal Schrödinger operator and the boundary condition of the wave functions of the Schrôdinger particle. We proved that the boundary conditions are classified into two types: one is characterized by the wave function's perfect reflection at the boundaries and the other by the wave function's imperfect reflection with penetration from one island to another island" [13]. To put this in simpler terms, the outcome was a graphene waveform packet conductor capable of transmitting state data between two subatomic particles whose states had become entangled, thus allowing them to share state data at a distance within a system. This capability is a fundamental part of what creates the conditions necessary for quantum computing.

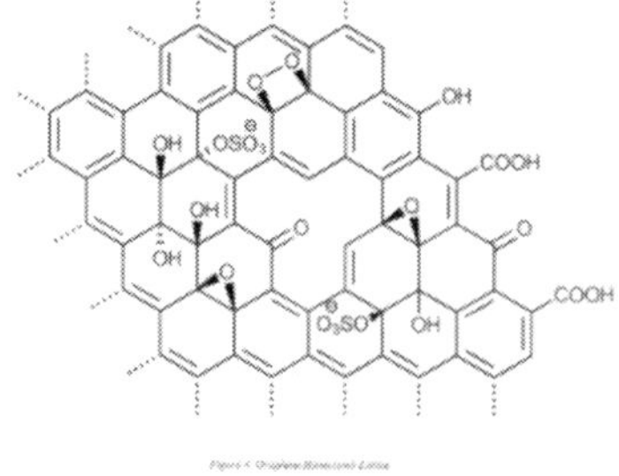

Figure 4. Graphene Honeycomb Lattice.

A separate technology also useful for data transmission is MOFs. "Thin films of inorganic porous crystals, zeolites and MOFs, have been developed for use as sensors, electronic materials, micro-reactors, and separation membranes. In particular, zeolite membranes have been attracting intense research interest as separation materials in the past decades. MOFs have also been studied in the field of membrane research in recent years" [14]. The ability to use these types of materials as sensors, reactors, and other electronic materials highlights their potential in systems architecture, especially in the area of power transfer, have wide applicability in the field of computing. While this technology has been used for decades in other areas, new applications for energy storage such as batteries and high-volume capacitors shows promise in the areas of cyber-enabled electronic drones as well as micro-drone clusters, not to mention portable computing devices.

More specifically as it relates to nanotechnology and nanomaterials is the question of their application to security within cyber systems. "Nanotechnology is expected to be a key enabling technology (KET) to sustain the development of future smart sensing systems and/or Cyber-Physical Systems (CPS) that will jointly integrate sensing, computation, communication and energy management functions" [15]. The applications vary widely with security applications at every layer of cyberspace. However, the most marked areas for advancement are probably authentication and cryptography systems. Currently, nano-optics are in development and have proven to be useful for the most sophisticated security authentication techniques. However, with the advancement of nano-enabled multi-parameter sensors, authentication may in the future include sophisticated access keys based on individualized multi-parameter techniques, including biological signals, which would be difficult to reproduce [15]. The complexity involved in producing authentication systems such as these rests heavily on nano capabilities as do those involved in cryptography. However, the encryption techniques and methods stem from a different angle. Since quantum computers are based on the fundamental information component of the qubit, they actually process information at the atomic level. As quantum technology and computing advance, so will the complexity of encryption, pattern recognition, and other security capabilities, making current cryptographic systems obsolete, if not in drastic need of reengineering [15].

Perhaps one of the most exciting and far reaching nano-enabled capabilities within the cyber meta-reality will be AI and ML. The United States, the National Strategic Computing Initiative (NSCI) made persistent demands on supercomputers to achieve incredible new levels of performance and power efficiency, insisting on the integration of new, more powerful exaflop supercomputers. Exaflop supercomputers will be about 30 times more powerful than today's fastest machines, and their graphics processing units will be able to handle up to ten times more operations per unit of energy compared to existing computers [15]. With processing capabilities like this, AI and ML computation, sorting, filtering, decision-making, and heuristics can be increased dramatically, allowing systems to learn and grow at an exponential rate.

The overall impact of nanotechnologies on the cyber meta-reality leads to amazing possibilities that are already breaching cyberspace and the physical domains as well. With such growth and impact, the introduction of the concept of a cyber microbiome may be of some interest and is worth additional thought and research beyond the scope of this paper. As the Earth and indeed human beings share their chemical/biological physicality with a host of enabling flora and fauna (Earth) and bacteria, fungi, protozoa, and even viruses (humans), the cyber meta-reality is growing into a type of non-physical, yet tangible sphere where stripping away or adding to it could have far-reaching ramifications yet understood. The human microbiome (Figure 5) has most recently been estimated to outnumber human cells by several orders of magnitude [16]. A cyber microbiome (Figure 6.) has already begun to take shape, characterized by viruses, archived data, dark Web outgrowths, and other symbiotic code and applications that will ostensibly grow rapidly as AI and ML begin to create additional code and data in the future. While the cyber microbiome may not be, in some cases, considered a direct part of the created domain we experience, it certainly must not be stripped away, eradicating the good along with the bad. The cyber microbiome is similar to its planetary and human corollaries in that it contains various undetectable components that serve to support its function in difficult to discern ways. For instance, the "dark web" as referenced in Figure 6 is much like the unseen portion of the iceberg under the surface. This indicates another way in which the cyber microbiome is so similar to its antecedents; the cyber microbiome is likely larger than visible cyberspace by many orders of magnitude. These basic understandings about the cyber microbiome serve as area of interest and concern and are worthy of further consideration.

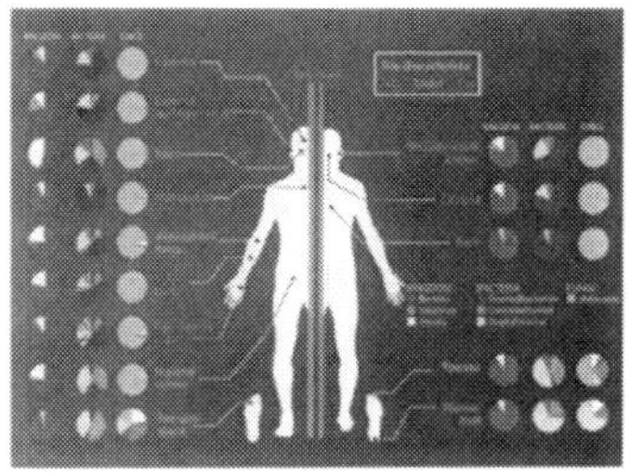

Figure 5. Human Microbiome.

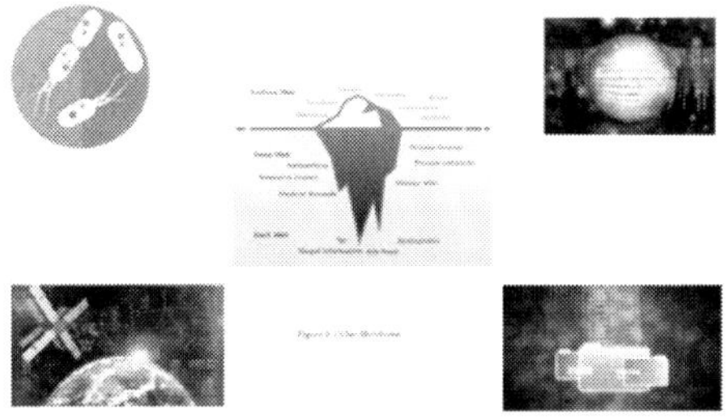

Figure 6. Cyber Microbiome.

VI. CONCLUSION

The world we encounter every day has an undercurrent of possibilities. There are new discoveries just below the skin of our reality and moving through and across what can be seen as the *cyber meta-reality*. With the rise of this cyber world of interconnections and technological upheaval, new capabilities are beginning to shape and expand the horizons of cyber and humans alike. AI and ML are reaching into areas and affecting systems in amazing and sometimes concerning ways. Quantum computing brings with it new capabilities including quantum encryption, enormous storage, unparalleled processing speeds, and seemingly infinite bandwidth. Nanotechnology and nanomaterials are critical enablers of all of these systems, providing the physical constructs to make them possible and practicable. Finally, with the almost organic, but silicone-based *cyber meta-reality* comes the emergence of a *cyber microbiome*; a symbiotic, construct yet unmapped that may lead to further understandings of the *cyber meta-reality* as well as our own physical one.

REFERENCES

[1] M. Guillot, "Emerging Technology: Creator of Worlds" *Strategic Studies Quarterly*, Emerging Technology Special Edition (FALL 2016), Vol. 10, No. 3, pp. 3-8, 2016.

[2] F. Maymí and S. Lathrop, 2018. "AI in Cyberspace: Beyond the Hype," *The Cyber Defense Review* (FALL 2018), Vol. 3, No. 3, pp. 71-82, 2018.

[3] A. Kott. Intelligent Autonomous Agents are Key to Cyber Defense of the Future Army Networks, *The Cyber Defense Review* (FALL 2018), Vol. 3, No. 3, pp. 57-70, 2018.

[4] L. Janssens, *A Prospect Of The Future: How Autonomous Systems May Qualify as Legal Persons*, Amsterdam University Press, 2018.

[5] Y. Wang, "Quantum Computation and Quantum Information," *Statistical Science* (August 2012), Vol. 27, No. 3, pp. 373-394, 2012.

[6] T. Waters, 2017. "Multifactor Authentication – A New Chain of Custody Option for Military Logistics," *The Cyber Defense Review* (FALL 2017), Vol. 2, No. 3, pp. 139-148, 2017.

[7] Y. Wang, "Quantum Computation and Quantum Information," *Statistical Science* (August 2012), Vol. 27, No. 3, pp. 373-394, 2012.

[8] M. Cuffaro, "How-Possibly Explanations in (Quantum) Computer Science," *Philosophy of Science* (December 2015), Vol. 82, No. 5, pp. 737-748, 2015.

[9] M. Guillot, "Emerging Technology: Creator of Worlds" *Strategic Studies Quarterly*, Emerging Technology Special Edition (FALL 2016), Vol. 10, No. 3, pp. 3-8, 2016.

[10] J. Porter, "Google may have just ushered in an era of 'quantum supremacy," *The Verge*, accessed 8 October 2019 from https://www.theverge.com/2019/9/23/20879485/google-quantum-supremacy-qubits-nasa, 2019.

[11] C. Fefferman and M. Weinstein. "Honeycomb Lattice Potentials and Dirac Points," *Journal of the American Mathematical Society* (OCTOBER 2012), Vol. 25, No. 4, pp.1169-1220, 2012.

[12] M. Ablowitz and Y. Zhu, "Nonlinear Waves in Shallow Honeycomb Lattices," *SIAM Journal on Applied Mathematics*, Vol. 72, No. 1, pp. 240-260, 2012.

[13] M. Hirokawa and T. Kosaka, "One-Dimensional Tunnel-Junction Formula for The Schrödinger Particle," *SIAM Journal on Applied Mathematics*, Vol. 73, No. 6, pp. 2247-2261, 2013.

[14] M. Sakai, M. Seshimo, and M. Matsukata. 2018. *Membrane Technology: How, Where, and Why*, Amsterdam University Press.

[15] A. Ionescu, "Nanotechnology and Global Security," *Connections* (Spring 2016), Vol. 15, No. 2, pp. 31-47, 2016.

[16] N. Fierer et al., "From Animalcules to an Ecosystem: Application of Ecological Concepts to the Human Microbiome," *Annual Review of Ecology, Evolution, and Systematics*, Vol. 43, pp. 137-155, 2012.

The Cyber Microbiome and the Cyber Meta-reality

Joshua A. Sipper
Air Force Cyber College
Air University
Maxwell AFB, AL, United States
Email: joshua.sipper.1@us.af.mil

Abstract— **The cyber realm as an entity continues to evolve and grow. As the Earth and indeed human beings share their chemical/biological physicality with a host of enabling flora and fauna (Earth) and bacteria, fungi, protozoa, and even viruses (humans), the cyber meta-reality (a reality of realities) is growing into a type of non-physical, yet tangible sphere where stripping away or adding to it could have far-reaching ramifications not yet understood. The human microbiome has most recently been estimated to outnumber human cells by several orders of magnitude. A cyber microbiome has already begun to take shape, characterized by viruses, archived data, Dark Web outgrowths, and other symbiotic code and applications that will ostensibly grow rapidly as Artificial Intelligence (AI) and Machine Learning (ML) begin to create additional code and data in the future. While the cyber microbiome may not be, in some cases, considered a direct part of the created domain we experience, it certainly must not be stripped away, eradicating the good along with the bad. The cyber microbiome is similar to its planetary and human corollaries in that it contains various undetectable components that serve to support its function in difficult to discern ways. For instance, the Dark Web is much like the unseen portion of the iceberg under the surface. This indicates another way in which the cyber microbiome is so similar to its antecedents; the cyber microbiome is larger than visible cyberspace by many orders of magnitude. This paper examines the concept of the cyber meta-reality with an in-depth analysis of the cyber microbiome and attempts to correlate the symbiotic relationships of these two entities through an examination of the cyberspace most people encounter and the vast underlying cyberspace of which most are oblivious.**

Keywords- cyber; microbiome; meta-reality; archive; code; malware.

I. INTRODUCTION

The cyber meta-reality we currently experience includes several realities being experienced simultaneously. From gaming realities, to research realities, to family realities, and even into the darker realities like pornography and cheating Websites, the cyber meta-reality (see Figure 1) continues to grow and deepen, offering escapes, adventures, and resources unimaginable just a couple of decades ago. However, what many have not realized is alongside this ever growing cyber meta-reality entity exists another, symbiont; a cyber microbiome (see Figure 2) often unseen, yet integral to the shaping and growth of the surface layer of the cyber meta-reality most inhabit. This underlying cyber space is similar in many ways to the Earth borne and human related microbiomes that flourish and support both systems respectively. The concept of the microbiome has its roots in the earliest theories of Macarthur in 1955 [2] and was later taken up by Savage in 1977 who stated, "In terms of numerical bacterial cells likely outnumber human cells by at least an order of magnitude." [3] This estimate was later extended by many orders of magnitude following further study. This concept usually shocks most people simply because the sheer enormity of microorganisms they suddenly realize inhabit and make up their bodies. We are under the impression that we are made up primarily of "human" cells, but this has been proven not only to be a false assumption, but the direct opposite with most of the body we share being made up of the microbiome. As scientists and medical professionals recognize, the human microbiome has fundamentally changed how they do research and practice medicine. Thus, this concept, while new to the formation and constitution of the cyber meta-reality is nevertheless one that must be considered, especially in light of the areas underlying and paralleling the cyberspace most see. The Dark/Deep Web alone accounts for a vast and overwhelming section of what can be termed the cyber microbiome, followed by malware, living archives, and code that populate the symbiotic Hadean realm we have yet to fully realize. In this paper, we will investigate these abysmal realms of the cyber meta-reality as we cross the digital River Styx.

Figure 1. Cyber Meta-reality.

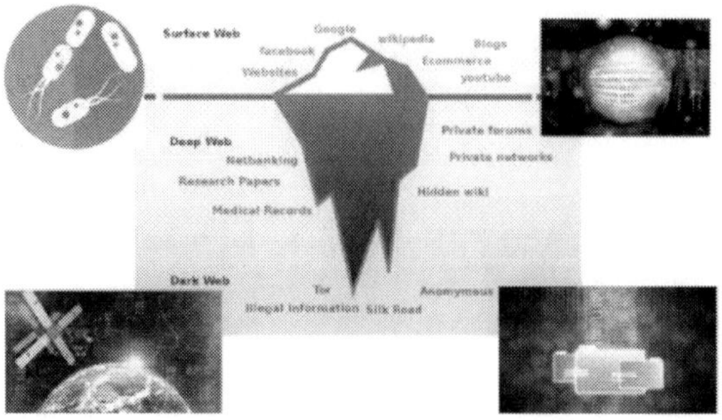

Figure 2. Cyber Microbiome.

II. THE DEEP DARK WEB

The Deep Web or Dark Web as some call it is known to relatively few but connects with and influences many people without them even realizing it. While not an illegal space itself, the "Dark Web" is known as a lawless realm leveraged by the dark cyber powers to conduct "Dark Market" activities of a less than savory nature. In this Underworld of viruses, Worms, Trojans, malware, ransomware, and a plethora of other malicious code for hire, hackers find community and items for sharing or purchase that may be added to their bag of tricks. Botnets can be hired for a mere few hundred dollars or less, passwords are sold on the cheap like crack cocaine, Bitcoin transactions traverse Virtual Private Networks (VPN), further obfuscating the already uber-secure blockchain mechanisms in place. And yet, this black cyber Gehenna is more spacious in data and global reach than any government or international enclave in existence. "The terms Deep Web, Deep Net, Invisible Web, or Dark Web refer to the content on the World Wide Web that is not indexed by standard search engines. The deepest layers of the Deep Web, a segment known as the Dark Web, contain content that has been intentionally concealed including illegal and anti-social information" [4]. As use of this shadowy enclave continues to grow, more and more capabilities are being created and leveraged. The growth of the Dark Web is so rapid that keeping up with its evolution is virtually impossible. Some predict "There will be more activity in darknets, more checking and vetting of participants, more use of cryptocurrencies, greater anonymity capabilities in malware, and more attention to encryption and protecting communications and transactions. Twitter is becoming a channel of choice; Tor and VPN services are finding increased use" [5]. Indeed this deepening of black and gray market transactions has been observed occurring at an alarming rate. "A recent study found that 57% of the Dark Web is occupied by illegal content like pornography, illicit finances, drug hubs, weapons trafficking, counterfeit currency, terrorist communication, and much more" [4]. This trend is likely to continue as more and more miners of the Dark Web find lucrative enterprises. This influx of additional Dark Web tourists and residents will no doubt expand this ever growing dark segment of the cyber microbiome. "People are becoming more technically sophisticated; younger generations are using technology on a daily basis in school, learning digital technology at a very early age. In the words of one expert, 'hacking has become little league: everyone starts out early, and spends a lot of time doing it'" [5]. Although the Dark Web has become a cyber reality associated with illegal activity and anti-social behavior, it did not begin this way. "To access material in the Dark Web, individuals use special software such as TOR (The Onion Router) or I2P (Invisible Internet Project). TOR was initially created by the U.S. Naval Research Laboratory as a tool for anonymously communicating online" [4]. The fact that TOR, now associated with and widely used by criminals, hackers, and terrorist groups to name a few, was originally created by a legitimate U.S. government entity is telling. The Dark Web and the bridges to and from it have evolved; morphed from one kind of thing into something entirely different and it continues to grow and change. This fact along with the imminent applications of technologies like AI, ML, quantum computing, and nanotech indicate a potential future growth of the Dark Web of astronomical proportions, indicating its continued significance as a fundamental part of the cyber microbiome.

III. MALWARE WITH A LIFE OF ITS OWN

What happens when a computer virus, Trojan, Worm, or other type of malware accomplishes its mission? Where does it go? Does it simply self-annihilate or does it live on as a part of the cyber microbiome underlying the cyber meta-reality? Of course, the answers to these questions usually depend on how the malware was designed and what its purpose is. However, these answers are becoming more subjective as the cyber meta-reality continues to change due to hackers' constantly fluctuating modus operandi and the impending implementation of AI and ML enabled malware that could lead to self-replication and even evolutionary code not yet fathomed. These kinds of effects can be seen in what are deemed "poisonous systems" where malware has infected and changed the most integral portions of said system. "Poisoned systems are distinct from systems infected with computer viruses, which allow malicious code to transfer to other systems when it meets various conditions through a self-replicating mechanism" [6]. The continued spread and replication in this case goes beyond such targeted malware as Stuxnet which had a specific purpose and target and was set to end once that objective had been met. Often, malware is also coded in such a fashion as to be easy to catch and defend against through patching and malware signature implementations. "[I]f an OCO capability is used against a target, several considerations must be considered. First, the capability cannot be used elsewhere globally as an anti-virus company will likely see it and create a signature for it" [7]. However, with the growth of malware, itself a persistent portion of the cyber microbiome, patching and signature implementation are becoming more and more difficult. "As one industry analyst observed: 'IT analyst forecasts are unable to keep pace with the dramatic rise in cybercrime, the ransomware epidemic, the refocusing of malware from PCs and laptops to smartphones and mobile devices, the deployment of billions of under-protected Internet of Things (IoT) devices, the legions of hackers-for- hire, and the more sophisticated cyber-attacks launching at businesses, governments, educational institutions, and consumers globally'" [8]. Other advances have already been incorporated into malware by hackers who understand the subtleties of signature-based algorithms and patching trends. The capabilities associated with advanced malware are concerning, but also fascinating in light of their ability to change, grow, and reproduce, thus adding another layer of complexity to their presence within the cyber meta-reality as a portion of the cyber microbiome. "[N]ew security products incorporating ML and AI are easily added to his or her testing cycle. The malware is validated against the test matrix, ensuring no tested product detects it" [9]. With the continued advancement of AI and ML functions, malware as part of the cyber microbiome will continue to expand and morph in myriad ways.

IV. Living Archives

As the cyber meta-reality and cyber microbiome continue to grow and deepen, questions concerning the nature of existence within these spheres arise. Ever since the discovery of the double-helix meta-molecule deoxyribonucleic acid (DNA) was discovered, the fundamental building blocks of life have been understood in terms of an extremely complex computer code that uses information to construct all organic, carbon-based life as we know it. This fact has profound application when considering the information environments we traverse daily, perhaps never comprehending the amount of information or how it is growing, changing, being shaped, and shaping us as information constructed entities. This confluence of carbon and silicon-based information hybridization can be seen in the experimentation taking place in the life of Finnish artist, engineer, and composer, Erkki Kurenniemi. A Belgian art and media group named Constant "foregrounds the digital life of an archive by practicing what it calls an 'active archive'. Unlike most online archive initiatives Constant places emphasis on the generative and active part of making an archive come alive" [10]. This living archive concept is based on recordings captured and archived that catalog and preserve Kurenniemi's life. This odd, but intriguing venture was undertaken by Kurenniemi in an effort to potentially resurrect himself at some point in the future by using this "file/life." "More precisely, Kurenniemi set out to create an archive of his own life for a possible artificial life resurrection in the future" [10]. Archives are seen by many as extensions of who we are individually and culturally. The information that makes up our personal and collective existence has now found itself displayed in many cases for the entire world to see. With social media and the internet in general, our lives are increasingly becoming an active archive. "[T]echnological advances in data collection and data science ... allow data to be transferred, stored, organized, and analyzed in an efficient and timely manner" [11]. In some cases, this data is being looked at for the purpose of customization of legal norms for individuals, but they are also being increasingly indexed as a means of understanding the most intricate habits and perspectives of singular humans. "[N]umerous firms are investing in collecting, organizing, and analyzing data or in creating products, services, and technologies that rely on such data, giving rise to data capitalism" [11]. Obviously, by capturing so much data, some information is subject to being misplaced, forgotten, or even put away for specific purposes be they good or evil. "Digital cloud storage simplifies our lives by releasing us from dependency on hardware we must manage ourselves. But we can get lost in the clouds. And a provider may decide, unbeknownst to us, not to archive our data beyond a few years. We change computers, we close accounts, time passes, and we lose entire portions of our memory" [12]. This loss of information identity leads back to the consideration of the living archive and what it would mean in the case of Kurenniemi if his data were lost, misplaced, or forgotten. "As Eugene Thacker has concluded in an overview of these tendencies, our notions of life underwent important changes during these post-war decades: 'the advances in genetic engineering and artificial life have, in different ways, deconstructed the idea that life is exclusively natural or biological.' This tendency in the sciences is crucial for understanding Kurenniemi's idea that an archive of files or information about a life as it is lived can actually also be or become a life form" [11]. This has further ramifications in the cyber meta-reality and cyber microbiome as all of the data and metadata associated with such archives lives in multiple places and within an indeterminate timeline. One need not look far before seeing the outgrowths of the living archive within the frameworks of the cyber meta-reality and microbiome.

V. Codenstein

Code is information. As mentioned above, information is the basic, fundamental chemical foundation of life in our physical reality. Within the *cyber meta-reality* and *microbiome* the same case can be made for an information-based, ever growing, reproducing, and self-perpetuating existence. For centuries, the definition of what makes something alive has been debated. Of course, life and intelligent life are different discussions, however from a basic point of view, life is defined as something that consumes, grows, and can reproduce without destroying itself in the process. Based on this simple definition, things like fire and viruses existing within our physical space are not considered to be alive since neither can reproduce without effectively destroying themselves. However, as an entity, the *cyber meta-reality* and *microbiome*, much like the human microbiome (see figure 3), both appear to consume energy in the form of electrons, grow in information proliferation and extensibility, and reproduce in the formation of additional information enclaves, forms, archives, and code. It is the latter of these progeny that seems to be the most prolific and analogous to the life, reproduction, and evolution we encounter as carbon-based life forms.

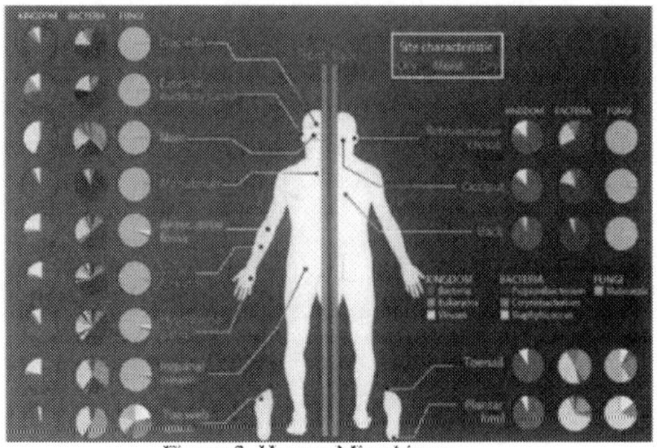

Figure 3. Human Microbiome.

Code is an information-rich, complex series of instructions that is used to create, control, and connect other information together in such a way to allow or make certain events occur. Just as animals sometimes do unexpected things *a la* the horse with the mind of its own, sometimes code is observed moving outside of its expected parameters. "It can be said that a computer can be both 'reliable' (but not infallible) and yet perform functions without the authority or knowledge of the owner or software writer. This may be when the code happens to execute in a way, because of a strange or unforeseen conjunction of inputs, which neither the owner nor the writer had imagined" [13]. This attribute of the unexpected nature of an information-constructed entity is tantamount to any other form of life behaving unpredictably. "Code can be used to create programs that provide insight into the universe, the human body, and efficiencies in transportation, finance, communications, and an almost infinite number of fields. The aggregate benefits of code are immense" [14]. The immensity of code capability in the hands of a skilled code creator is one thing, but one must also consider the trends and precedents that have been set in programs that create code autonomously. "Advanced development environments generate code automatically, although writing software to perform complex functions that works well in all circumstances remains exceedingly difficult and challenging" [13]. This is one step closer to the level of code being considered a type of life, but what about the possibility of intelligent life through code expansion and reproduction? "It should be observed that the increasing use of machine-learning systems complicates this issue, because the software code is instructed to make further decisions when running, which increases the complexity. In addition, the veridicality of machine-learning systems like neural nets cannot be easily understood or verified" [13]. While the autonomous decision-making capabilities of code generators using AI and ML are expanding rapidly, the question of ethical and moral agency may still be far off, if not possible. However, what is evident is code as an instrumental entity within the greater *cyber meta-reality* and *microbiome* is a category-shattering being on the verge of becoming something much larger and more complex.

VI. Conclusion

The *cyber microbiome* appears to be far more massive than anyone could have guessed. In this paper, we have only seen a few contributing areas that make up this symbiotic manifestation of the *cyber meta-reality*, but even then, the entity itself is enormous and extremely complex. As the interconnected cyber sphere continues to grow and change, so too will the Dark Web. In this dangerous, information-rich realm, people and machines will continue to create more narrow alleys of malware, code, and data that will potentially take on any number of byzantine existences. Malware that exists now and has been proliferated throughout systems will likely become smarter and more versatile, leaping into a new and more autonomous kind of existence that may grow into any number of malicious or potentially helpful expressions. As living archives continue to develop and evolve, the potential for advancement within this kind of file/life could be far-reaching, especially when factoring in AI and ML. Ultimately, all of these possibilities come down to code; the type, complexity, and growth of which could literally take on a life of its own. Through code that can write more code and learn and advance at rates soon to be enabled by quantum technology, nanotechnology, AI/ML, and any number of nascent capabilities, code will continue to develop through the seminal acts of human beings, potentially taking on a life of its own. All of these outgrowths and tectonic shifts only add to the propensity of the *cyber microbiome* to grow and change into the foreseeable future.

References

[1] N. Fierer et al., "From Animalcules to an Ecosystem: Application of Ecological Concepts to the Human Microbiome," *Annual Review of Ecology, Evolution, and Systematics*, Vol. 43, pp. 137-155, 2012.

[2] R. Macarthur. 1955. "Fluctuations of animal populations, and a measure of community stability," *Ecology*, 36:533- 536, 1955.

[3] D. Savage, "Microbial ecology of the gastrointestinal tract," *Annual Review Microbiology*, 31:107-33, 1977.

[4] G. Weimann, "Terrorist Migration to the Dark Web," *Perspectives on Terrorism* (June 2016), Vol. 10, No. 3, pp. 40-44, 2016.

[5] L. Ablon, M. Libicki, and A. Golay, "Projections and Predictions for the Black Market," RAND Corporation, 2014.

[6] R. Stevens and J, Biller. 2018. "Offensive Digital Countermeasures: Exploring the Implications for Governments," *The Cyber Defense Review* (FALL 2018), Vol. 3, No. 3, pp. 93-114, 2018.

[7] M. Klipstein, "Seeing is Believing," *The Cyber Defense Review* (SPRING 2019), Vol. 4, No. 1, pp. 85-106, 2019.

[8] C. Downes, "Strategic Blind–Spots on Cyber Threats, Vectors and Campaigns," *The Cyber Defense Review* (SPRING 2018), Vol. 3, No. 1, pp. 79-104, 2018.

[9] B. Bort, "There IS No Cyber Defense," *The Cyber Defense Review* (SPRING 2018), Vol. 3, No. 1, pp. 41-46, 2018.

[10] E. Røssaak, *FileLife: Constant, Kurenniemi, and the Question of Living Archives*, Amsterdam University Press, 2017.

[11] N. Elkin-Koren and S. Gal, "The Chilling Effect of Governance-by-Data on Data Markets," *The University of Chicago Law Review*, Vol. 86, No. 2, Symposium: Personalized Law, 2019.

[12] S. Abiteboul. *Memory: The Digital Shoebox*, Peter Wall Institute for Advanced Studies, 2018.

[13] S. Mason, "The Presumption That Computers Are 'Reliable'," *School of Advanced Study*, University of London, Institute of Advanced Legal Studies, 2017.

[14] A. Brantly, "The Violence of Hacking: State Violence and Cyberspace," *The Cyber Defense Review* (WINTER 2017), Vol. 2, No. 1, pp. 73-92, 2017.

DISCLAIMERS:

The views expressed are those of the author and do not necessarily reflect the official policy or position of the Air Force, the Department of Defense, or the U.S. Government.

DoD School Policy. DoD gives its personnel in its school environments the widest latitude to express their views. To ensure a climate of academic freedom and to encourage intellectual expression, students and faculty members of an academy, college, university, or DoD school are not required to submit papers or material that are prepared in response to academic requirements and not intended for release outside the academic institution. Information proposed for public release or made available in libraries or databases or on web sites to which the public has access shall be submitted for review.

Dismissing Poisoned Digital Evidence from Blockchain of Custody

David Billard

University of Applied Sciences in Geneva
HES-SO
Geneva, Switzerland
Email: David.Billard@hesge.ch

Abstract—**This paper presents a solution to dismiss a digital evidence from a permissioned blockchain-based legal system, serving as evidence chain of custody. When challenged into court, a digital evidence can be entirely dismissed, as well as all the procedural acts originating from this evidence, including personal gathered data. Since a blockchain, by design, cannot be altered, this paper proposes an alternative solution based on an access control to the blockchain. This solution relies on an additional structure, linked to the blockchain, representing the history and current legal state of the case. Access to the blockchain is controlled by first interrogating this additional structure in order to serve only legally accepted evidence. Therefore, an evidence stored into the blockchain is not destroyed, but is no longer visible nor accessible. Furthermore, evidence data is separated from the blockchain transaction's payload, that holds only metadata, and this separation reinforces privacy protection. The solution presented in this paper is explainable to all parties to a court trial.**

Keywords–Digital Evidence; Blockchain; Chain of custody; Privacy.

I. Introduction

This paper focuses on an often-forgotten aspect of digital evidence handling, when a court dismisses an evidence from a trial. Multiple reasons can lead to dismiss an evidence: it can be challenged by a party during an investigation or in front of the court, have an expired delay if it is time-bounded, or simply dropped by the prosecutor.

Of course, different countries apply different laws, but let's take a simple example, quite universal. Bob is suspected to hold illegal child pornography material. A warrant is issued and a police search is conducted at Bob's house. During the search, a hard drive is seized and following police procedure, the drive is registered. Since this police body is a modern one, a chain of custody is initiated into the blockchain-based evidence inventory software.

Digital forensics experts examine the drive and find connections with Alice, who seems deeply involved in child pornography. A police search is therefore triggered on Alice and a USB stick with a lot of inculpatory evidence is found at Alice's home. As required by the procedure, the USB stick is registered into the same blockchain-based software.

Much later in the investigation, a defense lawyer raises the legality of the first police search on serious grounds. The court follows the motion and the first police search is dismissed. Since the second police search is a direct offspring of the first, it is also dismissed from the case.

Now let's have a look at how to implement the dismissing of evidence when it is stored into a blockchain, since the blockchain does not allow for alteration, deletion or cancellation. Having a unique structure at hand, there exist at least two possible options in order to dismiss transactions.

The first one is to delete the whole blockchain and to issue a new blockchain, without the dismissed evidence. In practice, it means to start from the root block and re-issue all the subsequent transactions (excepted transactions linked to the dismissed evidence of course). Although it is theoretically doable, it means a huge effort of transaction and block validation, involving voting algorithms, and keeping track of all the blockchain intra references. This option is studied further in this work, but the reader can already notice that the computational complexity is quite significant.

The second option is to issue undo-transactions whose purpose is to indicate that the referenced transaction is void and cannot be used anymore. It means that the blockchain contains two categories of transactions:

- transactions for registering evidence;
- undo-transactions for dismissing evidence.

This technique of using undo-transactions is widely used in DataBase Management Systems (DBMS) for recovery or rollback purposes. Unfortunately, while it is well suited for DBMS, it brings some issues in blockchain-based systems.

The major issue concerns the verification of transaction validation. For a user to check if a transaction is valid, the user will have to verify if the chain of hashes and signatures has not been broken since a particular point in time (usually the begin of the blockchain). This check means that the transaction has been correctly entered into the system and has been validated following the rules.

But this check does not prove that the transaction is valid from a legal point of view: the evidence linked to the transaction may have been dismissed later. Therefore, the check process must continue until either: (1) it finds the undo-transaction, in which case the transaction is not legally valid or (2) it reaches the end of the blockchain, in which case the transaction is legally valid. The reader will notice that the computational complexity of this check is significantly higher than the single transaction verification protocol usually observed in blockchain.

There exists another perspective for solving this problem, with manageable complexity, relying on an additional structure recording the invalidated transactions, and a controlling structure granting or denying access to the blockchain.

When a transaction is invalidated, an undo-transaction is inserted into a *new distinct blockchain structure*, that holds all undo-transactions. The system is then composed of the evidence blockchain and the undo-transactions blockchain.

In order to verify the validity of a transaction, the system first look into the undo-transaction blockchain if an undo-transaction exists for this particular transaction. If it exists, then the system returns an error and exits. If it does not exist, the system proceeds with the verification in the evidence blockchain. Checking *a priori* the undo-transaction blockchain has a lower overhead, directly connected to the number of invalidated transactions.

Solving the invalidation of transactions related to dismissed evidence is still not complete, since transactions' payload may contain sensitive data, which is considered as a privacy issue. This paper advocates that the blockchain storing the evidence should know only signatures, hashes and metadata about a case. All the content should be taken out from the transaction payload and kept in distinct, encrypted and secured structures. Thus, when a transaction is invalidated, its content can be safely erased without compromising the blockchain structure.

This paper is organized as follows: section II introduces some related works about blockchain-based systems designed for digital forensics. Then, in section III, the notion of tainted evidence, and what it implies, is presented. Further, section IV presents several solutions for dealing with dismissed evidence and their degree of workability. Section V exposes a solution based on two blockchains and an access control and, in section VI, the identification of tainted transactions is specified. Then, in section VII, the paper studies the privacy protection for this solution before concluding, in section VIII, with future works.

II. Related Work

The idea of storing the chain of evidence into a blockchain has recently sparked a lot of attention from the digital forensics community. The blockchain is ideally fitted for legal evidence because the properties attached to legal evidence are embedded into the blockchain properties. In [1], the author lists the desirable properties of a blockchain transaction:

- *Immutability*. The blockchain cannot be tampered with, otherwise the tampering is detected. Although in [2] the authors are cautiously advising that immutability can only hold up to the cryptographic strength of the hash function used, it is still one of the major blockchain properties.
- *Provenance*. The assets embedded into a transaction have a provenance and any authorized reader can know where the asset comes from and how its ownership has changed over time. Data provenance is the representation of the origin of data, and its subsequent alterations.
- *Finality*. The blockchain holds all the references to an asset, its ownership, its validity.
- *Consensus*. When digital evidence is added to the blockchain, as a transaction, it is validated by the users of the blockchain. At that peculiar moment, all (or a vast majority) of voters agreed on the transaction outcome.

These properties adhere well to the concept of "chain of custody". The NIST, in [3], defines the *chain of custody* as *"A process that tracks the movement of evidence through its collection, safeguarding, and analysis lifecycle by documenting each person who handled the evidence, the date/time it was collected or transferred, and the purpose for any transfers."*

Therefore, many authors tried to propose blockchain mechanisms in order to capture the chain of custody / evidence and to offer associated services.

In [4]–[7], the authors use blockchain in the context of Internet of Things forensics, in particular aboard intelligent cars. The blockchain purpose is to record data about navigation and provide evidence should accident occurs.

In [8]–[10] the authors propose architectures based on blockchain and smartcontrats in order to store evidence, or evidence metadata, into the blockchain.

In [11] the authors advocate for a loose coupling structure in which the evidence reference and its content are maintained separately. Only the evidence reference is stored into the blockchain, and the evidence data is stored on a trusted storage platform. this paper thrives for the same separation, in order to avoid privacy issues when facing deletion of evidence.

In [12], the author describes an architecture where evidence is stored in a Digital Evidence Inventory blockchain, and additional structures provide a global timeline to order evidences and a tentative of evidence rating. Each transaction is expressed as a CASE object [13] or an XML token [14].

Many researches [8], [10], [15]–[17] propose blockchain for holding evidence. However, none of these papers address simultaneously two important specificities of digital forensics: 1) evidence can be dismissed by court order and 2) evidence cannot be inserted or viewed by everyone.

III. Dismissing Tainted Evidence

An investigation or a trial is not a straightforward process and dismissing of evidence can be triggered by several causes, for instance a procedural issue like a 4th amendment violation for the USA, which in short states that any evidence illegally obtained should be excluded from a case.

Therefore, an evidence can be tainted by a breach of rights, and derivative evidence have to be dismissed, since it becomes "tainted" too. Some jurists refer to that situation as the *"fruit of the poisonous tree"*.

A famous example is the *Mapp v. Ohio, 367 U.S. 643* [18] in 1961. In this case, Dollree Mapp's house was searched because it was assumed that a bombing suspect was hiding there. During the search, the police found a small number of pornographic books and pictures. Ms Mapp was arrested, prosecuted for possession of the books and found guilty (sentenced to one to seven years in prison). She appealed to the U.S. Supreme Court because the warrant was concerning the hiding of the bombing suspect, not the possession of pornographic books. The Court overturned the conviction, and five Justices held that the states were bound to exclude evidence seized in violation of the Fourth Amendment.

This case can easily translate into modern days with possession of pedo-pornographic material in a digital form. But besides the case itself, it's the impact of such decision on computerized systems, and especially when cases are large ones, that interests this paper.

With the current technology, the blockchain records evidence that is dismissed, which is not correct. The transactions related to the dismissed evidence must be deleted or made non-reachable. Some work, at Interpol in 2018 [19], but most notably in 2019 [20], devised a schema in a permissionless blockchain, like the bitcoin's one, in order to alter a block.

However, this scheme cannot apply easily in a permissioned blockchain because alterations have to be recorded and not all the transactions can be altered by anyone. An authorization mechanism must exist, thus the use of permissioned blockchain, which unfortunately prevent the use of the mechanism depicted in [20]. In [21], the authors review some ways of modifying the blockchain structure to allow mutability for GDPR (General Data Protection Regulation) constraints, alas destroying the alteration information.

The reader can imagine an Enron-like investigation put into a blockchain. The number of evidence items is staggering, and the number of people having access to the evidence is also very high. But the blockchain is precisely designed to hold a large number of evidence, as well as many users at the same time.

But how to prevent tainted evidence to be used by one party or another when the information of which evidence is tainted dissolves into the sheer number of evidence to process? How to prevent names and private data to be used when included into a tainted evidence?

The answer to those questions is a system that *controls the distribution of evidence data with respect to its legitimacy*.

IV. BLOCHAIN STRUCTURE V/S BLOCKCHAIN ACCESS

The blockchain, by definition, is immutable. Immutable roughly means that validated transactions cannot be modified without the alteration being detected. Therefore, how to proceed to undo a transaction, or a set of transactions?

This paper presents three scenarios that are feasible, at different costs: (1) rewriting the whole blockchain, (2) issuing undo transactions, (3) working on the blockchain access, not on its structure.

A. Rewriting the blockchain

Although ludicrous it seems at first, this option might be exploited in some blockchain implementations.

The validation of a transaction is done by consensus, more rarely by proof-of-work in the case of evidence blockchains. Consensus property originally means that more than a sufficient percentage of certified voters agreed on the outcome of a transaction. It's the turning point when a transaction, or more precisely the block containing the transaction, is validated. When a block is added to the system, it is unmovable.

Of course, in case of proof-of-work, with enough computing power and cryptographic effort, a majority of the voters can twist the system and prevent a block from being validated. It's a common threat in the crypto-currency world, and it is a real danger. But this attack is more an idle-threat in the case of blockchain used in digital forensics. As a matter of fact, legal systems rely on permissioned blockchains with voting algorithms and certificates, and no on mining and proof of work.

However, the problem at hand is not to modify the future chain, but to rewrite history, which means to re-validate every transaction block that was entered into the system since the block containing the transactions associated to the tainted evidence. That means to force the certified voters to vote again the same transactions which is doable if a blockchain is devoted to only one case and the voters are still the same and available. Which is not the usual setup seen in several related works, since a blockchain may contain information from several cases.

However, if doable, the cost of this operation is a one-time $O(n)$ where n is the length of the blockchain since the first transaction related to the tainted evidence. It means also that the blockchain is unavailable for use during this cleaning operation and the duration of the cleaning process might be long, depending on the validation schema used for transactions and blocks. It also means that the decision of justice to dissmiss an evidence is lost.

B. Issuing undo transaction

In DBMS systems, where ACID transactions are a central part, a committed transaction can be undone only by issuing a new transaction voiding the effects of the committed transaction. Undoing a committed transaction is far from trivial and leads to interesting problems, especially when failure occurs.

In the case of a blockchain holding evidence, one solution is to consider a "dismiss evidence" transaction or undo-transaction, in order to remove the evidence from the case.

Alas, it means that when a user wants to access an evidence, the system has to parse all the subsequent transactions in order to detect if a "dismiss evidence" transaction has been issued for this transaction. Practically speaking, it means that for each transaction T that is searched, or for validating a new transaction that references T, one need to parse the whole blockchain in order to eventually find if T is valid. The cost of this search is $O(n)$ where n is the number of transactions in the system. And this additional cost will occur whether there are, or not, invalidated transactions in the blockchain. It also means that if a user wants to have access to each transaction of the system, it will cost $O(n^2)$ in terms of verification.

C. Controlling the blockchain access

Instead of modifying the structure of the blockchain or its purpose, another way is to prevent a user to access tainted evidence. Let's name the evidence blockchain *InventoryTX*.

This paper proposes to add an additional structure, *InvalidatedTX*, that records the invalidated transactions, and a controlling structure *AccessTX* which is the access point to *InventoryTX*.

In order to access a transaction from the *InventoryTX* blockchain, the request goes through the *AccessTX* access point that first parses the *InvalidatedTX* blockchain. The cost for parsing *InvalidatedTX* is $O(m)$ where m is the number of invalidated transactions. In usual cases, m will be close to zero, thus the search overhead will be insignificant.

When a transaction is returned from the *InventoryTX* blockchain, it has the properties inherited from being in a blockchain, and the additional property that the transaction is legally sound and has not been voided.

V. THE ACCESS-BASED SOLUTION

This solution works with a majority of blockchain implementation because it does not modify the blockchain structure.

The payload of every transaction in *InvalidatedTX* contains the transaction ID related to a tainted evidence. It is recommended that each transaction in *InvalidatedTX* is signed by the jurisdiction issuing the removal of the tainted evidence.

The validation of each invalidating transaction is processed as in a normal blockchain, since the root of *InvalidatedTX*. Only the nature of the invalidating transaction differentiates it from a traditional blockchain.

An example might be the best way to illustrate the different components of the proposed solution. In this fictious case, the police searches Ms Marple's home. This woman is suspected to host a suspected man running from the police. Three evidence items are found at her home:

- Agent *Poirot* found a USB key with the searched man identity documents and 1000 bitcoins;
- Agent *Ness* found a notebook with pornographic contents and a hyperlink to a web server;
- Agent *Loch* found a love letter from the suspected man to Ms Marple.

Later, the web site is investigated by agent *Chris* and it contains drug recipes.

The *InventoryTX* blockchain is built and has the look of Figure 1. The reader will notice that it is a generic representation of a blockchain and that different authors in the literature may have additional features.

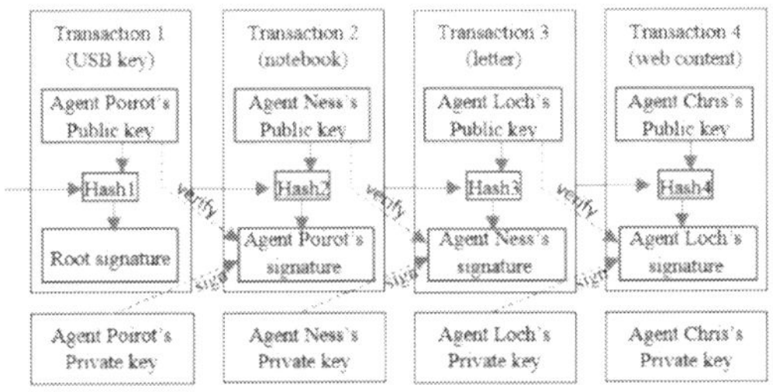

Figure 1. InventoryTX for the Marple case

In this fictious example, the defense argues that pornographic materials and drug recipes are not the subject of the search and should be dismissed. The court follows this request and judges *Roy* and *Prince* update the *InvalidatedTX* blockchain which is depicted in Figure 2.

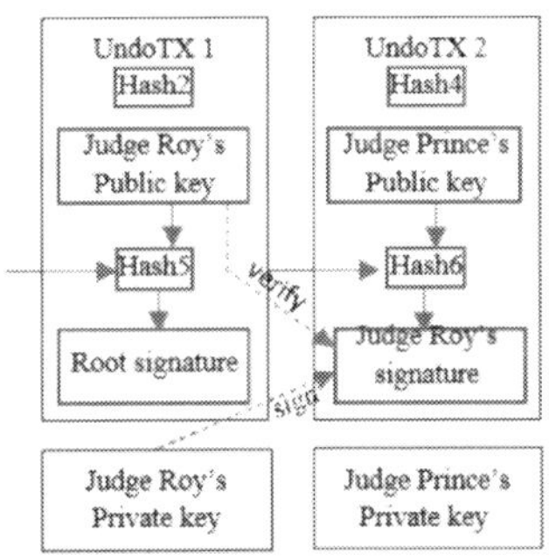

Figure 2. InvalidatedTX for the Marple case

When parties will access the evidence stored into the *InventoryTX*, the system will first look into the *InvalidatedTX* to verify if the transaction concerning the evidence is legally sound. Three scenarios are then possible:

- If the transaction hash is absent from *InvalidatedTX*, and present in *InventoryTX* then the system will serve the transaction payload, which is usually a reference to a safe storage entity holding the content, or a description, of the evidence.
- If the transaction hash is absent from *InvalidatedTX*, and also absent from *InventoryTX* then the system will raise a "Transaction not found" exception.
- If the transaction hash is present in *InvalidatedTX* then the system will raise a "Transaction invalidated by court order #xxx" exception.

This system possesses the advantage of being very lightweight. In the absence of dismissed evidence, the cost for the lookup is $O(1)$, since *InvalidatedTX* is empty. In the presence of dismissed evidence, the cost for the lookup is in $O(m)$ with m the total number of dismissed evidence records. A broader overview of the system is depicted in Figure 3.

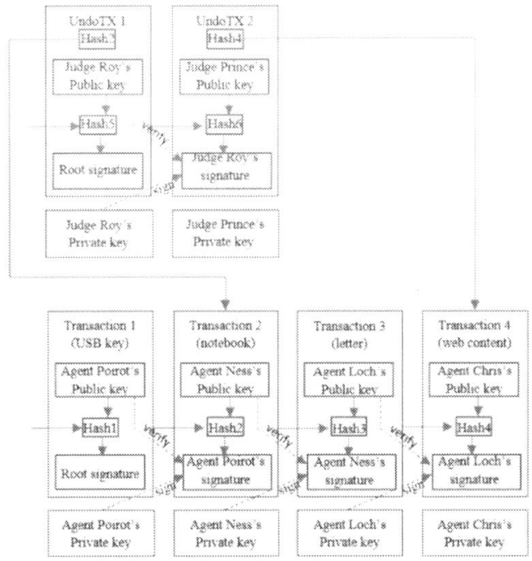

Figure 3. Overview of the two structures

The algorithm used to access a transaction of the blockchain can be summarized as in Figure 4. T references the transaction to be accessed, $hash(T)$ represents the transaction hash (its ID) and $payload(T)$ is the transaction's payload.

```
if (hash(T) ∉ InvalidatedTX) then
  if (hash(T) ∈ InventoryTX) then
    return payload(T)
  else
    return "Transaction not found"
  end if
else
  return "Transaction invalidated by court order #xxx"
end if
```

Figure 4. AccessTX: Controlling access to a transaction

This algorithm, which is simple enough and explainable to parties concerned by a trial, should help in the adoption of blockchain solutions by providing more flexibility in the evidence management.

VI. IDENTIFYING DISMISSED TRANSACTIONS

Works related to blockchain use in digital forensics are different in many respects. But usually, the transaction payload refers to the evidence. For instance, in [9], the author expressed each transaction as a CASE object [14] using XML. Therefore, mentioning the evidence into the transaction payload can be achieved quite simply with an XML tag.

An example can illustrate a simplified blockchain, using the CASE format. Table I is the result of examining the USBSTOR

Windows registry hive of the suspect computer *AliceComputer*. This table shows that three USB devices have been connected to the computer at different times.

It is worth noting that XML allows for missing or partial element. For instance, the first entry from the USBSTOR hive has no registered user and no first connection date.

TABLE I. CONTAIN OF USBSTOR

Serial #	Name	User	Last conn.	First conn.
42014287	S3300		04.11.2016 08:52:50	
7299803F	Kingston Data-Traveler 2.0 USB Device	BadGuy	08.11.2016 12:30:11	2016.05.17 12:45:57
182127000	USB Flash Memory USB Device	BadGuy	18.07.2016 12:15:16	2016.07.18 08:39:50

Table II is a simplified version of a transaction representing the USBSTOR in the blockchain. In this example, the transaction payload contains a reference to *AliceComputer*.

TABLE II. TRANSACTION FOR THE USBSTOR IN INVENTORYTX


```
<Transaction>
<TransactionID>0001</TransactionID>
<EvidenceID>AliceComputer</EvidenceID>
<USBSTOR>
<Holder>\\SecureServer\AliceCase\usbstor</Holder>
<Access key>Decyphering Element</Access key>
<Element hash>0x123423e234fdaa5787e</Element hash>
</USBSTOR>
</Transaction>
```


The important element is that the reference to the digital evidence is present in the payload. Here, <EvidenceID> will be used to parse the blockchain for transactions to dismiss.

By using the CASE format, parsing for the transactions issued from a tainted evidence EvidenceID is straightforward: all the transactions are checked and the transactions referring to the tainted transaction are added to InvalidatedTX.

VII. Privacy protection

Privacy protection has gained momentum in the public and in particular in the processing of evidence or police files. When investigating digital evidence, scores of names are retrieved and recorded. Some names will lead to persons that will be investigated, but other names will be cleared. This puts forward how personal data is stored and managed in investigations.

Some research works, like [9], advocate for information to be stored inside the blockchain, in the transaction payload. Unfortunately, if the personal information is recorded into a blockchain, it will stay in the blockchain forever. And if a transaction needs to be dismissed because it is linked to a tainted evidence, then its payload needs to be deleted.

So, this paper advocates for a model where evidence contents is stored inside an encrypted and secured vault. The blockchain transaction payload will store only the evidence hash, or series of hashes, in addition to the location information and the deciphering key. In case of a transaction being voided via a legal order, the evidence content can be safely deleted, without any modification to the transaction.

An example of such a transaction is depicted in Table II, where the transaction data (the USBSTOR content) is stored at: `\\SecureServer\AliceCase\usbstor` and the hash of USBSTOR is: `0x123423e234fdaa5787e`.

An example of the undo-transaction added to the *InvalidatedTX* blockchain is provided in Table III, where <OrigTransactionID> is the ID of the original transaction.

TABLE III. UNDO-TRANSACTION FOR USBSTOR IN INVALIDATEDTX


```
<Transaction>
<TransactionID>00034</TransactionID>
<OrigTransactionID>0001</OrigTransactionID>
<EvidenceID>AliceComputer</EvidenceID>
</Transaction>
```


Therefore, the system offers a double privacy protection:

- The access control provided by *AccessTX* that will prevent the transaction payload to be disclosed;
- In case *AccessTX* is bypassed by a malevolent user, the information from the payload will lead to nowhere.

To summarize, when an evidence is dismissed from a case, following a court order, or a procedural decision, the following process is followed:

- Parsing of the *InventoryTX* transactions in order to identify the transactions linked to the tainted evidence;
- For each of these transactions, atomically execute:
    - issue undo transaction into *InvalidatedTX*,
    - delete the content referred by transaction payload.

This scheme ensures that information which is outside the scope of a case is definitely erased from the case and cannot be accessed anymore by the parties. The algorithm to dismiss transactions is summarized in Figure 5.

for all transaction T **do**
  if EvidenceID(T) = EvidenceID **then**
    Add a new transaction to InvalidatedTX
    Delete referenced content
  end if
end for

Figure 5. Dismissing transaction from a tainted evidence

VIII. Conclusion and Future Works

This paper presents a cost-effective solution for obliterating blockchain transactions from a case, in the presence of tainted evidence. The algorithms are simple enough to be explainable to all parties concerned by a trial, and should help in the adoption of blockchain solutions by providing more flexibility in the evidence management.

The presented solution for dismissing tainted evidence does not erase the fact that the evidence was once part of the procedure, but it will prevent the use of this evidence by the parties.

When a transaction is added to a case, its payload includes at least a reference to the evidence, a reference to the storage location of the evidence data, as well as its hash value. The payload does not contain evidence data.

When a court rules that a digital evidence has to be dismissed, our solution proceeds in three steps:

1) The transactions originated from tainted evidence are detected via the reference included in their payload.
2) Each time a transaction is positively checked:

a) an undo-transaction is added to an *InvalidatedTX* blockchain, holding all the undo-transactions
b) the evidence content referred by the transaction is erased from its secure storage.

Steps 2a and 2b need to be executed atomically in order to guarantee that when a transaction is erased, all its content is erased as well.

When a transaction is requested by a party, a component *AccessTX* does a first lookup in the *InvalidatedTX* blockchain in order to verify if the transaction has been previously dismissed. If the transaction is absent from *InvalidatedTX*, its payload is served to the party, otherwise an exception is raised, mentioning that the evidence was dismissed by court order.

As a matter of fact, the system will not serve a transaction which is linked to a tainted evidence, and in the case of a malevolent bypassing of the controlling mechanism, the digital evidence content is unavailable since 1) the transaction payload is only a reference to evidence data and 2) the evidence data has been erased from storage.

In short, this solution helps in the management of tainted digital evidence by removing the dismissed transactions while providing privacy protection over personal data that may appear in criminal investigations.

The solution presented in this paper can be improved in many ways. For instance, it does not take into account the cascading nature of the dismissal. As a matter of fact, the dismissal of a legal evidence should automatically lead to the dismissal of all the legal evidences which are an offspring. Unfortunately, to determinate if an evidence is an offspring of exactly one and only one evidence is not trivial: two distinct procedure acts may lead to obtain the same evidence. In this paper, it is assumed that the list of dismissed evidence is provided by the court. The automatization of the dismissed evidence list is the subject of a future work.

This work is now being considered for implementation, by using the IBM blockchain framework [22] on top of Hyperledger Fabric developed by Linux Foundation [23], which offers an extensive framework for permissioned blockchain.

REFERENCES

[1] M. Gupta, *Blockchain for Dummies, vol. 51*. John Wiley & Sons, Inc., ibm limited edition ed., 2018.

[2] Conte de Leon Daniel, "Blockchain: properties and misconceptions," *Asia Pacific Journal of Innovation and Entrepreneurship*, vol. 11, pp. 286–300, Jan. 2017.

[3] R. Ayers, S. Brothers, and W. Jansen, "Guidelines on Mobile Device Forensics," NIST Pubs 800-101 Rev 1, May 2014.

[4] M. Cebe, E. Erdin, K. Akkaya, H. Aksu, and S. Uluagac, "Block4Forensic: An Integrated Lightweight Blockchain Framework for Forensics Applications of Connected Vehicles," *IEEE Communications Magazine*, vol. 56, pp. 50–57, Oct. 2018.

[5] K. Decoster and D. Billard, "HACIT: a privacy preserving and low cost solution for dynamic navigation and Forensics in VANET," *Proceedings of the 4th International Conference on Vehicle Technology and Intelligent Transport Systems (VEHITS 2018)*, pp. 454–461, 2018.

[6] C. Oham, S. S. Kanhere, R. Jurdak, and S. Jha, "A Blockchain Based Liability Attribution Framework for Autonomous Vehicles," *arXiv:abs/1802.05050*, 2018.

[7] H. F. Atlam, A. Alenezi, M. O. Alassafi, and G. Wills, "Blockchain with Internet of Things: Benefits, challenges, and future directions," *International Journal of Intelligent Systems and Applications*, vol. 10, pp. 40–48, June 2018.

[8] A. H. Lone and R. N. Mir, "Forensic-chain: Blockchain based digital forensics chain of custody with PoC in Hyperledger Composer," *Digital Investigation*, vol. 28, pp. 44–55, Mar. 2019.

[9] D. Billard, "Weighted forensics evidence using blockchain," *International Conference on Computing and Data Engineering*, pp. 57–61, May 2018.

[10] S. Brotsis, N. Kolokotronis, K. Limniotis, S. Shiaeles, D. Kavallieros, E. Bellini, and C. Pavue, *Blockchain Solutions for Forensic Evidence Preservation in IoT Environments*. Mar. 2019.

[11] Z. Tian, M. Li, M. Qiu, Y. Sun, and S. Su, "Block-DEF: A secure digital evidence framework using blockchain," *Information Sciences*, vol. 491, pp. 151 – 165, 2019.

[12] D. Billard, "Blockchain-Based Digital Evidence Inventory," *Journal of Advances in Information Technology*, vol. 10, pp. 41–47, May 2019.

[13] E. Casey, G. Back, and S. Barnum, "Leveraging CybOX™ to standardize representation and exchange of digital forensic information," *Digital Investigation*, vol. 12, pp. S102–S110, 2015.

[14] E. Casey, S. Barnum, R. Griffith, J. Snyder, H. v. Beek, and A. Nelson, "Advancing coordinated cyber-investigations and tool interoperability using a community developed specification language," *Digit. Investig.*, vol. 22, no. C, pp. 14–45, 2017.

[15] G.S.Harihara, S. S. Akila, Ashmithashree, Gayathri, and A. Jebin, "Digital Forensics Using Blockchain," *International Journal of Recent Technology and Engineering (IJRTE)*, pp. 182–184, Sept. 2019.

[16] S. Bonomi, M. Casini, and C. Ciccotelli, "B-CoC: A Blockchain-based Chain of Custody for Evidences Management in Digital Forensics," *ArXiv*, 2018.

[17] H. Al-Khateeb, G. Epiphaniou, and H. Daly, "Blockchain for Modern Digital Forensics: The Chain-of-Custody as a Distributed Ledger," Apr. 2019.

[18] "Mapp v. Ohio, 367 U.S. 643 (1961)."

[19] G. Tziakouris, "Cryptocurrencies—A Forensic Challenge or Opportunity for Law Enforcement? An INTERPOL Perspective," *IEEE Security Privacy*, vol. 16, pp. 92–94, July 2018. Conference Name: IEEE Security Privacy.

[20] D. Deuber, B. Magri, and S. A. K. Thyagarajan, "Redactable Blockchain in the Permissionless Setting," in *2019 IEEE Symposium on Security and Privacy (SP)*, pp. 124–138, May 2019. ISSN: 2375-1207.

[21] E. Politou, F. Casino, E. Alepis, and C. Patsakis, "Blockchain Mutability: Challenges and Proposed Solutions," *IEEE Transactions on Emerging Topics in Computing*, pp. 1–1, 2020. Publisher: Institute of Electrical and Electronics Engineers (IEEE).

[22] IBM, "IBM Blockchain Platform.," *https://ibm-blockchain.github.io/develop/*, 2017. Retrieved: 09-2020.

[23] L. Foundation, "HyperLedger Fabric docs," *https://hyperledger-fabric.readthedocs.io/en/release/*, 2016. Retrieved: 09-2020.

A Privacy-Preserving Architecture for the Protection of Adolescents in Online Social Networks

Markos Charalambous[1], Petros Papagiannis[1], Antonis Papasavva[1], Pantelitsa Leonidou[1], Rafael Constaninou[2], Lia Terzidou[3], Theodoros Christophides[1], Pantelis Nicolaou[2] Orfeas Theofanis[4], George Kalatzantonakis[4], Michael Sirivianos[1]

[1]Cyprus University of Technology, Limassol Cyprus

[2]Cyprus Research and Innovation Center, Nicosia, Cyprus

[3]Aristotle University of Thessaloniki, Thessaloniki, Greece

[4]LSTech LTD, Milton Keynes, United Kingdom

Email: {marcos.charalambous, petros.papagiannis, t.christophides, michael.sirivianos}@cut.ac.cy, {as.papasavva, pl.leonidou}@edu.cut.ac.cy, {r.constantinou, p.nicolaou}@cyric.eu, lterz@csd.auth.gr, {orfetheo, george}@lstech.io

***Abstract*—Online Social Networks (OSN) constitute an integral part of people's every day social activity. Specifically, mainstream OSNs, such as Twitter, YouTube, and Facebook are especially prominent in adolescents' lives for communicating with other people online, expressing and entertain themselves, and finding information. However, adolescents face a significant number of threats when using online platforms. Some of these threats include aggressive behavior and cyberbullying, sexual grooming, false news and fake activity, radicalization, and exposure of personal information and sensitive content. There is a pressing need for parental control tools and Internet content filtering techniques to protect the vulnerable groups that use online platforms. Existing parental control tools occasionally violate the privacy of adolescents, leading them to use other communication channels to avoid moderation. In this work, we design and implement a user-centric Cybersafety Family Advice Suite (CFAS) with Guardian Avatars aiming at preserving the privacy of the individuals towards their custodians and towards the advice tool itself. Moreover, we present a systematic process for designing and developing state of the art techniques and a system architecture to prevent minors' exposure to numerous risks and dangers while using Facebook, Twitter, and YouTube on a browser.**

Keywords–online social networks; online threats; cybersecurity risks; privacy; minors.

I. INTRODUCTION

The majority of teens (85%) use more than one social media site according to a Pew Research Center [1] survey ($N = 743$). A 2018 poll ($N = 1001$) [2] found that the average 5 to 15 year-olds spend about 15 hours online every week. Additionally, 90% of the 11 to 16 year-olds surveyed said that they have an online social network account. These numbers illustrate that the overwhelming majority of young people use OSNs, even if they are not old enough to legally register accounts for most mainstream OSNs, like Facebook, Instagram, Twitter, YouTube, and Snapchat. Alarmingly, there are many risks adolescents are exposed to when using OSNs. Specifically, a 2019 study [3] of 21.6K primary school children and 18.1K secondary school children found that 16% and 19%, accordingly, had seen content that encouraged people to hurt themselves. The same study reports that 11 to 18 year-olds reported seeing sexual content in the most popular OSNs. Last, reviews from over 2K young people aged 11 to 18, show that the 16% witnessed violence and hatred, 16% encountered sexual content, and the 18% witnessed others being victims of cyberbullying. A different study conducted in 2018 found that 59% of U.S. teens have been victims of cyberbullying or harassment online. Additionally, about a third (32%) of teens report that someone has spread false rumors about them on the Internet, while smaller shares (16%) have been the target of physical threats online. Notably, the majority of the victims tend to be females. The study concludes that 59% of the parents worry that their child might be getting bullied online, but most are confident they can teach their teen about acceptable online behavior [4].

Overall, the popularity of the Internet, and OSN usage in particular, is very high and with an increasing tendency among youngsters. Thus, the online risks for these sensitive age groups received increased awareness. To design an architecture for the protection of youngsters in OSNs, we list the most frequent dangers the young users might encounter. Existing literature [4]–[6] agrees to the following distinctive threats: i) cyberbullying; ii) cyberpredators; iii) sensitive information leakage; iv) manipulated content and pornography; and v) offensive images and messages.

Contributions. In summary, this work makes the following contributions:

1) The design and implementation of a privacy-preserving CFAS that utilizes machine learning classifiers and other filters to protect minors when using OSNs.
2) CFAS makes efforts to keep the minors fully aware of what their custodians and what the Family Advice Suite can monitor, filter, and analyze about their online activity.
3) CFAS employs fine-grained tools to spread awareness to the custodians and the minors about the various threats they face when using OSNs. It also utilizes the Guardian Avatar that interacts and advises the adolescents in a direct and user-friendly way.
4) The proposed architecture can accurately detect: (i) cyberbullying; (ii) sexual grooming; (iii) abusive users; (iv) bot accounts; (v) personal information exposure; (vi) sensitive

content in pictures; (vii) hateful and racist memes; and (viii) disturbing videos.

Paper Organization. The rest of the paper is organized as follows. First, we provide a detailed demonstration of the proposed architecture in Section II, followed by our design principles in Section III. Then, we list and discuss how the classifiers hosted on the Intelligent Web-Proxy (IWP) work in Section IV. We also provide an early evaluation of the system via a virtual environment, and physical experiments with beta testers (Section V), before discussing existing related work on parental control tools in Section VI. Last, we conclude this work in Section VII.

II. Architectural Overview

In this section, we describe the main pillars of our architecture. This architecture comprises the following: 1) OSN Data Analytics Software Stack (Back-End); 2) Intelligent Web-Proxy; and 3) browser add-on. For the tool to work efficiently, all three components interact with each other, but none depends on the other to function. Figure 1 depicts the proposed architecture of the CFAS framework, including its main components and the interfaces that interconnects them. We describe the main purposes and functionalities of each component below.

A. OSN Data Analytics Software Stack

The first component of the CFAS architecture is the OSN Data Analytics Software Stack, referred to as the *Back-End* henceforth. This is a single machine, which is responsible to train machine learning algorithms for the detection of threats in OSNs. The trained classifiers and detection rules created on this machine are sent automatically to the registered Intelligent Web-Proxies (IWP) when available (see # in Figure 1). In addition, the Back-End stores anonymized OSN traffic data from the registered IWPs, *only* if both the custodian and the minor give their explicit consent (4* in the figure). These anonymized data are used to retrain the machine learning algorithms hosted in the Back-End to extract more accurate and intelligent classifiers, which are sent back to the IWPs to replace the existing classifiers, as shown in step # in Figure 1.

B. Intelligent Web-Proxy

The Intelligent Web-Proxy (IWP) is a small device that is connected to the router of the service provider in the house of the protected family. We note that every different network needs its own IWP to be protected as a single IWP supports only one network. The IWP consists of three modules that handle specific tasks, as described below.

1) DOM Tree Analysis: This part of the IWP captures all the incoming and outgoing traffic of the user (child). Note that the word *user* refers to the child protected by our architecture henceforth. First, the user requests a webpage using their browser (see 1 at Figure 1). The response of this request is sent to the IWP: the DOM Tree Analysis module, specifically (step 3 in the figure). After capturing the traffic, the DOM Tree Analysis module handles TLS connections and performs TLS termination to decrepit HTTPS websites (only Facebook and Twitter currently). Importantly, the IWP is tested to manage high network traffic load and extract the webpage content from the captured DOM tree. At the same time, the same data are sent to the Data Access Layer for analysis (see 4 in Figure 1). We describe how the Data Access Layer (DAL) works below.

2) Data Access Layer: The Data Access Layer hosts all the trained classifiers and detection rules generated from the Back-End that are used to check all the received captured traffic.

Figure 2 demonstrates the functionality of the Data Access Layer, which is the main storage unit hosted in the IWP and the Back-End of the CFAS infrastructure. First, the data captured by the DOM Tree Analysis are sent to the *Decision Mechanism* of DAL (step 1 in Figure 2). Every bit of information (Facebook chat, Facebook news-feed pictures, Facebook posts created by the user, Facebook pictures uploaded by the user, visited YouTube videos, and visited Twitter user profiles) is sent individually. Upon reception of this data, the Decision mechanism creates a unique Execution ID (ExecID), see step 2 in the figure. This unique string is used by the Decision mechanism to define the job number of the trained classifier, which is used to analyze the data.

Then, the Decision mechanism requests the Data Access API to store this data in the database: a MongoDB (step 3). Once the data are stored, the Data Access API binds them with a unique number, which is used as a primary key to identify these data: DataID. The DataID is sent back to the Decision mechanism (step 4), which is combined with the ExecID to call the suitably trained classifier to detect suspicious behavior (see step 5). Once the trained classifier receives the ExecID and the DataID, it sends the DataID to the Data Access API to request the retrieval of data for analysis (step 6), which in return are sent back to the trained classifier (step 7). Once the trained classifier finished the analysis of the data, it sends its results to the Data Access API, along with the ExecID and DataID to be stored in the database (step 8). Then, the trained classifier sends the ExecID and DataID back to the Decision Mechanism to inform it that the analysis finished (step 9).

In response, the Decision Mechanism requests the results of the job from the Data Access API (step 10), and the Data Access API responds with the results of the analysis (step 11). Last, based on the results of the trained classifier, and thresholds set in the Decision mechanism, the Decision mechanism is responsible to decide whether a notification needs to be sent to the user via the CFAS browser add-on, and to the custodian of the user, via the Parental Console. If this is the case, the Decision Mechanism triggers an event via the Notification Module (step 12). Note that step 12 in Figure 2 is the same as step 5 and step 5* in Figure 1.

3) Parental Console: The last component hosted in the Intelligent Web-Proxy is the Parental Console. The Parental Console is a fine-grained web-based platform that enables the custodian of the user to manage which data of the user (child) he/she and the IWP can see. Also, via the Parental Console, the custodian can choose what the IWP filters, protects, and blocks. Additionally, custodians can set the level of the child's cybersafety. To set these options in operation, the child receives notifications on their browser add-on through the Notification Module, informing them that their custodian has made some changes in the options.

We highlight that for these options to operate, the child needs to approve them via their browser add-on. This way, we ensure that the child gave their consent about what the IWP captures, analyzes, filters, and blocks. At the same time, this functionality ensures that the child knows exactly what notifications their custodian will be receiving about the

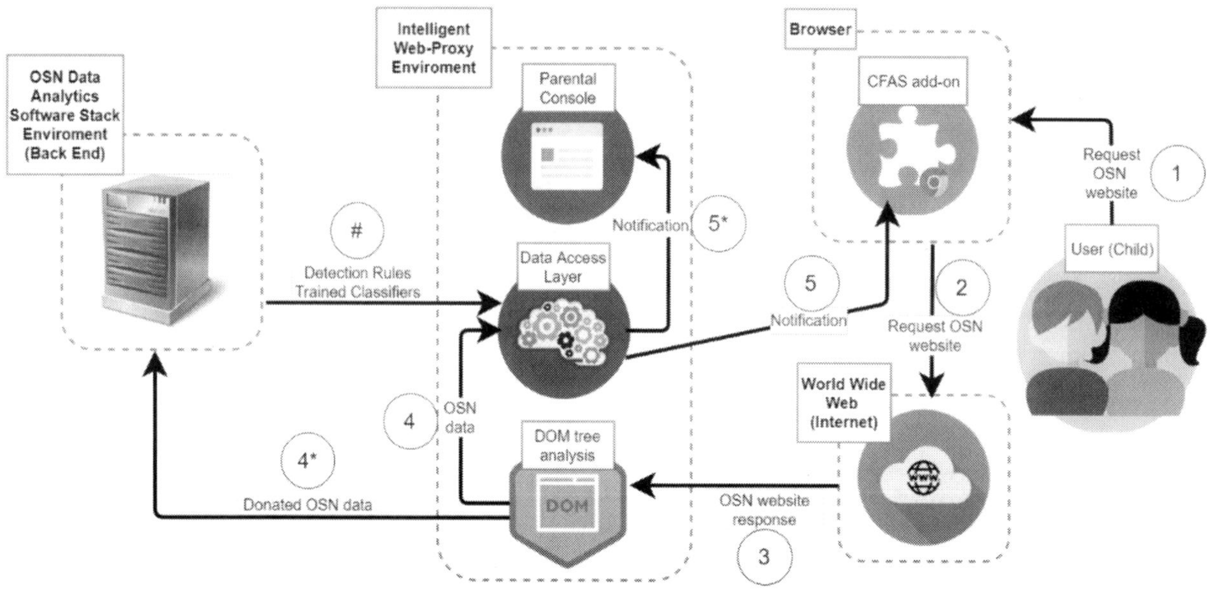

Figure 1. Cybersafety Family Advice Suite Architecture

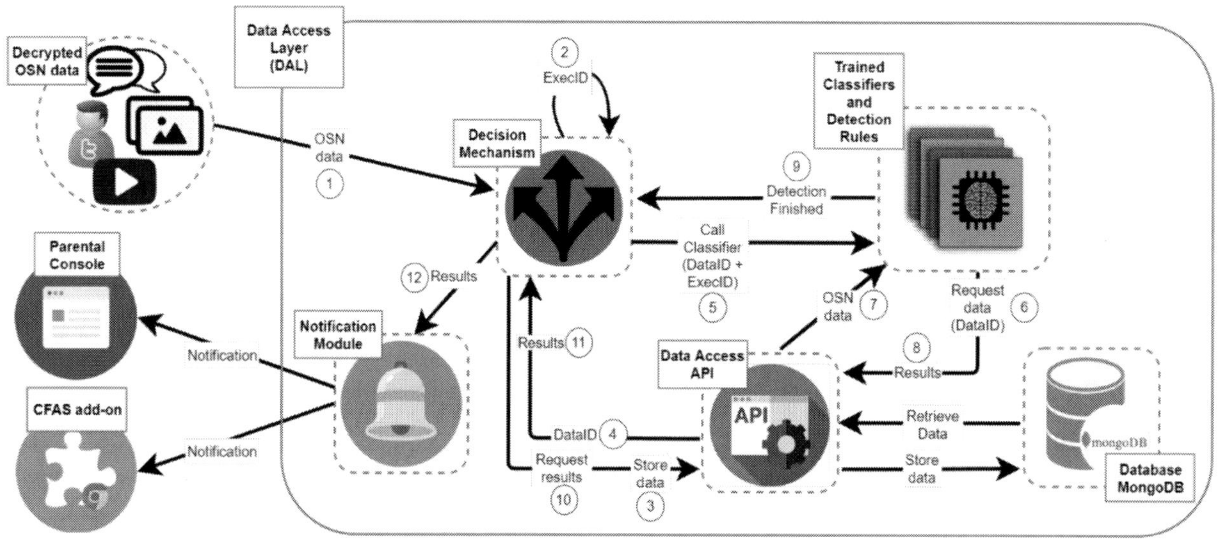

Figure 2. Data Access Layer (DAL) processes. DAL is the main storage unit of the IWP and the Back-End of the CFAS infrastructure.

online activity of the child, and what OSN traffic activity the custodian can see. We note that our proposed architecture promotes a conversation and close communication between the custodian and the child. This way, the family protected by CFAS can agree on what online activity of the child the custodians need to monitor, and what are the main risks and threats involved in using OSNs. Moreover, this architecture promotes OSN threat awareness, hence enforcing a culture of safe OSN usage. To achieve this, we introduce specific Parental and Back-End visibility options and Cybersafety options.

1) Parental Visibility Options: These options define what the custodian of the user can see, while enabling various levels of monitoring for the custodians, always with the explicit consent of the user. We define three Visibility Levels:

- Level 1: This is the lowest level of parental visibility, meaning that the custodian cannot see any data regarding the OSN traffic of the user. We note that the custodian still receives notifications regarding the threats detected by the trained classifiers hosted in the IWP, without mentioning the name of the perpetrator or revealing any OSN data. For the sake of the following examples, we assume that the protected child's name is *John*: "John might be a victim of cyberbullying."
- Level 2: This level of visibility allows the custodian to select some of the following OSN activity of the child to be visible to them: suspicious Twitter usernames the child

visited, disturbing YouTube videos the child watched, Facebook wall, photos, and friends of the child. Once the user gives their consent via their browser add-on for this data to be visible to the custodian, the visibility option is operational. A notification example: "John might be a victim of cyberbullying by Eve", where John is the protected child, and Eve is the perpetrator.

- Level 3: This is the default and highest level of parental visibility. When this option is selected, it adds all the options from Level 2, along with data regarding the user's Facebook chat. So at this level, the custodian of the child can see all the incoming and outgoing traffic of the child's Facebook wall, photos, notifications, friends, and chat, *only* in case of an incident. A notification example: "John might be a victim of cyberbullying by Eve. Click here to see the suspicious chat". This way, the custodian can see *portions* of the chat between the user and the perpetrator that show signs of cyberbullying.

We note that these options expire once every six months, so the custodian and the child can reset them as they wish. All the above levels of visibility can be set up after a mutual agreement between the custodian and the user while keeping the user fully aware of what their custodian can see.

2) Back-End Visibility options: Through the Back-End Visibility options, the Cybersafety Family Advice Suite offers options regarding which OSN traffic data is sent to the Back-End. OSN data sent to the Back-End are used to retrain the machine learning algorithms and detection rules hosted there to make them more accurate in future predictions. The custodian can choose among the child's Facebook wall, photos, notifications, friends, and chat. We note that the user needs to give their consent for the data to be sent to the Back-End. We define the following Back-End Visibility Levels:

- Level 1: This is the lowest level of Back-End visibility. If this option is set, no data is sent to the Back-End.
- Level 2: In this level, the custodian allows the IWP to send data to the Back-End regarding the child's Facebook wall, friend's Facebook wall, and the child's Facebook friends profiles. The custodian may select one or all of the above. Also, these data may be sent anonymized or not.
- Level 3: This is the highest level of Back-End visibility. When this option is set, it allows the IWP to send all the data from level 2, in addition to the child's Facebook chats. Once again, these data may be sent anonymized or not, and always with the consent of both the custodian and the child.

3) Cybersafety Options: Last, the Parental Console allows the custodian to choose the child's level of Cybersafety. These options define how aggressive the IWP can be, regarding the protection of the user: what the IWP can filter, protect, block, replace, encrypt, or watermark. This options can be configured at two different levels:

- Level 1: This is the lowest level of cybersafety. If set, the IWP only pushes notifications to the user explaining that certain suspicious or malicious activity is detected. This means that the IWP still detects suspicious activity, but it does not hide, protect, encrypt, blocks, or watermarks any content. Via the Parental Console, the custodian can choose the notifications they wish for the child to receive for each detection mechanism. The detection mechanisms include: a) cyber grooming; b) hate or inappropriate speech (cyberbullying); c) distressed behavior (when the child is suicidal, scared, depressed); d) fake activity (fake OSN profiles); e) personal information exposure (when the child is about to publish personal information); f) hateful memes; g) inappropriate YouTube videos; and h) sensitive content in pictures (when the child is about to share a benign picture that includes nudity without protection, like a picture in a swimsuit).
- Level 2: At this level, the custodian may choose any of the above IWP detection mechanisms to take action and filter, replace, protect, encrypt, or block content before it reaches the browser of the protected child. The detection mechanisms remain the same as level 1, but the custodian needs to select at least one to be operational for this level to hold.

Overall, the IWP is responsible for capturing the incoming and outgoing traffic of Facebook, Twitter, and YouTube of the user and send it to the locally hosted trained classifiers to detect malicious activity. In case the suspicious activity is detected by one or more trained classifiers, the IWP pushes a notification to the browser add-on of the user to inform them about the imminent threat detected. At the same time, the suspicious malicious content is blocked or filtered by the browser add-on to protect the minor, given that the Cybersafety Option Level 2 is set by the custodian and the user. The IWP hosts trained classifiers and detection rules to perform the following actions:

1) detect nudity in images included in the captured traffic;
2) encrypt sensitive images with steganography;
3) detect and warn the minor in case they are about to share personal information;
4) detect cyberbullying in Facebook conversations;
5) detect sexual grooming in Facebook conversations;
6) detect hateful and racist memes in Facebook feed;
7) detect bot, aggressive, bully, and spam Twitter users;
8) detect inappropriate videos for children on YouTube;
9) provide sentiment analysis of the chat of the minor;
10) generate informative notifications to the minor;
11) push notifications to the custodian about an incidence (e.g., sexual grooming);
12) push notifications to the child via the browser add-on;
13) submit data to the Back-End through a secure tunnel; and
14) block adult, or any other site, defined by the custodian.

C. Browser add-on

The last component of our architecture is the browser add-on (CFAS add-on in Figure 1). The browser add-on is the gateway between the IWP and the user, responsible to inform the user about the threats detected from the IWP, and the Visibility and Cybersafety options set by their custodian.

Importantly, our browser add-on operates as a Guardian Avatar that the child may interact with to ask for advice. Our avatar operates as the *guardian angel* of the user while using different OSN platforms (Facebook, Twitter, and YouTube only, currently). By following the Guardian Avatar approach as a gamification feature [7], CFAS aims to encourage the users to use it and interact with it because of its extended usability and improved user experience functionalities.

In addition, the user can select their favorite avatar icon from a list of icons. The Guardian Avatar "follows" the user in their online-activities as a virtual friend. When the IWP detects any malicious behavior or incidents, the notifications (warnings, advice, etc.) appear as chat bubbles of the avatar, in a friendly and encouraging text. An example of the avatar notifying the minor about a detected incident is depicted in Figure 3. With the addition of the avatar, it is expected that the CFAS warnings and advice will be less disturbing for children (especially for the adolescents) and will make users more willing to use it.

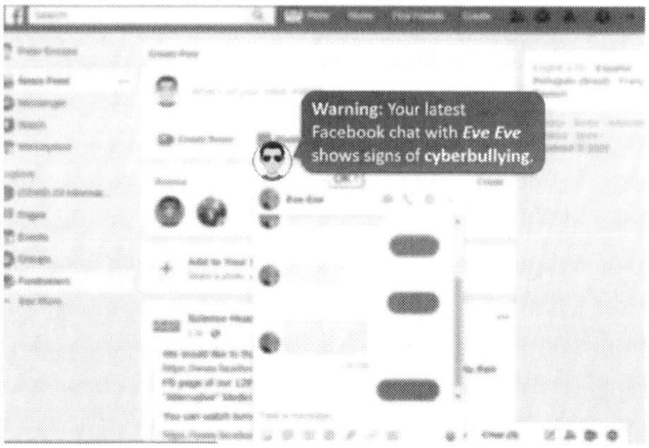

Figure 3. Guardian Avatar notifies the minor of any detected incidents

The browser add-on can:

1) notify the user about the activity detected by the IWP;
2) notify the user about what their custodian can see based on the preferences (Parental Visibility options) applied;
3) notify the user about what data is sent to the Back-End to aid the machine learning classifiers to become more accurate (Back-End Visibility options);
4) let the user change the options about what OSN traffic activity their custodian can see;
5) let the user change the options about what data is sent to the Back-End;
6) let the user flag content/text as cyberbullying activity, sexual cyber grooming activity, aggressive behavior activity, fake identity activity, and false information activity in case the IWP failed to detect so;
7) let the user flag sensitive or nudity content in case the IWP failed to detect so; and
8) let the user flag content/text as an incorrect sensitive content, cyberbullying, sexual grooming, aggressive behavior, fake identity, and false information activity in case the IWP detected so.

Overall, we propose a fully privacy-preserving architecture for the protection of minors when they use OSNs, both towards their custodians and towards the system itself. First, the minor is empowered to choose the online activity and warnings that their custodian receives in case a threat is detected by the IWP. This can be done via the Parental Visibility Options. Second, the user can choose which online activity the IWP filters, captures, and protects via the Cybersafety Options. Also, the IWP, the device that is responsible for capturing and analyzing the online activity of the minor to detect online threats, is connected and physically exists within the network of the user. Thus, the online activity of the minor is captured and analyzed locally and is isolated within the network of the user. In addition, the IWP never makes any data visible to the rest of the system (Back-End or other IWPs) without the explicit authorization and consent of both the user and their custodian via the Back-End Visibility Options.

III. Design

We now detail the design of the proposed architecture. Instead of simple rule-based filters, our architecture utilizes advanced machine learning algorithms. The downside of having rule-based filters is that they are blunt. There are situations where there is a particular piece of content that technically does not violate the specified policies, but when this content is analyzed with advanced machine learning techniques, it might turn out to be hate speech, sarcasm, sexual grooming, etc. Such techniques allow us to detect bullies or predators that are close to the line. To sum up, the aim is to have these granular standards so that our design can control for bias. Our design approach is based on the following design principles:

1) We place all functionalities (filters, text replacement, notifications, data submission to the Back-End, etc.) in the IWP instead of the browser add-on when it can be correctly and efficiently implemented. This way, we prevent a minor from modifying or disabling the system's functionality through the browser add-on. For example, in case a minor accidentally or willingly disables the browser add-on, the IWP does not get affected, and all the processes and functionalities can continue their operation normally. We assume that the device of the minor is still configured to route social network services through the IWP and that the child does not have the permission, knowledge, or access to alter the configuration of the IWP or their personal device. Also, the IWP can notify the custodian through the Parental Console that the browser add-on of the minor is not responding anymore.

This architecture aims to provide the ability to seamlessly support multiple types of clients (desktop browsers, mobile apps, etc.) with a minimal client or client platform configurations or modifications. Moreover, the browser add-on does not support complex functionalities other than javascript and HTML scripts. For example, functionalities, like text replacement, picture encryption, filtering, etc., are too complex to be implemented and run on a browser add-on.

In case the IWP is down, the browser add-on calls REST API requests from the Back-End, and the Back-End DAL is employed to identify suspicious content. This means that the OSN traffic activity of the user is sent outside of the network, to the Back-End, for analysis. Whether a suspicious activity is detected by the Back-End or not, all the user OSN traffic data is automatically deleted from the Back-End. Having some functionalities on the IWP prevents it from calling REST API requests from the Back-End every time it needs to analyze OSN traffic activity. In addition, placing some functionalities on the IWP, solves the potential problem of the whole system being down in case of Back-End unavailability, thus solving the problem of single-point failure. Examples: i) The IWP can push notification to the browser add-on without the need of the Back-End. ii) Before any content reaches the minor's device, the IWP can replace cyberbullying content without calling REST API requests from the Back-End, using the functionality installed on it already.

2) Rules and trained classifiers are generated in the Back-End. Trained classifiers are placed in the IWP only if they can

run efficiently. The Back-End collects data from all the IWPs to generate detection rules and trained classifiers. Data collected from the IWPs are used to generate cyberbullying, sexual cyber grooming, distressed behavior, aggressive behavior, fake identity, and false information detection rules.

3) Warning, flagging, and feedback functionality is placed on the browser add-on. The Guardian Avatar displays notifications in dialogue boxes after the IWP detects suspicious behavior and pushes a notification to the browser add-on. The user can flag content as cyberbullying activity, sexual cyber grooming activity, aggressive behavior activity, fake identity, false information, and sensitive picture through the browser add-on in case the IWP failed to detect so. The user can also give feedback based on the activity detected by the IWP. For example, in case the IWP detects cyberbullying, it pushes a notification to the browser add-on. The Guardian Avatar shows the notification/warning to the user explaining that cyberbullying was detected (Figure 3). Then, the user can provide feedback on whether this detection is accurate or not.

4) The minor can check the content their custodian, the IWP, and the Back-End can see. The custodian can set up the Visibility settings in a fine-grained way and always with the consent of the minor. This way, we enable various levels of monitoring for parents and the Back-End with the child's consent, while keeping the child fully aware of what their custodians and the Back-End can see, e.g., chat messages.

Overall, we propose a system that eases the tension of ensuring the safety of minors while respecting their privacy with respect to what their custodians and third parties can see. By automating the detection of malicious communication, we enable custodians to be continuously aware of their child's safety. This is achieved without the parent having to go through the minor's online communication manually, thus, without having to invade the minor's privacy. Our approach aims to warn the custodians about the suspicious online activity that was detected, without violating the privacy of the minor. For example, if the minor has a Facebook online conversation with sexual content with somebody, the custodian of the minor will receive a warning that such a conversation is taking place, once the IWP captures it. Still, the parent won't be able to see the actual content because that would violate the teenager's privacy. Instead, the parent can only see the actual conversation through their Parental Console once the explicit consent of the child has been granted. To sum up, our design principles intend to encourage custodians to have a conversation with the minor; thus, bringing families closer and spreading awareness about the numerous threats that exist in contemporary OSNs.

IV. IMPLEMENTATION

We implement all the architecture components, and integration's that we describe in Sections II and III. In this section, we provide the details of the prototype implementation. Note that we employ classifiers created in previous work for the detection of threats in OSNs. We note that these classifiers are generated on the Back-End and hosted on the IWP. In case the classifiers detect suspicious activity, the IWP pushes notifications to the browser add-on of the user, and the Parental Console.

A. Detection of Abusive Users on Twitter

When the minor visits a Twitter user account, the IWP captures the username of the visited user, and it calls the Twitter API to collect the last 20 tweets (including retweets) of that user [8]. This information is then sent to a classifier developed by Chatzakou et al. [9] for analysis. The developed classifier is trained with Twitter annotated data [10] [11] and analyzes the last 20 tweets of the visited Twitter user to detect whether it is an aggressive, bully, spam, or normal account.

B. Fake and Bot user detection on Twitter

When the minor visits an account on Twitter, the IWP captures the username of the Twitter account and sends it for analysis via a REST API call developed by [17] and Echeverria et al. [18]. This API returns True if the Twitter user account is a bot, and False otherwise. In case of the former, the IWP pushes a notification to the browser add-on of the minor, and to the Parental Console of the custodian (based on the Parental Visibility options).

C. Detection of Hateful and Racist memes on Facebook

The IWP captures the Facebook incoming and outgoing traffic of the minor and performs TLS termination of the DOM tree. All the images that are extracted from the DOM tree are sent to the classifier developed by Zannettou et al. [12] to be labeled as a hateful meme or not. This classifier is trained using images from Twitter, Reddit, 4chan's Politically Incorrect board [13], and Gab [14]. In case the detection is positive, the picture will be automatically replaced by the IWP with a static image to inform the minor.

Similarly, when the minor uploads an image on Facebook, the picture is analyzed by the aforementioned classifier to detect whether that image is hateful or racist. If so, then the IWP pushes a notification to the guardian avatar to advise the minor that the image they try to upload contains hateful content, and they shouldn't upload it.

D. Sexual Predator Detection on Facebook

When the minor is chatting with a friend on Facebook, the conversation is captured by the IWP and is sent to the classifier developed by Partaourides et al. [15] for analysis. A previous version of this classifier was trained with data from Perverted Justice website [16] to recognize patterns similar to the ones from convicted sexual predators. Upon positive detection, the IWP pushes a notification to the browser add-on of the minor, notifying them that signs of sexual predator have been detected. The custodian can see only portions of the chat between the minor and the predator via the Parental Console, only if the minor consents so via the Parental Visibility options explained in Section II. We note that the custodian can only see portions of the chat that the classifier detects as a sexual grooming pattern.

E. Cyberbullying Detection on Facebook

Similar to the Sexual Predator detection, when the minor is chatting with a friend on Facebook, the conversation is captured by the IWP and is sent to the classifier developed by Partaourides et al. [15] for analysis. This classifier returns percentages of how angry, frustrated, and sad the minor is during the Facebook chat conversation, using sentiment analysis. If any of these three feelings exceed 65%, the IWP pushes a notification to the browser add-on of the child to warn them that the Facebook chat they are having seems to be toxic for them. Similar to the sexual predator detection above, the custodian is only able to see portions of the suspicious chat, only if the minor gave their consent beforehand.

F. Personal Information Leakage Detection on Facebook

When the user tries to make a post on Facebook, the IWP captures the text written by the user and analyzes it to detect dates, times, phone numbers with or without extensions, links, emails, IP and IPv6 addresses, prices, credit card numbers, street addresses, and zip codes. We implement this detection technique using existing Python libraries [19]. In case any of the above personal information is detected, the IWP pushes a warning to the minor to remove the sensitive information from their post. In case the minor dismiss these warnings, a notification is sent to the Parental Console of the custodian (in accordance with the Parental Visibility options).

G. Watermarking and Steganography

For the purposes of this detection mechanism, we consider any image that includes nudity (topless images of boys, or swimsuit images) as sensitive content images. When the minor tries to send a sensitive image to a friend over Facebook chat, the image first passes in the IWP for analysis. We followed similar techniques to Ghazali et al. [20] and Kolkur et al. [21] to develop our skin and nudity detection techniques. In case the image contains sensitive content, the IWP watermarks it [22]. Then, the IWP hides the original image in another static image using steganography. This way, only the person that the picture was sent to is allowed to see the hidden original image. We note that for this to work, the receiver needs to be part of the Cybersafety Family Advice Suite network as decryption keys hosted on the Back-End are requested from the IWP to decrypt the image. Similarly, if the minor tries to post an image that contains sensitive content on their Facebook wall, the IWP watermarks and performs steganography techniques to the image before posting it on Facebook. The minor, using the browser add-on, can set who is able to see (decrypt) this picture (family members, friends, classmates, etc.). For this scenario, we assume that the minor allows the image to be visible to family members only, and that their family members are registered CFAS members and have their own IWP set up at home. When a family member of the minor scrolls Facebook, their IWP captures that image and communicates with the CFAS Back-End to check if they have permission to see this image. If this is the case, then the IWP decrypts the image automatically. In case the image does not contain sensitive content, the IWP only applies watermarking on it before posting it. The receivers that are not part of the CFAS network can only see the static encrypted image.

H. Disturbing videos on YouTube

Our architecture also detects disturbing YouTube videos for young children, using the developed classifier by Papadamou et al. [23]. This classifier was trained using YouTube videos [24] and can discern inappropriate content with 84.3% accuracy. When a minor visits a YouTube video, the IWP captures the YouTube link, which includes the YouTube video ID, and it calls the YouTube API to collect the video features [25]. These features include the video upload date, likes, tag, title,

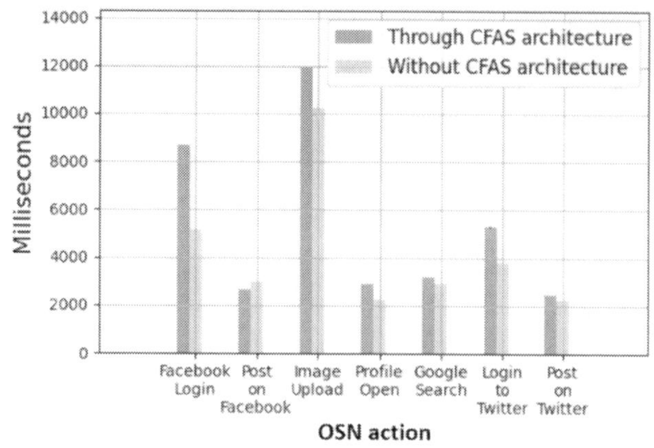

Figure 4. OSN actions with CFAS & without CFAS

thumbnail, etc. The IWP then sends these video features to the developed classifier for analysis. In case the classifier returns positive detection (inappropriate), then it warns the minor that the video they are watching is not suitable for them via the browser add-on.

V. EVALUATION

In this section, we evaluate the performance of the prototype implementation of the Cybersafety Family Advice Suite.

A. Performance Evaluation

To test the performance in regard to the number of concurrent users, we set a small home cluster using a laptop with 4GB Ram, a quad-core Intel Core i5 processor that is running Ubuntu 18.04 64bit and Google Chrome Version 80.0.3987.162 (64 Bit), which is used as the minor's laptop that hosts the browser add-on. In addition, we set up two virtual machines with 2GB RAM each, and one tablet of 3GB RAM: 4 users in total. The IWP is a virtual machine hosted on the Google cloud, configured with 4GB RAM, a dual-core Intel Xeon CPU, running Centos 7 (64 Bit), and it is using the mitmproxy [26]: the HTTPS proxy. Also, the IWP hosts a MongoDB for Data storage and Python3 for the API Calls. We run the experiments with a downlink of $\sim$20 Mbps and an uplink of $\sim$5 Mbps.

Figure 4 depicts the time in milliseconds needed for OSN actions to be executed with and without CFAS. Each machine executes the OSN actions using a JavaScript automated method in a serial manner. Then, we calculate the average time that each machine needed to finish each action using the start time and end time of each action. We observe that with CFAS, there are reasonable delays regarding the execution of some actions (e.g., Facebook Login, Image Upload, Twitter Login). This delay is acceptable since extra processing is needed to load and execute the CFAS tools. Other actions' delay is negligent ($\sim$1 second).

B. User Experience

In this section, we present the results of a user experience evaluation questionnaire given to minors and custodians after interacting with CFAS. The participation of minors required their custodians' consent. The sample consists of 30 minors and 12 custodians that had no knowledge or experience of the CFAS tools. The questionnaires were GDPR-compliant and

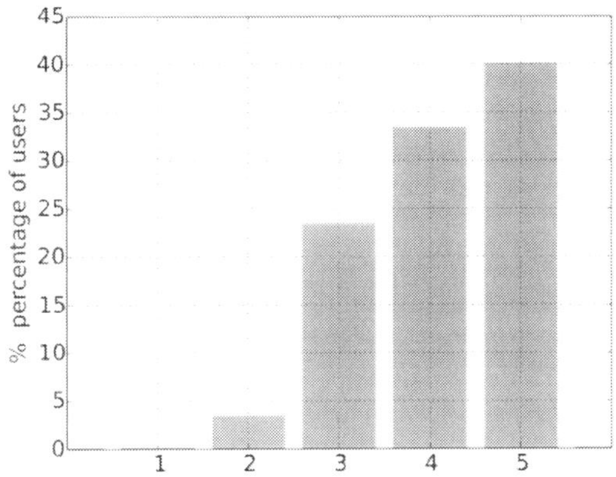

Figure 5. (Minors) Would you allow CFAS to send notifications to your custodian regarding suspicious detection? (1: Totally Disagree, 5: Totally Agree)

anonymous. The study has received data protection approvals by the Ethics Committee of the Cyprus University of Technology, and by the Office of the Commissioner for Personal Data Protection of the Republic of Cyprus.

To evaluate our tools, the minors had to answer a variety of questions regarding their usability, accessibility, and performance. The minors were between 12 to 16 years old and reported using the Internet daily for entertainment and education purposes. The percentages of minors in our sample that have a registered Facebook, Instagram, and YouTube account are 53.3%, 33.3%, and 13.3%, respectively.

We report some of the results we obtained from the questionnaires given to minors and their custodians after they used the CFAS tools. When minors asked whether they would allow CFAS to send notifications to their custodians, the majority reported high, and complete agreement (Figure 5). In addition, the majority of minors believe that these tools could improve their safety when using OSNs, as depicted in Figure 6. Importantly, all of the minors report being very happy with the capabilities of CFAS (Figure 7). Alarmingly, Figure 8 depicts that many minors had their personal data (24%) and photos (7%) misused, being a victim of cyberbullying (7%), and witnessing inappropriate speech and racism (37%) on social networks. Note that the minors could select any that applied to them for this question.

On the other hand, the overwhelming majority of the custodians report that their child never complained of being a victim or a spectator of such threats online (Figure 9). Although this is a small number of participants, it depicts that it is usually the case that minors don't report the threats they face on OSNs to their custodians. Last, all of the custodians agree that CFAS could improve the safety of minors online (Figure 10), and the overwhelming majority of custodians report that they would install CFAS at home (Figure 11).

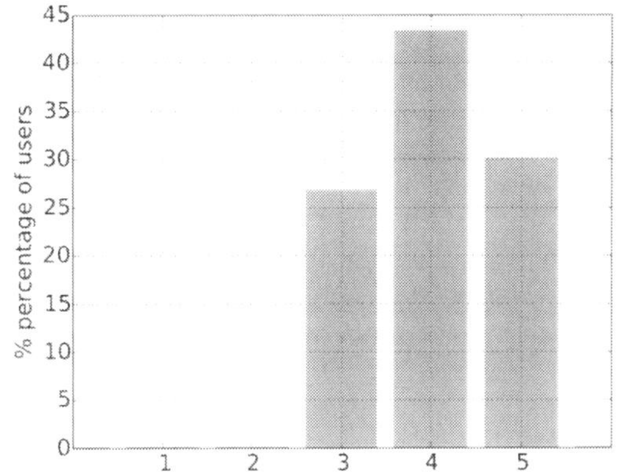

Figure 6. (Minors) Do you believe CFAS would improve your safety when using OSNs? (1: Totally Disagree, 5: Totally Agree)

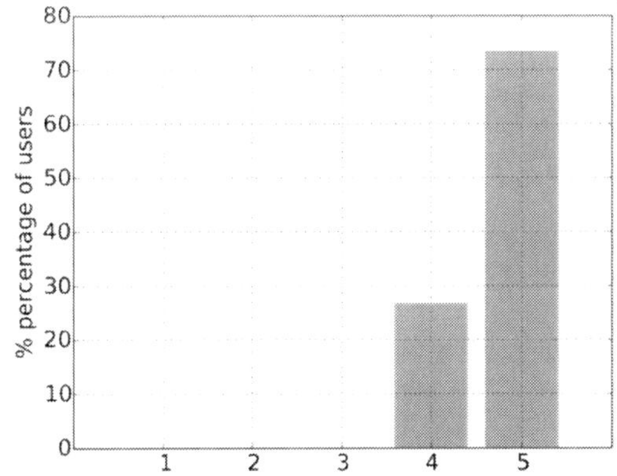

Figure 7. (Minors) Are you satisfied with CFAS capabilities? (1: Totally Disagree, 5: Totally Agree)

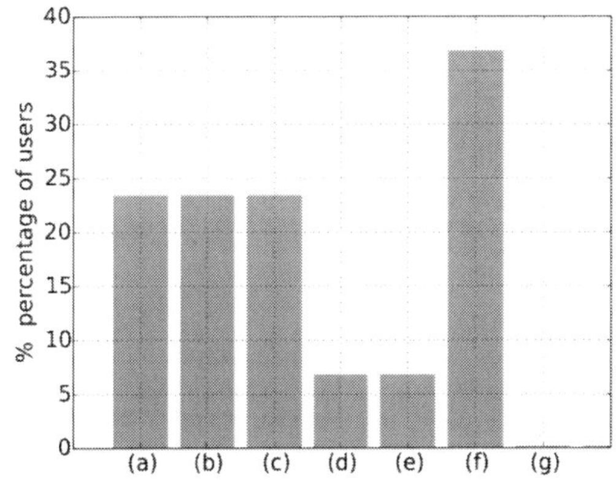

Figure 8. (Minors) Have you ever experienced the following online-threats? Select all that apply to you: (a) I prefer not to say; (b) None; (c) Personal data misused; (d) Personal photo misused; (e) Cyberbullying; (f) Inappropriate speech and racism; and (g) Sexual grooming

VI. Related Work

This section reviews some web-based and mobile applications that try to protect adolescents on the Internet and OSNs. We list the ones most relevant to the concepts of CFAS.

Qustodio is a parental control software [27] that enables parents to monitor and manage their kids' web and offline activity on their devices. It also tracks with whom the child communicates on various OSNs and can be used as sensitive content detection and protection tool (using filters). Last, it monitors messages, calls, and the location of the minor's device. Kidlogger allows custodians to monitor what their children are doing on their computer or smartphone [28]. It performs keystroke logging, keeps a schedule of which websites the minors visit and what applications they use, and with whom they are communicating on Facebook. Also,

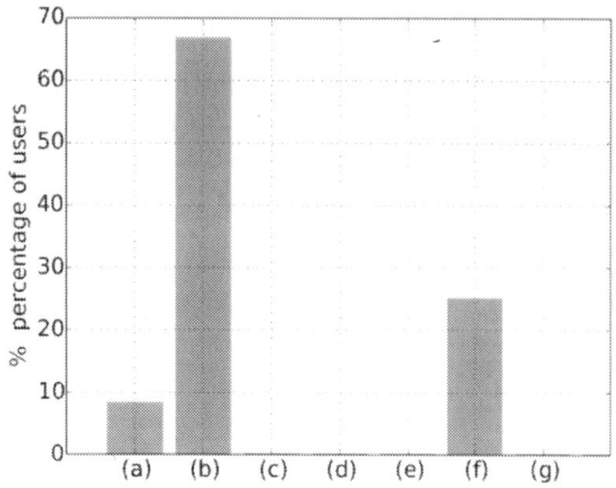

Figure 9. (Custodians) Has your child ever reported to you being a victim of the following? (a) I prefer not to say; (b) None; (c) Personal data misused; (d) Personal photo misused; (e) Cyberbullying; (f) Inappropriate speech and racism; and (g) Sexual grooming

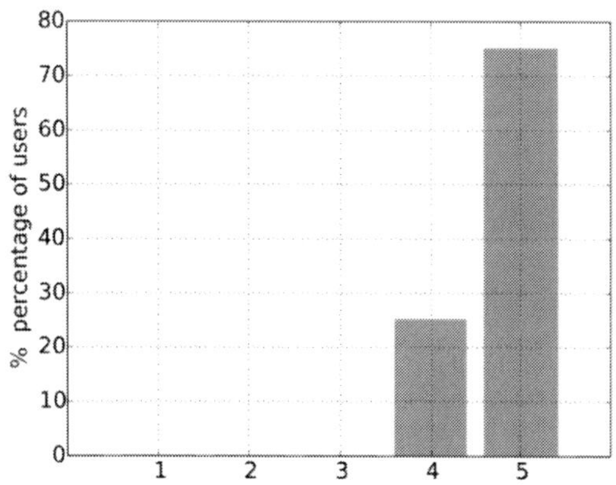

Figure 10. (Custodians) Do you think that CFAS would improve the safety of minors when using OSNs? (1: Totally Disagree, 5: Totally Agree)

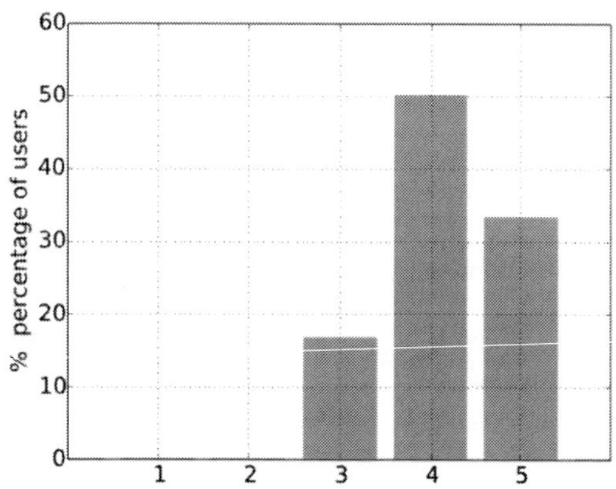

Figure 11. (Custodians) Would you install CFAS at home? (1: Totally Disagree, 5: Totally Agree)

Kidlogger offers sound recording of phone and online calls, smartphone location tracking, and photo capture monitoring. Web of Trust (WoT) is a browser add-on and smartphone application for website reputation rating that warns users about whether to trust a website or not [29].

Mspy is a smartphone application that monitors almost all the applications and activities on the smartphone of the minor [30]. Alarmingly, the application may be installed on the smartphone of the minor by the custodian and remain hidden, so the minor cannot know they are being monitored. Syfer [31] is a device, still in production, that can be plugged into the router of the house network and analyses the traffic activity for possible threats. It protects against cyber threats in realtime, stops invasive data collection, offers a VPN, has artificial intelligence for enhanced security, and blocks advertisements. It doesn't log any information, and it offers encrypted activity. It restricts inappropriate content with real-time website analysis provided by their AI engine. Bark [32] monitors text messages, YouTube, emails, and 24 different social networks for potential safety concerns. Bark looks for activity that may indicate online predators, adult content, cyberbullying, drug use, suicidal thoughts, and more. In case anything suspicious is detected, the custodians receive automatic alerts along with expert recommendations from child psychologists for addressing the issue. They offer an application for iOS, Android, Kindle, browser add-ons for Google chrome on PC and Safari on Mac, and Kindle. The user has to allow the Bark application to send all the traffic data to Bark's Back-End for analysis and detection.

The majority of the existing applications follows a more traditional approach (monitoring, restrictions over online activities). Most applications consider parents or custodians as the end-users, instead of the children [33] [34]. Many of the applications do not have interfaces for children but are just installed as services running in the background [35]. A new notion suggests designing and developing tools and software that is more "children-aware" and "children-friendly". Online safety applications should consider the child as the major user and try to enrich children's self-regulation and their risk coping skills in cases of online dangers [36]. By enforcing this child-friendly approach, we achieve a collaboration where parents and children need to communicate and discuss online risks and behavior in contrast with the approach of restriction and monitoring. We aim to teach children how to cope with online threats and use social media with responsibility and self-awareness. CFAS follows this approach by involving the child in the process of setting the filters, and parental and Back-End visibility options. In addition, the cybersafety tools require the child's consent to be activated. Last, we note that this work is a follow up of the work presented by Papasavva [37].

VII. CONCLUSION

In this paper, we present the architecture of a user-centric privacy-preserving advanced family advice suite for the protection of minors on OSNs. The architecture comprises three main components, namely, the Data Analytics Software Stack, the Intelligent Web-Proxy, and a browser add-on, which operates as a guardian angel of the child while using OSNs. This architecture aims to protect minors when using OSNs while preserving their privacy. We propose Guardian Avatars that interact with, warn, and advise adolescences when they face threats on OSNs. Also, the custodian of the adolescent receives notifications on their Parental Console in case a malicious activity is detected by the classifiers hosted on the IWP to be aware of the threats their child was exposed to. Importantly, the custodian can only see the relevant content, which indicated to be suspicious, only if the minor had previously given their explicit consent.

Blocking content from the minors or thoroughly monitoring

their every online-move should not be the solution as it violates the privacy of the adolescents. The proposed architecture advertises the collaboration between parents and children and aims at bringing the family to work together to protect the vulnerable groups of the Internet while using OSNs.

ACKNOWLEDGMENTS

This project has received funding from the European Union's Horizon 2020 Research and Innovation program under the Marie Skłodowska-Curie ENCASE project (Grant Agreement No. 691025), and the CYberSafety II project (Grant Agreement No. 1614254). This work reflects only the authors' views.

REFERENCES

[1] M. Anderson and J. Jiang, "Teens, Social Media & Technology 2018," *Pew Research Center: Internet, Science & Tech*, vol. 31, 2018.

[2] "Children and parents media use and attitudes: annex 1," 2019, URL: https://bit.ly/2JIshIk [accessed: 2020-08-25].

[3] "Online Abuse - How safe are our children?" 2019, URL: https://bit.ly/390zOhO [accessed: 2020-08-25].

[4] "Pew Research Center. A Majority of Teens Have Experienced Some Form of Cyberbullying," 2018, URL: https://pewrsr.ch/32o2AHY [accessed: 2020-08-25].

[5] "EU Kids Online II Dataset: A cross-national study of children's use of the Internet and its associated opportunities and risks," 2017, URL: https://ab.co/30dr3NB [accessed: 2020-08-26].

[6] T. Andreas, T. Nicolas, S. Makis, P. Kwstantinos, and S. Michael, "Cyber Security Risks for Minors: A Taxonomy and a Software Architecture," in *11th International Workshop on Semantic and Social Media Adaptation and Personalization (SMAP)) July 12–14, 2013, Thessaloniki, Greece*. SMAP, Nov. 2016, pp. 93 – 99, ISBN: 978-1-5090-5246-2, URL: https://ieeexplore.ieee.org/abstract/document/7753391 [accessed: 2020-08-26].

[7] S. Deterding, M. Sicart, L. Nacke, K. O'Hara, and D. Dixon, "Gamification: Using game design elements in non-gaming contexts," *ACM CHI*, vol. 125, pp. 2425–2428, 2011, ISBN: 9781450302685.

[8] "Twitter API," 2020, URL: https://developer.twitter.com/en/docs [accessed: 2020-08-25].

[9] D. Chatzakou *et al.*, "Mean Birds: Detecting Aggression And Bullying On Twitter," in *Proceedings of the 2017 ACM on Web Science Conference (WebSci) June, 2017, New York, NY, United States*. ACM, Jun. 2017, pp. 13–22, ISBN: 9781450348966,URL: https://dl.acm.org/doi/pdf/10.1145/3091478.3091487 [accessed: 2020-08-26].

[10] "Restricted Dataset for "Large Scale Crowdsourcing and Characterization of Twitter Abusive Behavior"," 2020, URL: https://zenodo.org/record/3706866 [accessed: 2020-08-25].

[11] "Dataset for "Mean Birds: Detecting Aggression and Bullying on Twitter"," 2018, URL: https://zenodo.org/record/1184178 [accessed: 2020-08-25].

[12] S. Zannettou *et al.*, "On The Origins Of Memes By Means Of Fringe Web Communities," in *Proceedings of the Internet Measurement Conference 2018 (IMC) October, 2018, New York, NY, United States*. ACM IMC, Oct. 2018, pp. 188—202, ISBN: 9781450356190, URL: https://dl.acm.org/doi/pdf/10.1145/3278532.3278550 [accessed: 2020-08-26].

[13] A. Papasavva, S. Zannettou, E. De Cristofaro, G. Stringhini, and J. Blackburn, "Raiders of the lost kek: 3.5 years of augmented 4chan posts from the politically incorrect board," in *Proceedings of the International AAAI Conference on Web and Social Media (ICWSM) 8-11 June, 2020, Atlanta, Georgia, US*, vol. 14, Jun. 2020, pp. 885–894, URL: https://www.aaai.org/ojs/index.php/ICWSM/article/view/7354 [accessed: 2020-08-26].

[14] "Dataset for "On the Origins of Memes by Means of Fringe Web Communities"," 2018, URL: https://zenodo.org/record/3699670 [accessed: 2020-08-25].

[15] H. Partaourides, K. Papadamou, N. Kourtellis, I. Leontiades, and S. Chatzis, "A Self-Attentive Emotion Recognition Network," in *IEEE International Conference on Acoustics, Speech and Signal Processing (ICASSP) 4-8 May, 2020, Barcelona, Spain*. IEEE, May 2020, pp. 7199–7203, ISBN: 978-1-5090-6631-5, ISSN: 2379-190X, URL: https://ieeexplore.ieee.org/stamp/stamp.jsp?tp=&arnumber=9054762 [accessed: 2020-08-26].

[16] "Perverted Justice Data," 2019, URL: http://www.perverted-justice.com/ [accessed: 2020-08-25].

[17] "Astroscreen," 2019, URL: https://www.astroscreen.com/ [accessed: 2020-08-25].

[18] J. Echeverria *et al.*, "LOBO: Evaluation Of Generalization Deficiencies In Twitter Bot Classifiers," in *Proceedings of the 34th Annual Computer Security Applications Conference (ACSAC) December, 2018, New York, NY, United States*. ACM, Dec. 2018, pp. 137–146, ISBN: 9781450365697, URL: https://dl.acm.org/doi/pdf/10.1145/3278532.3278550 [accessed: 2020-08-26].

[19] "GitHub - madisonmay/CommonRegex: A collection of common regular expressions bundled with an easy to use interface," 2019, URL: https://bit.ly/2Zu4gh8 [accessed: 2020-08-26].

[20] G. Osman, M. S. Hitam, and M. N. Ismail, "Enhanced skin colour classifier using RGB ratio model," *arXiv*, 2012.

[21] S. Kolkur, D. Kalbande, P. Shimpi, C. Bapat, and J. Jatakia, "Human skin detection using RGB, HSV and YCbCr color models," *arXiv*, 2017.

[22] "Watermark with PIL," 2005, URL: http://code.activestate.com/recipes/362879/ [accessed: 2020-08-25].

[23] K. Papadamou *et al.*, "Disturbed YouTube For Kids: Characterizing And Detecting Inappropriate Videos Targeting Young Children," in *Proceedings of the International AAAI Conference on Web and Social Media 26 May, 2020, Palo Alto, California USA*. AAAI, May 2020, pp. 522–533, ISBN: 978-1-57735-823-7, ISSN: 2334-0770, URL: https://www.aaai.org/ojs/index.php/ICWSM/article/view/7320 [accessed: 2020-08-26].

[24] "Dataset: "Disturbed YouTube for Kids: Characterizing and Detecting Inappropriate Videos Targeting Young Children"," 2020, URL: https://zenodo.org/record/3632781 [accessed: 2020-08-25].

[25] "YouTube API," 2020, URL: https://developers.google.com/youtube/v3 [accessed: 2020-08-25].

[26] "mitmproxy HTTPS proxy," 2020, URL: https://mitmproxy.org [accessed: 2020-08-25].

[27] "Qustodio," 2020, URL: https://www.qustodio.com/en/ [accessed: 2020-08-26].

[28] "KidLogger parental control," 2016, URL: http://kidlogger.net [accessed: 2020-08-26].

[29] "Web of Trust," 2020, URL: https://www.mywot.com [accessed: 2020-08-26].

[30] "mSpy," 2020, URL: http://www.spyrix.com/android-monitor.php [accessed: 2020-08-26].

[31] "SYFER Complete Cybersecurity," 2020, URL: https://mysyfer.com [accessed: 2020-08-26].

[32] "Bark," 2020, URL: https://www.bark.us [accessed: 2020-08-26].

[33] K. Badillo-Urquiola *et al.*, ""Stranger Danger!" Social media app features co-designed with children to keep them safe online," in *Proceedings of the 18th ACM International Conference on Interaction Design and Children (IDC)) July 19, 2019, New York, NY, United States*. ACM, Jun. 2019, p. 394–406, ISBN: 9781450366908, URL: https://dl.acm.org/doi/pdf/10.1145/3311927.3323133 [accessed: 2020-08-26].

[34] B. McNally *et al.*, "Co-designing mobile online safety applications with children," in *Proceedings of the 2018 CHI Conference on Human Factors in Computing Systems(CHI)) July 19, 2018, New York, NY, United States*. ACM, Apr. 2018, p. 523, ISBN: 9781450356206, URL: https://dl.acm.org/doi/pdf/10.1145/3173574.3174097 [accessed: 2020-08-26].

[35] P. Wisniewski, A. K. Ghosh, H. Xu, M. B. Rosson, and J. M. Carroll, "Parental control vs. teen self-regulation: Is there a middle ground for mobile online safety?" in *Proceedings of the 2017 ACM Conference on Computer Supported Cooperative Work and Social Computing (CSCW)) February 25, 2017, New York, NY, United States*. ACM, Feb. 2017, pp. 51—69, ISBN: 9781450343350, URL: https://dl.acm.org/doi/pdf/10.1145/2998181.2998352 [accessed: 2020-08-26].

[36] A. K. Ghosh, C. E. Hughes, M. B. Wisniewski, Pamela J, and J. M. Carroll, "Circle of Trust: A New Approach to Mobile Online Safety for Families," in *Proceedings of the 2020 CHI Conference on Human Factors in Computing Systems (CHI)) April 21, 2020, New York, NY, United States*. ACM, Apr. 2020, p. 1–14, ISBN: 9781450367080, URL: https://dl.acm.org/doi/pdf/10.1145/3313831.3376747 [accessed: 2020-08-26].

[37] A. S. Papasavva, "A Privacy-preserving Architecture for Parental Control Tools for the Protection of Minors on Online Social Networks," 2019.

Resilient Communications Availability

Inverting the Confidentiality, Integrity, and Availability Paradigm

Steve Chan
Decision Engineering Analysis Laboratory, VT
San Diego, USA
e-mail: schan@dengineering.org

***Abstract*—Communications networks are subject to degradation due to a variety of factors from the cyber electromagnetic spectrum. Interference may be unintentional and/or intentional, but the consequences are comparable; communications availability may be affected. Although cellular carriers must abide by the Federal Communications Commission's Enhanced 911 (E911) rules, poor radio frequency cellular coverage and intermittent connections remain problematic. As numerous communications networks transition to Internet Protocol-based operations, new service reliability vulnerabilities have emerged for, by way of example, 911 location services, and poor wireless internet network (a.k.a. wi-fi) coverage may cause availability issues for 311 (e.g., reportage of road damage), and 211 (e.g., facilitation for essential community services), among others. As society becomes more dependent upon wireless communications networks, it is vital to maintain acceptable service availability levels under prototypical circumstances as well as amidst incidents, including disruptions emanating from within the cyber electromagnetic spectrum ecosystem. In several cases, public safety systems, which have gone through full acceptance testing, have been adversely affected due to interference stemming from known systems (e.g., as they expand) as well as unknown systems (e.g., unregistered). Dropped calls, garbled messages, and blocked messages have been among the reported effects. Given these known phenomena, it is possible to interfere with both cellular and Voice over Internet Protocol (VoIP) 911 and first responder-related calls by the strategic placement of interfering nodes in the form of misused cellular boosters and/or strategically positioned femtocells, deliberate Bluetooth congestion so as to limit the number of frequency channels available and interfere with wi-fi and cellular network technologies (including spread spectrum), thereby affecting the involved communications paradigm. This string of effects has segued into a potential cyber kill chain (which comprise the phases of a cyberattack from reconnaissance to exploitation) paradigm, which is examined in this paper. Among other items presented, an alarming spike in the prevalence of non-compliant boosters is noted. In addition, the increasing number of incidents as pertains to "incidental radiators" and "unintentional emitters" of Radio Frequency Interference (RFI) is also noted. Overall, as the potential for RFI has increased, the potency of the described cyber kill chain also increases. An outcome of the paper is the recognition of this potential blindspot within current communications architectural paradigms.**

Keywords-Communications networks; Cyber electromagnetic spectrum; Radio frequency cellular coverage; Internet Protocol-based coverage; Signal boosters; Oscillation detection; Oscillation prevention; Spectrum analyzer; Smart auto switching; Non-bonded single channel; Bonded multi-channel; Cyber kill chain.

I. INTRODUCTION

Various government organizations, such as the U.S. Cybersecurity and Infrastructure Security Agency (CISA) Emergency Communications Division (ECD), have provided guidance (e.g., route diversity) for communications resiliency. In essence, it is vital to maximize both the reliability and resiliency of the involved communications network. While reliability represents the ability to continue operating at acceptable service availability levels, resiliency deals with the ability to recover from adversity. This paper will examine the notions of reliability and resiliency for communications networks amidst some known cyber electromagnetic spectrum phenomena, which can readily segue to a cyber kill chain. Indeed, the cyber kill chain described in the abstract has become even more potent amidst COVID-19 times. Misconfigured and/or poorly manufactured boosters can cause extensive interference, and the number of non-compliant boosters has increased dramatically. The Federal Communications Commission (FCC) notes that, "Although signal boosters can improve cell phone coverage, malfunctioning, poorly designed, or improperly installed signal boosters can interfere with wireless networks and cause interference to a range of calls, including emergency and 911 calls." With the increase in mobile phone usage during COVID-19 times, it should be of no surprise that the market demand for boosters has increased dramatically. Along with the COVID-related increase in online purchases, e-commerce sites have been selling a high volume of signal boosters; however, not all of these signal boosters comply with FCC standards. Alarmingly, these non-FCC-compliant boosters have been noted as being top sellers in the signal booster category. To even further fuel this trend, there is an e-commerce tactic utilized, wherein sellers use reviews from other low-cost products to make the boosters appear more popular than they are, thereby inducing even more sales. As a further accelerant, on a related front of goods sold, some of the keiretsu-like structured manufacturers also sell equipment into the electrical grid sector. While the substantive portion of the Radio Frequency Interference (RFI) noise emanating from the electric utility equipment are construed as emanating from "incidental emitters," it should be noted that there are no specific limits on the conducted or radiated emissions [1]; this represents a potential blindspot.

This section introduced the subject matter. The remainder of this paper is organized as follows. Section II describes cellular and non-cellular communications coverage. Section III presents regulatory compliance and adherence considerations. Section IV discusses communications architectures that endeavor to mitigate against the interference issue and maintain acceptable service availability. Section V features the trend of ongoing societal predilection towards availability. Section VI goes into finer details with respect to some known cyber vulnerabilities within this facet of the communications ecosystem. Section VII presents some preliminary experimentation/simulation. Section VIII puts forth some concluding thoughts and the acknowledgement closes the paper.

II. Communications Coverage

A. Cellular Coverage

While a substantive portion of developed country internet users depend on hard-wired internet connections, the shift to wireless has increased tremendously over the past several years. According to a 12 June 2019 Pew Research Center Internet/Broadband fact sheet, approximately one-in-five American adults is dependent strictly upon smartphones for online access and no longer has traditional home broadband service. This phenomenon had transpired even prior to the advent of the first fairly substantial Fifth Generation (5G) technology standard for cellular network deployments in April 2019. To date, the attractiveness of relying upon smartphone cellular services to connect to the internet is the relative ubiquity of a cellular signal; however, the quality of the cellular signal varies greatly, and this is particularly noticeable with higher bandwidth digital media-related activities (e.g., watching streaming video, uploading pictures for social media, etc.), particularly when only one bar of a Fourth Generation (4G) cellular signal (in terms of the commonly accepted Received Signal Strength Indicator or RSSI, a signal typically ranges from full bars at -50db to no bars/dead zone at -120db) is available.

The degradation in signal strength should be of no surprise. Cellular signals are radio waves, and as with all types of radio frequency waves, they are readily susceptible to interference. Outside Radio Frequency Interference (RFI) can be caused by, among others, mountains, hills, valleys, trees, and tall structures. The transition from an outside to an inside environs also experiences RFI; certain construction materials, which are the primary cause of poor cellular service, include concrete, brick, metal, glass, various energy-efficient materials (e.g., foam board, fiberglass batts, Leadership in Energy and Environmental Design or LEED certified glass), and conductive material (e.g., copper), among others. Internal interference can be caused by wood, plaster, drywall, plywood, electrical devices, and clutter.

In addition to the exemplar cellular signal blocking materials provided, weather also has a tremendous impact on cellular coverage as does distance from a cellular base station (a.k.a. cell tower or cell site). For these cases, a cellular signal booster (a.k.a. amplifier or repeater) can assist matters by amplifying the weak signal. Typically, the Federal Communications Commission (FCC) has no issue with cellular signal repeaters extending the range of a cellular network in areas that, historically, receive poor cellular service [2].

B. Non-Cellular Coverage

In addition to cellular means, non-cellular wi-fi is a method for devices, such as smartphones, to connect wirelessly to the internet via radio frequency waves. Generally speaking, wi-fi is faster than Third Generation (3G) and is sometimes faster than 4G mobile data; typically, bottlenecks stem from bandwidth limitations on the landline internet connection side. In contrast to cellular signals, wi-fi signals can readily pass through many materials (e.g., plywood, plaster, and drywall) that pose a problem for cellular signals. However, for certain cases, some walls are quite thick and may utilize reinforced concrete or other materials that block some of the signals. Hence, similar to cellular, as a radio wave, wi-fi is also susceptible to interference, such as from other wi-fi networks and other usages within the utilized bands. For these cases, a wi-fi repeater or extender can assist matters. As a wi-fi extender makes no use of a cellular signal, there must be an existing wi-fi signal for an extender to work.

III. Regulatory Compliance and Adherence

The FCC has endeavored to ensure that cellular booster equipment does not interfere with the carrier network that it supports, and boosters must undergo a series of tests to be certified by the FCC. Carrier-specific boosters must adhere to a particular set of regulations while carrier-agnostic boosters adhere to a separate set of regulations. By way of example, for carrier-specific boosters, the amplifier gain (e.g., FCC-approved commercial cellular signal boosters are restricted to +70 dB gain), downlink output power (FCC-approved boosters are restricted to 12 dBm) [3], and other technical limits are set by 47 CFR Ch. 1 §20.21. For carrier-agnostic boosters, these characteristics, as well as other technical limits, have also been established. With a surge in the use of boosters, an interesting phenomenon has arisen.

Malfunctioning and misused boosters have posed substantial interference problems for the cell tower sites of cellular carriers as well as the public safety emergency radio traffic that utilize the same frequency bands that signal boosters occupy. For this reason, various cellular carriers have lobbied the FCC so as to curtail the use of boosters and have requested the following constraints: (1) signal boosters are subject to the wireless licensee's presumptive authorization (i.e., the booster is registered and able to be controlled by the licensee in the form of dynamic control over the booster's transmit power for any reason at any time), (2) signal boosters may only be operated on a channelized basis on the proscribed frequencies utilized by the wireless licensee whose signal is being boosted (i.e., carrier-specific narrowband booster), (3) signal boosters are designed with oscillation detection and will terminate transmission when oscillation occurs, and (4) signal boosters are subject to the FCC's equipment certification process, an industry certification process, and approval by the individual licensee.

Section 510 of the International Code Council's (ICC) 2018 International Fire Code (IFC) affirms these points for signal boosters, such as: (1) Bi-Directional Amplifiers (BDAs) used in emergency responder radio coverage systems shall have oscillation prevention circuitry, and a spectrum analyzer or other suitable test equipment shall be utilized to ensure that spurious oscillations are not being generated by the subject signal booster, as well as (2) signal boosters shall have FCC or other radio licensing authority certification and be suitable for public safety use prior to installation. Despite the actions taken by the FCC and the guidance provided by the IFC, the preference of cellular carriers is to sell/provide femtocells (for use in a home or office) to customers. Interference remains a complex issue, and phenomena, such as inter-cell site and intra-cell site interference, remain problematic. Interference can be caused by a call on the same frequency from a neighboring cell, or a call on an adjacent channel in the same or neighboring cell [4]. For 4G, intra-cell interference is reduced by, among other techniques, Orthogonal Frequency-Division Multiplexing (OFDM) digital modulation and Orthogonal Frequency Division Multiple Access (OFDMA). In comparison, inter-cell interference, which is caused by frequency reuse (the process of utilizing the same radio frequencies at cell sites within a geographic area that are separated by sufficient distance so as to minimize interference) and increased femtocell deployment.

IV. Communications Architectures

As is evidenced, cellular interference is a major issue, thereby necessitating a robust, reliable, and resilient communications architecture. In many cases, a layered approach is employed, and non-cellular wi-fi may be leveraged.

A. Network Topology

Although non-cellular wi-fi, particularly public wi-fi, is not necessarily stable in many cases (this often stems from congestion on the network), most of the time, non-cellular wi-fi tends to be faster than cellular [mobile] data connections. For this reason, contemporary smartphones employ smart auto switching between non-cellular wi-fi and mobile data. This smart network switching (a.k.a. adaptive wi-fi), in essence, connects to a wi-fi network and a cellular network concurrently. In some cases, instead of bonding them into a single channel (i.e., non-bonded single channel), traffic is sent on whichever connection is faster at the moment (i.e., switches back and forth between non-cellular wi-fi and cellular [mobile] data). Alternatively, multi-channel bonding (i.e., bonded multi-channel) can be used, which leverages multiple internet connections (mobile data, wi-fi, Bluetooth, etc.) concurrently for increased throughput and redundancy.

1) Types of Networks Leveraged:

Accordingly, three types of networks are often leveraged: (1) Wireless Personal Area Networks (WPANs), which are short-range networks that utilize Bluetooth technology to connect a smartphone to a device (e.g., desktop computer, which has an Internet Protocol or IP connection); (2) Wireless Local Area Networks (WLANs), which are medium-range networks that typically utilize wi-fi technology and provide wireless access points that are connected to a wired network; and (3) Wireless Wide Area Networks (WWANs), which are long-range networks that typically utilize cellular technology and leverage the backbone provided by cellular service providers.

2) Striving for Reliability and Resiliency:

In addition, contemporary communications architectures might leverage three different layers for reliability and resiliency: (1) Cellular booster layer, which — depending upon the manufacturer — can boost 4G coverage ranging from 50,000 to 200,000 square feet with a potential +70 dB gain (for U.S. carriers) at various levels of signal strength (i.e., 5 bars, 3-4 bars, 1-2 bars) (the coverage will depend on the strength of the original signal, and the commonly accepted inflection point for booster viability is at about -105 dB outside signal); (2) Lorawan Wi-Fi layer, which can provide coverage ranges from the gateway ranging from about 800 meters at 100% data packets received to approximately 1500 meters at 98% data packets received in an urban environment [5]; and (3) 5G layer with three versions of wireless technology: low-band (part of the nationwide coverage), mid-band (faster speeds at longer ranges and limited indoors functionality), and millimeter-wave (mmWave) (for extended indoors functionality, albeit walls, glass, and even a hand can block mmWave signal) [6], as well as spread spectrum technologies (e.g., chaotic sequence) combined with generalized frequency division multiplexing.

B. The Amalgam of Network Layers

Smart switching leverages both non-cellular wi-fi and cellular. Macrocells cover about 30 kilometers (km) radius. Microcells cover about a 2 km radius and lessen the load of the macrocell network as well as provide capacity and in-building penetration. A metrocell covers about a 300 meter radius. A picocell covers about a 200 meter radius, and femtocells cover about a 10 meter radius (although the AT&T femtocell covers about a 12 meter radius). The irony of carriers preferring femtocells is that they are designed to maintain a connection to the femtocell as much as possible, but risk dropping a call, particularly if the call needs to be switched to a picocell, metrocell, microcell, or macrocell (which can readily occur for callers on the move). Hence, the barrier to entry to disrupt a call is rather low. For example, interfering with the wi-fi would obligate the smart switching to devolve to cellular; then, interfering with the femtocell (as just one example) can induce a dropped call or even prevent a 911 call.

V. Predeliction Towards Availability

The 9/11 Commission Report, originally published on 22 July 2004, had recommended that the U.S. Congress provide for "the expedited and increased assignment of radio spectrum for public safety purposes," as various blindspots in emergency communications infrastructure were illuminated when first responders from varying jurisdictions were unable to communicate with each other due to differences in equipment [7]. Furthermore, cellular service was quickly overwhelmed from use by both first responders and civilians. In the absence of a dedicated public safety network, first responders predominantly communicated, via Land Mobile Radios (LMRs) (wireless communications systems that support low-speed data communications and voice) and commercial cellular networks (wireless communications systems that support voice and high-speed data communications and access to communications, but cannot substantively deliver the equivalent security standards that LMRs can for "mission critical voice" communications). Traditionally, LMRs have been the most reliable and secure method of voice communications. However, LMRs operate on thousands of different networks, are often not interoperable because they operate on different spectrum frequencies, are encrypted in different ways, are non-standardized (i.e., customized) by vendors and/or agencies, and newer LMRs are often not backwards compatible.

In 2008, the FCC auctioned licenses for segments of the 700 MHz Band for commercial purposes. Carriers began using these segments of the spectrum to offer mobile broadband internet access services for smartphones, tablets, laptop computers, and other mobile devices. On 22 February 2012, the U.S Congress enacted the Middle-Class Tax Relief and Job Recovery Act of 2012 (a.k.a. Spectrum Act), which directed the FCC to allocate the D-Block (758-763 MHz/788-793 MHz) for a public safety nationwide broadband network. Title IV of the Spectrum Act formed the First Responder Network Authority (a.k.a. FirstNet) (an independent authority charged with establishing "a nationwide, interoperable public safety broadband network") within the National Telecommunication and Information Administration (NTIA), an agency of the U.S. Department of Commerce.

Initially, public safety officials endeavored to have a "dedicated public safety network" that was distinct and disparate from any commercial provider. However, while the U.S. Congress had allocated USD $7 billion to build a network, it turned out to be insufficient funding for the construction of a distinct and disparate network [8]. The estimated cost for constructing a new nationwide 4G network for the FirstNet system ranged up to USD $40 billion, as infrastructure, such as cell towers, had to be built not only in dense urban areas, but also across all of rural America [9]. The magnitude of the project hinted at the need for public-public and/or public-private partnerships. In March 2017, FirstNet formed a public-private partnership with AT&T and awarded AT&T a 25-year contract to build out the network. Pursuant to this public-private partnership, AT&T obtained access to the 20 MHz segment of the Band 14 spectrum (758–768 MHz/788–798 MHz) (a highly desirable segment of spectrum in the 700 MHz band that facilitates good propagation in urban/rural areas as well as penetration into buildings) allocated to FirstNet and can receive up to USD $6.5 billion by operationalizing network deployment milestones in a timely fashion; in turn, AT&T agreed to provide access to its existing infrastructure and to "spend about $40 billion over the life of the contract to build, deploy, operate and maintain the network" [10]. Please refer to Figure 1 below.

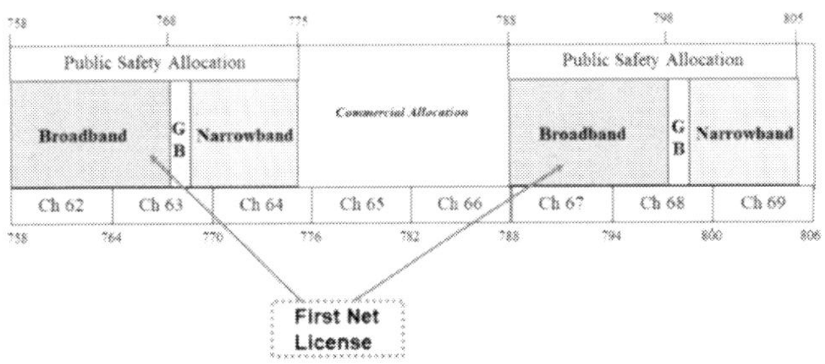

Figure 1. FirstNet Licensed Portions of the 700 MHz Spectrum [11]

As the main backbone of AT&T's Long-Term Evolution (LTE) network (which has substantial nationwide coverage) previously consisted of a superset of Band 17 and Band 12 (699-716 MHz/729-746 MHz), AT&T's FirstNet cellular network soon comprised both Bands 12 and 14.

First responders have priority on AT&T's FirstNet cellular network, but the underlying legislation that created FirstNet allows for much more pervasive usage; any government user and certain commercial entities, under specific circumstances, have priority usage. According to the National Institute of Standards and Technology (NIST), "public safety practitioners utilizing the forthcoming Nationwide Public Safety Broadband Network will have smartphones, tablets, and wearables at their disposal" ... "although these devices should enable first responders to complete their missions, any influx of new technologies will introduce new security vulnerabilities" [12]. Near the turn of the year, NIST had noted that there were 163 FirstNet-ready (capable of accessing the private core FirstNet network running on Band 14) and FirstNet-capable devices (designed to share wireless space with AT&T's commercial customers, whereby FirstNet users receive priority and preemption access over non-FirstNet users). According to NIST and cyber practitioners, the preference towards availability and the looming vulnerabilities of having Band 14 in so many devices (e.g., iPhone, iPad, Samsung Galaxy, Dell, etc.) constitutes a large attack surface area. Also, if the network is overloaded with public-safety use, it would not be available for citizen 911 calls or alerting by citizens, such as in accordance with "If You See Something, Say Something" [13]. Historically, high-profile networks have been subject to such cyberattacks. For example, Romanian hackers took over 123 of the 187 Washington D.C. police department's outdoor surveillance cameras from 12-15 January, just days before the U.S. presidential inauguration on 20 January 2017 [14].

For modern society, availability is central. For example, customers are increasingly influenced by the availability and Quality of Service (QoS) of high-speed wi-fi. Several studies shows that about two thirds of businesspeople assert that they would refuse to return to a location with sub-standard wi-fi, and the dependencies upon availability seem to persist across the enterprise, small medium businesses (SMB), industrial, residential sectors, etc. Providing free wi-fi service also has the complications of contending with squatters (people that "camp out" to gain access to the free wi-fi, but purchase very little, if anything), who impact the bandwidth; there is even the further complication of having squatters that may be infringing/downloading illegal content (albeit there are certain "safe harbor" provisions under §512 of the Digital Millennium Copyright Act or DMCA for the provider of the free wi-fi) and even launching cyberattacks from the wi-fi network.

VI. KNOWN CYBER VULNERABILITIES

To demonstrate how Distributed Denial of Service (DDoS) or Telephony Denial of Service (TDoS) attacks could affect 911 call systems (and putting aside the known vulnerabilities of TeleTYpewriter or TTY services), researchers created both a detailed simulation of North Carolina's 911 infrastructure as well as general simulation of the U.S. 911 infrastructure; the researchers reported that with only 6,000 infected phones, it was possible to effectively block 911 calls from 20% of the state's landline callers, half of the mobile customers, and per the simulation, although people called back four or five times, they still could not reach a 911 operator [15].

By way of background information, when 911 is called, via a landline or mobile phone, the carriers facilitate the connection to an appropriate call center. Over time, to increase the capacity and avoid bottlenecks, carriers have transitioned from circuit-switched 911 infrastructure to packet-switched Voice over Internet Protocol (VoIP) infrastructure, which is referred to as Next Generation 911 (NG911). Within the NG911 paradigm, load balancing among the approximately 6,200 public-safety answering points (a.k.a. Public-Safety Access Points) (PSAPs) improves reliability, and callers can also transmit text, images, video, and other data to the PSAPs. While the NG911 can indeed help mitigate against the DDoS problem by dynamically connecting to PSAPs around the country, the rate at which callers give up trying to call 911 (a.k.a. the "despair rate"), amidst a TDoS attack, is significant [15].

Beyond being vulnerable to DDoS attacks, there are other attack vectors. For example, for those areas, wherein Band 14-related towers for the FirstNet system are not viable to be deployed, it is envisioned that satellite systems will be deployed for the "last mile" [16]. However, satellite vulnerabilities have been of concern for quite some time. The issue of Assured Positioning, Navigation and Timing (A-PNT) (related to Global Positioning System or GPS/location spoofing) had been raised in the National Defense Authorization Act (NDAA) for Fiscal Year 2019 and prior. Indeed, one of the central features of Enhanced 911 (E911) (for Basic 911 service, the caller must inform the emergency operator as to the location, whereas for E911, the location is automatically displayed on the emergency operator's screen) is location-determination. Yet, phenomenon, such as swatting (a tactic of deceiving emergency services to respond to a particular location via location spoofing) have been prevalent for quite some time. Typically, swatting involves calling 911 with a non-serviced "burner" or anonymous pre-paid phone; the burner phones are neither enabled nor linked to any account. Yet, under federal law, these Non-Service Initiated (NSI) devices (with no service plan) are still able to call 911. The popularity of VoIP has segued to an interesting vulnerability for the 911 system; VoIP users manually provide their address (e.g., billing address) so as to populate the database of the VoIP service provider (VSP). When a 911 call is placed, the call is sent to an Emergency Services Gateway (ESG). Automatic Number Identification (ANI), and for some cases a pseudo-ANI (pANI) is involved, processes the number, and the ESG performs a search of the VSP database to ascertain the assigned PSAP. The call is forwarded to the assigned PSAP, which receives the location information provided by the VSP database. Automatic Location Information (ALI) returns an address (which might be false) that is associated with the number. Compromising location-determination systems (e.g., modifying the VSP, ANI, or ALI records) could lead to first responders being directed to the wrong location. Altering the VSP, ANI, and/or ALI databases or denying service to the databases could also increase the credibility of the swatting call [17]. By misdirecting resources, swatters could delay first responders to a planned physical attack; in addition, a swatter could create an incident, which concentrates first responders in a specific location for the purposes of an ambush [18].

As an alternative to calling 911, the swatter could simply call one of the approximately 4,000 PSAPs (of the approximately 6,200), which serve as primary 911 call centers, whereby operators dispatch first responders directly [15]. Calls made directly to the PSAP do not use the VSAP, ANI, and/or ALI databases; rather, the operator simply asks the caller for the address. Please refer to Figure 2 below, which summarizes some of the described attack vectors.

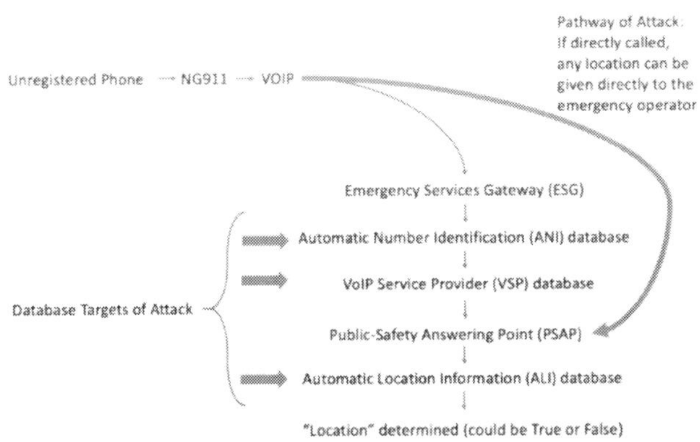

Figure 2. Potential Attack Vectors to Spoof Location

Generally, the phone numbers for PSAPs are closely held information. However, recorded 911 calls obtained by Freedom of Information Act (FOIA) or the relevant public records act (e.g., for a particular state) contain the Dual-Tone Multi-Frequency (DTMF) tones for the number of the PSAP when a call is transferred [19]. There are various DTMF decoders available on GitHub and other open source repositories to determine the numbers for the PSAPs. The National Emergency Number Association (NENA), an organization that serves as a public safety committee with regards to 911, is endeavoring to have the PSAP numbers protected (i.e., redacted) and non-extractable for 911 recordings. In any case, the Confidentiality, Integrity, and Availability (CIA) triad must be carefully considered. A disclosure of previously private information or communications to unauthorized parties is a breach of confidentiality (e.g., the VSP, ANI, and/or ALI databases are compromised). A violation of the intended function of a system by unauthorized parties is a breach of integrity (e.g., misdirecting of emergency services by swatters). An attack (e.g., DDoS or TDOS) that leads to an unavailability issue (e.g., PSAPs being made unavailable to handle 911 calls) is a breach of availability, which seems to be of the highest concern amidst contemporary times.

VII. Experimentation/Simulation

Beyond the described attack vectors, limiting the frequency channels available for use also creates honeypot observational space opportunities for a potent cyber kill chain, and this notion is shown in Figure 3 and 4 below.

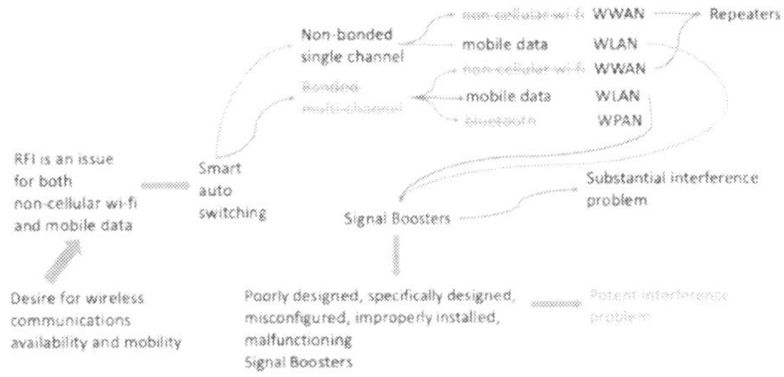

Figure 3. Limiting the channels available for use to create a more potent honeypot observational space cyber kill chain

The described scenario was simulated on a GNU Octave platform, which is a numerical computation platform that is mostly compatible with MATLAB. However, as GNU Octave is released under a GNU GPLv3 license, the source code was modified so as to take advantage of Compute Unified Device Architecture (CUDA) multi-threaded parallel computing accelerants for the utilized Semi-Definite Programming (SDP) solver so as to quickly address the involved convex optimization problems.

A. Cyber Kill Chain

The simulation involved Bluetooth Adaptive Frequency-Hopping (AFH) spread spectrum on twenty collocated WPANs. The Bluetooth usage engaged in changing channels up to 1600 times per second among 79 channels on the 2.4 GHz band. The simulation also involved wi-fi networks on twenty collocated WLANs. With the 2.4 GHz band heavily congested with Bluetooth traffic, the wi-fi networks were constrained to only a single channel on the 2.4 GHz band (e.g., Channel 40) and the 5 GHz band. The emulated FirstNet-capable devices (which share wireless space with commercial customers) included cellphones (which generally have very weak Wi-Fi radios to maximize battery life and small antennas to minimize device size), tablets (compared to cellphones, they have have stronger Wi-Fi radios and better antennas), and laptops (compared to tablets, they have stronger Wi-Fi radios and better antennas). The specified effective range for the devices were as follows: 200 meters from a hub for cellphones, 400 meters from a hub for tablets, and 900 meters from a hub for laptops. The effective range between a hub to another hub (i.e., remote hub) was established as 3 km. At 1.5 km, the bandwidth was 10 Million bits per second (Mbps); at 3 km, the bandwidth is < 5 Mbps. Every "hop" across a remote hub cut the available bandwidth in half (single radio hubs were emulated, and these cannot send and receive at the same time). More than three hops resulted in a bandwidth < 1 Mbps. The urban/rural demarcation was set at 1.5 km. As the "urban" area was congested with Bluetooth traffic, the wi-fi avoided the 2.4 GHz and endeavored to utilize the 5 GHz band. However, with twenty WLANs competing for the 5 GHz band, the lower portion of the Unlicensed National Information Infrastructure (U-NII-1) and upper portion (U-NII-3) quickly became congested. For the simulation, the remaining U-NII-2 was congested with portable weather radar (IEEE channel numbers 120, 124, 128). IEEE channel numbers 52, 56, 60, 64, 100, 104, 108, 112, 116, 132, 136, 140, and 144 of U-NII-2 was congested (at spreading factor 7, no packets were received, and even at spreading factor 12, no packets were received) so that communications, via smart auto switching, devolved to cellular mobile data, such as described in Figure 3.

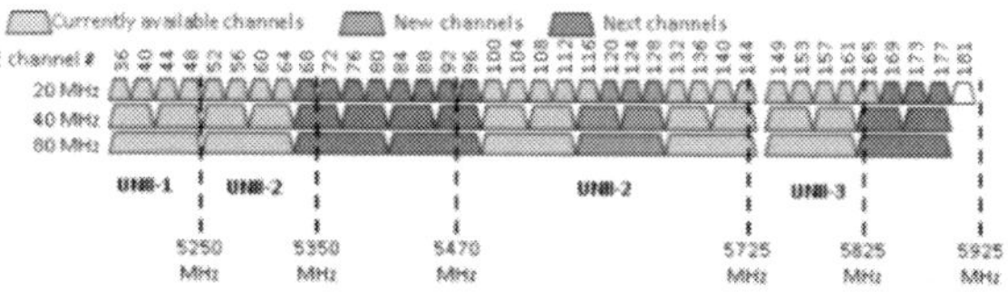

Figure 4. Unlicensed National Information Infrastructure (U-NII) Segments and IEEE Channels on the 5GHz Wi-Fi Spectrum [20]

Co-tier interference (between neighboring femtocells) and cross-tier interference (among different tiers of the network, such as between femtocell and picocell, metrocell, microcell, or macrocell) were also emulated so as to force the communications to return to Channel 40 (between 5170 and 5250 MHz) on U-NII-1. The Berkeley Packet Filter (BPF) was utilized to monitor the channels, specifically Channel 40. Hence, the cyber kill chain was complete.

B. An Even More Potent Cyber Kill Chain

Industrial Systems (IS) are heavily dependent upon communications so as to be "smart." As many IS are in remote areas, the communications is sparser and infrastructure deployment can be costly. Hence, signal boosters have been utilized to bridge the gap for this "last mile" paradigm. Ironically, these boosters can readily interfere with the existing communications used by system operators and linemen, who are servicing the involved critical infrastructure. It should also be noted that, in some cases, the keiretsu-like structured manufacturers of the non-FCC-compliant are some of the more predominant purveyors of equipment into the electrical grid sector in certain locales. The ensuing risk is that these represent nodes/clusters of potential interference; two types are discussed briefly.

1) Incidental Emitters: Generally speaking, the substantive portion of the noise emanating from electric utility equipment stems from incidental emitters. Yet, there are no specific limits on the conducted or radiated emissions. There are guidelines for these unlicensed emitters of Radio Frequency (RF) energy to not deliberately cause harmful interference [21], and the Federal Communications Commission (FCC) has mandated that utility companies rectify powerline-related interference problems within a reasonable time, particularly if the interference is caused by faulty electric utility equipment. Under FCC rules, most powerline and electric utility-related equipment are classified as "incidental radiators [22]," as the RF energy or noise created is simply an incidental part of its intended operation. However, historically, a number of electric utility chief executive officers have received letters from the FCC Enforcement Bureau pertaining to this type of violation [22].

2) Unintentional Emitters: A portion of the noise emanating from electric utility equipment stems from unintentional emitters; while this type of emitter intentionally generates an internal radio signal, it does not intentionally radiate/transmit it. Examples include some types of switched-mode power supplies (an electronic power supply that incorporates a voltage switching regulator — which transforms the incoming power supply into a pulsed voltage that is then smoothed, via the utilization of capacitors, inductors, and other elements — to convert electrical power efficiently) as well as microprocessors utilized within some of the electric utility equipment.

Depending upon the locale, the RFI emitters from the electrical grid can constitute a substantive source of interference and is clearly discernible, via a spectrum analyzer. Taking just one example of a potential impact, according to the FCC, location information must be available for at least 70% of wireless emergency assistance 911 calls or location information must be accurate to within 50 meters for 2020, and the requirements increase for 2021 [21]. Yet, given the vulnerabilities and cyber kill chain described, the true operationalization of this mandate needs to be further explored, particularly as the simulated interference precluded this.

VIII. CONCLUSION

Modern communications architectures have shifted to accommodate the societal predilection for availability. The prototypical techniques for reliability (e.g., bonded multi-channel communications) is well understood. The resiliency pathways (e.g., frequency hopping to available frequency channels) are also well understood. An attack (e.g., DDoS) that leads to PSAPs being made unavailable to handle 911 calls is a breach of availability for emergency services, which seems to be of paramount importance in modern society. Yet, the bur availability architectures has not slowed; indeed, the architectures have greatly increased in number, and the described privatization of communications backbones has fueled the use of privately-owned signal boosters. Although boosters should adhere to a set of regulations (e.g., +70 dB gain, 12 dBm downlink output power), it is possible for rogue boosters to ignore these regulations, effectuate communications interference, and wreak havoc during emergencies. Likewise, congesting channels would rate limit the channels available/utilized for non-bonded single channel and bonded multi-channel communications alike. In particular, while the intent of NG911 is to facilitates 911 callers reporting incidents and the conveying of information (e.g., text, images, video) to the PSAPs, disruption of such communications networks would create a large blindspot for first responders. While the described preliminary experimentation/simulation involved WPANs and WLANs, future work will build upon the described experimentation/simulation by congesting WWANs as well. In this way, the notion of available for the various simulated resilient communications architectures can be better explored and examined.

Overall, given the situation that communication networks are subject to degradation due to a variety of factors, it is possible to interfere with both cellular and voice over Internet Protocol (VoIP) 911 and/or first responder-related calls by the strategic placement of interfering nodes in the form of misused cellular boosters and/or strategically positioned femtocells, deliberate Bluetooth congestion so as to limit the number of frequency channels available and intentionally interfere with wi-fi and last-mile communications technologies, thereby affecting the communications paradigm.

Acknowledgment

This research is supported by the Decision Engineering Analysis Laboratory, an Underwatch initiative, which has previously supported the FTA Program under the Assistant Secretary of Defense for Research and Engineering, via participation at certain venues (e.g., IARIA). This is part of a VT white paper series on 5G-enabled defense applications, via proxy use cases, to help inform Project Enabler.

References

[1] S. Chan, "Detecting Powerline Noise with Low-Cost Noise Sensors for Power Outage Mitigation," 2020 IEEE Sensors Applications Symposium, Kuala Lumpur, Malaysia, 2020, pp. 1-6, doi: 10.1109/SAS48726.2020.9220027.

[2] Federal Communications Commision. *Indoor Location Accuracy Benchmarks.* [Retrieved September 10, 2020] from: https://www.fcc.gov/wireless/bureau-divisions/mobility-division/signal-boosters/signal-boosters-faq

[3] Federal Communications Commision. *Indoor Location Accuracy Benchmarks.* [Retrieved September 10, 2020] from: https://www.fcc.gov/document/use-and-design-signal-boosters-report-and-order

[4] Y. A. Adediran, H. Lasisi, and O. B. Okedere, "Interference management techniques in cellular networks: A review," Cogent Engineering, 4:1, DOI: 10.1080/23311916.2017.1294133

[5] Smartmakers. *LoRaWAN Range Part 2: Range and Coverage of LoRaWAN in Practice (Updated).* [Retrieved September 10, 2020] from: https://smartmakers.io/en/lorawan-range-part-2-range-and-coverage-of-lorawan-in-practice/

[6] M. Yoshida, "MWC: Are Your 5 Fingers Blocking Your 5G?" EE Times. [Retrieved September 10, 2020] from: https://www.eetimes.com/mwc-are-your-5-fingers-blocking-your-5g/#

[7] National Commission on Terrorist Attacks Upon the United States. *The 911 Commission Report.* [Retrieved September 10, 2020] from: https://www.9-11commission.gov/report/911Report.pdf

[8] National Telecommunications and Information Administration. *Public Safety.* [Retrieved September 10, 2020] from: https://www.ntia.doc.gov/category/public-safety

[9] A. Loh, "The State of FirstNet, America's Public Safety Broadband Network," Lawfare [Retrieved September 10, 2020] from: https://www.lawfareblog.com/state-firstnet-americas-public-safety-broadband-network

[10] U.S. Government Accountability Office. *Public-Safety Broadband Network.* [Retrieved September 10, 2020] from: https://www.gao.gov/assets/710/704058.pdf

[11] Federal Communications Commision. *700 MHz Public Safety Spectrum.* [Retrieved September 10, 2020] from: https://www.fcc.gov/700-mhz-public-safety-narrowband-spectrum

[12] J. Franklin, G. Howell, S. Ledgerwood, and J. Griffith, "Security Analysis of First Responder Mobile and Wearable Devices," NIST, pp. ii, May 2020, doi:10.6028/NIST.IR.8196

[13] Federal Emergency Management Agency. *Integrated Public Alert & Warning System.* [Retrieved September 10, 2020] from:https://www.fema.gov/emergency-managers/practitioners/integrated-public-alert-warning- system.

[14] R. Weiner, "Romanian hackers took over D.C. surveillance cameras just before presidential inauguration, federal prosecutors say," *The Washington Post*, December 28, 2017. [Retrieved September 10, 2020] from: https://www.washingtonpost.com/local/public-safety/romanian-hackers-took-over-dc-surveillance-cameras-just-before-presidential-inauguration-federal-prosecutors-say/2017/12/28/7a15f894-e749-11e7-833f-155031558ff4_story.html

[15] M. Goebel, C. Dameff, and J. Tully, "Hacking 9-1-1: Infrastructure Vulnerabilities and Attack Vectors," J Med Internet Res. 2019 Jul; 21(7), Jul. 2019, doi: 10.2196/14383

[16] Senate Hearing 115-153. Investing in America's Broadband Infrastructure: *Exploring Ways to Reduce Barriers to Deployment.* [Retrieved September 10, 2020] from: https://www.govinfo.gov/content/pkg/CHRG-115shrg28640/html/CHRG-115shrg28640.htm

[17] 2019 Michigan State Law Review 1133. *Combatting the Swatting Problem: The Need for a New Criminal Statute to Address a Growing Threat.* [Retrieved September 10, 2020] from: https://digitalcommons.law.msu.edu/cgi/viewcontent.cgi? article=1251&context=lr

[18] Director of National Intelligence, *Persistent Threat of Terrorist Ambush Attacks on First Responders.* [Retrieved September 10, 2020] from: https://www.dni.gov/files/NCTC/documents/jcat/firstresponderstoolbox/81_NCTC_DHS_FBI_-_Ambush_Attacks.pdf

[19] Federal Communications Commision. *Task Force on Optimal PSAP Architecture.* [Retrieved September 10, 2020] from: https://docs.fcc.gov/public/attachments/DA-16-179A2.txt.

[20] C. Spain, "Winning Back the Weather Radio Channels Adds Capacity to 5GHz Wi-Fi Spectrum," [Retrieved September 10, 2020] from: https://blogs.cisco.com/networking/winning-back-the-weather-radio-channels-adds-capacity-to-5ghz-wi-fi-spectrum

[21] "Part 15-Radio Frequency Devices § 15.3," [Retrieved September 10, 2020] from: https:// www.ecfr.gov/cgi-bin/text-idx?node=pt47.1.15&rgn=div5

[22] M. Marcus, J. Burtle, B. Franca, A. Lahjouji, N. McNeil, "Federal communications commission spectrum policy task force," E&UWG, 2002.

Mitigation Factors for Multi-domain Resilient Networked Distributed Tessellation Communications

Steve Chan
Decision Engineering Analysis Laboratory, VT
San Diego, USA
e-mail: schan@dengineering.org

***Abstract*—Numerous technical calls have converged upon an overarching goal of Resilient Networked Distributed Tessellation Communications (RNDTC) so as to provide long-range communications through the notion of "tessellation" antennas, which are comprised of spatially distributed low Size, Weight, Power, and Cost (SWaP-C) transceiver "polygons." At its core, this approach supplants higher powered amplifiers and large directional antennas with various tessellations of spatially dispersed transceiver polygons. In essence, the transmit power is spatially distributed amongst the polygons, and gain is achieved, via signal processing rather than the use of, by way of example, an antenna aperture so as to concentrate energy. Therefore, signal processing functions enable the various polygons to self-form into an array and enable beamforming, among other techniques, thereby enhancing the desired signals and somewhat obviating intentional/unintentional interference. However, the algorithmic approaches to date have varied pros and cons (e.g., the attainment of reduced sidelobes at the expense of the mainlobe, wherein interference suppression is achieved at the cost of the resolution of the signals). There are promising interference mitigation factor pathways, such as adaptive weight shifting, during the analyzing, transforming, and synthesizing of such signals. However, despite the advantages of adaptive weighting techniques, the computational complexity is extremely high, and the ensuing complexity reduction processes are subject to adversarial exploitation. Accordingly, this paper proposes mitigation factors by way of Artificial Intelligence (AI)-centric Genetic Algorithm (GA) approaches amidst the analysis, transformation, and synthesis amalgam. In particular, preliminary experimental results (to be furthered in future work) indicate promise for the auto-tuning of the Steady State Genetic Algorithm (SSGA) compression factor ζ for more optimal convergence.**

Keywords—Transceiver polygons; Signal processing; Beamforming; Non-permissive cyber electromagnetic environment; 5G networks; Smart grids; Covariance matrix; Spatial filtering algorithms; Convex optimization problems; Semidefinite programming solvers; Space-Time Adaptive Processing; Heuristical vulnerability.

I. Introduction

Traditional long-range communications are achieved by using high-powered Radio Frequency (RF) communications. However, the static RF footprint exposes these long-range oriented communications nodes to adversarial jamming, eavesdropping, and other Advanced Persistent Threat (APT) vectors. This problem is especially compounded amidst an Anti Access/Area Denial (A2/AD) environs. To mitigate against this exposure, the notion of a more agile and Resilient Networked Distributed Tessellation Communications (RNDTC) has been proposed by a variety of agencies and organizations. One of the challenges, among others, is to achieve distributed beamforming without the benefit of apriori information as pertains to the involved constituent nodes. To date, spatial diversity has been assumed and relied upon for clustering purposes. However, practically speaking, as information is obtained in real-time, hitherto heuristically designated single clusters may actually turn out to be comprised of multiple distinct and disparate clusters, and in some cases, the constituent clusters may even represent adversarial organizations (e.g., "blue" units have been engulfed by "green" units, thereby making cluster identification much more complex). Given these nuances of cluster identification, the complexity of interference suppression also greatly increases.

Clearly, operating within contemporary cyber electromagnetic environments necessitates incorporating various Electronic Warfare (EW) countermeasures, and transceiver polygons must contend with interference intrusions amidst a non-permissive environs. The envisioned signal processing (and constituent self-forming array), as construed by many, segues into the promulgation of nulls in the direction of interference so as to effectuate a suppression/mitigation mechanism in the spirit of anti-jamming. Practically speaking, particularly in a battlefield environment, the involved continual relative motion results in a constantly shifting interference direction. To further complicate matters, jamming typically involves dynamic interference source(s). Hence, the null promulgated by a spatial filtering algorithm may not be able to sufficiently suppress the interference. Given the constantly shifting arrival angle of the interference signal and the dynamism involved, computing the pertinent anti-jamming vector from simply a sample covariance matrix derived from a sampled signal, for most cases, proves to be an ineffectual approach vector. This is particularly pertinent in the realm of multi-domain cyber electromagnetic spectrum vulnerabilities for fifth generation (5G) technology standard for cellular networks. Consequently, mitigation factors for the realm of multi-domain RNDTC (e.g., 5G) might be apropos, particularly as several technical calls (e.g., Defense Advanced Research Projects Agency or DARPA) have converged upon an overarching goal of RNDTC so as to provide long-range communications through the notion of tessellation antennas, which are comprised of spatially distributed low Size, Weight, Power, and Cost (SWaP-C) transceiver polygons.

This section introduced the problem space. Section II discusses some of the related work in the literature, the operating environment, such as a potentially contested and non-permissive battlespace, and the state of the challenge. Section III discusses the signal processing intent of various RNDTC initiatives and provides some background information regarding a true adaptive beamforming approach. Section IV discusses the selective updating of the Adaptive Weight Vector

(AWV), the platform utilized for the involved high-performance Semi-Definite Programming (SDP) solvers, and the strategy for transforming optimization problems to convex form so as to reduce the complexity class from Non-deterministic Polynomial-time Hardness (NP-Hard) to polynomial time, such as for Signal-to-Interference-plus-Noise Ratio (SINR)-related computations. Section V discusses enhancing the maximized SINR, via multi-dimensional Space-Time Adaptive Processing (STAP). Section VI discusses structure exploitation of the covariance interference matrix. Section VII highlights a potential STAP heuristical vulnerability exploitation and posits an experimental mitigation factor for the STAP vulnerability of RNDTC. Section VIII presents some preliminary experimental results. Section IX concludes with some observations, and the acknowledgements close the paper.

II. Related Work in the Literature, The Operating Environment, and the State of the Challenge

As part of a resilient communications paradigm, particularly for the upcoming 5G paradigm, Ultra Reliable Communication (URC) is construed to constitute a core gauge for performance metrics. The studies available in the corpus of literature tend to examine dependability in the time domain, and only select studies scrutinize dependability in the space domain. Yet, the communications service demand is heterogeneous, non-uniformly distributed, and highly dynamic; axiomatically, the ensuing networks have irregular topologies, and while the majority of the literature focuses upon the adaptation of the network to time-varying conditions, the treatment of the reduction of computational complexity, particularly as pertains to the non-uniformity of the service demand in the spatial domain, has been less prevalent [1].

A. Related Work in the Literature

Certain studies in the literature certainly contend with the issue, via a proxy domain (e.g., electrical grid domain), whose Radio Frequency Interference (RFI) and communications performance characteristics are more clearly discernible [2]. The probabilistic availability of URC in such a proxy network are generally analyzed "cell-wise and/or system-wise," and Poisson point process and Voronoi tessellation tend to be utilized in the modeling of the spatial characteristics of cell deployment in both homogeneous and heterogeneous networks [3][4]. By way of example, several approaches involve the notion that for a node *n* that is a constituent element of a set *S*, the set of all nodes closer to node *n* than to any other node of *S* is the interior of a bounded convex polytope (a special case of a polytope with the property that it is also a convex set contained in the d-dimensional Euclidean space R^d) Voronoi cell for *n*, and the set of such Voronoi cells is the Voronoi tessellation corresponding to *S*. This approach, among others, treats resiliency inherently, as it presumes node failures.

B. The Operating Environment

To highlight some of the complexities of these networks, among a variety of sources, the U.S. Army Cyber Warfare Field Manual (FM) 3-38 [5], "Cyber Electromagnetic Activities" (supplanted by FM 3-12 "Cyberspace and Electronic Warfare" and others) contends that "Cyber Electromagnetic Activities" encompasses not only the conventional activities involving electronic warfare and spectrum management operations, but also elements of cyberspace operations. The various involved domains of the potentially contested and non-permissive battlespace can be recast as in Figure 1 below.

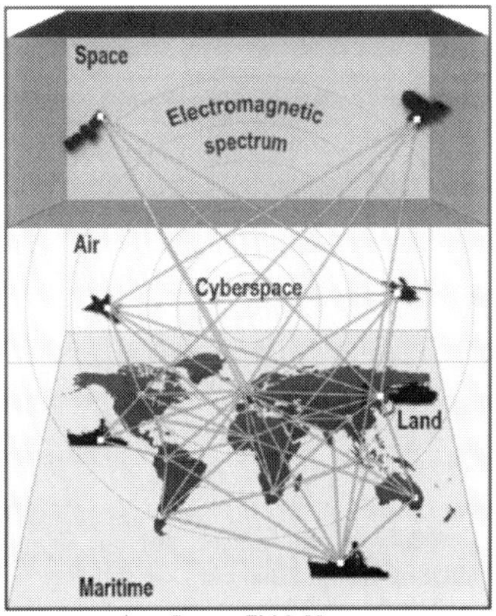

Source: FM 3-38

Fig. 1. Potential Non-permissive Domains

Accordingly, the envisioned transceiver polygons can be recast for the applications alluded to, among others, in Figure 2 below.

Fig. 2. Potential Transceiver Polygon Applications

The resolution of the challenge for transceiver polygon applications has far-reaching implications for a variety of sectors (e.g., defense, intelligent transportation systems, etc). The cascading effects on the related supply sectors (e.g., semiconductor industry for the implementation of these applications) are quite profound.

C. The State of the Challenge

The nature of the challenge centers upon a core need to reduce computational complexity when considering the myriad of system parameters interplaying into the achievable link availability. While existing approaches may touch upon complexity reduction processes during the analyzing, transforming, and synthesizing of such signals, to date, they have not robustly addressed adversarial exploitation of the complexity reduction processes. Although some exploration of unbounded polytopes has been conducted, principally, the research has been constrained to that of bounded convex polytopes.

III. The Signal Processing Intent of Resilient Networked Distributed Tessellation Communications (RNDTC) and a True Adaptive Beamforming Approach

Among the core specifications of various transceiver polygon approaches, and temporarily setting aside Size, Weight, Power, and Cost (SWaP-C) considerations, the overall intent is scrutinized. The asserted "Big Idea" for the various transceiver polygon approaches (such as delineated by the Defense Advanced Research Projects Agency or DARPA) center upon the following goal — enhanced robustness against failure/attack and enhanced stealthiness.

A. The Signal Processing Intent of Resilient Networked Distributed Tessellation Communications (RNDTC)

This translates, technically, into the following signal processing tasks, among others, for the approach vector delineated herein (all the following six signal processing tasks should be advanced to Technology Readiness Level or TRL 3+): (1) Advance an adaptive beamforming algorithm that will enhance the beamforming and endeavor to mitigate against interference morphological adjustments, (2) Advance a hybridized Adaptive Weight Vector (AWV) algorithm conjoined with a decomposition-based evolutionary algorithm (a.k.a. Genetic Algorithm or GA), which are both supported by an Artificial Intelligence (AI)-based prioritization algorithm for selective continual updating of the AWV, (3) Advance a Semi-Definite Programming (SDP) algorithm, which can transform the AWV derivation, via maximizing a recast Signal-to-Interference-plus-Noise Ratio (SINR) criterion subject to a similarity constraint, that can be recast as a convex optimization problem, (4) Advance a Quadratically Constrained Quadratic Programming (QCQP) step-down algorithm, which will compute the QCQP special class convex optimization problem in polynomial time, (5) Advance, via a multi-dimensional Space-Time Adaptive Processing (STAP) algorithmic solution set, an enhancement of the maximized SINR, and (6) Advance a structural exploitation of the covariance interference matrix so as to leverage SDP Solvers and ascertain optimal pre-processors.

B. True Adaptive Beamforming Approach

For this discussion, beamforming will refer to the self-forming adaptive array. Axiomatically, the simplistic notion of beam steering (i.e., mechanical positioning to alter the antenna orientation, fixed phase offsets, etc.) will be bypassed, and the discussion shall proceed to true adaptive beamforming. The first priority of an adaptive beamforming algorithm is signal extraction while concurrently suppressing interference as well as noise. The differentiation between the involved methodological approach, as contrasted to conventional approaches (which often experience non-graceful performance degradation) is that of hybridizing, via a prioritization engine, signal-subspace projection (eigenspace-based beamformers, via orthogonal projection of signal subspace, can reduce a substantive portion of noise), diagonal loading (incongruity between the posited and actual array response can be mitigated, via automatic computations), and other methodological approaches to reduce noise, interference, and performance degradation. Collectively, these methods will be selected (based upon the time involved) to enhance the beamforming and endeavor to mitigate against interference morphological adjustments (e.g., propagation channel varying, interference dynamism, etc).

IV. Selective Updating of the Adaptive Weight Vector, a High-Performance Semi-Definite Programming (SDP) Solver, and Reduction from Non-deterministic Polynomial-time Hardness (NP-Hard) to Polynomial Time for Signal-to-Interference-plus-Noise Ratio (SINR) Computations

A particular triumvirate approach has been shown to be effective in prosecuting the task of achieving the described intent: (1) selective updating of the adaptive weight vector, (2) utilizing a high-performance SDP Solver, and (3) reducing the complexity class from NP-Hard to polynomial time for the involved SINR computations.

A. Selective Updating of the Adaptive Weight Vector

Fortunately, the computational availability of Field Programmable Gate Arrays (FPGAs) can facilitate the selective updating of the optimal adaptive weight vector (AWV). Concurrently, derivative null broadening algorithms (the imposition of nulls toward the regions of the nonstationary interference, predicated upon the reconstruction of the interference-plus-noise covariance matrix) offset the need for continuous updating and can move the paradigm towards selective updating. In essence, the AWV can be derived, via maximizing a recast SINR criterion subject to a similarity constraint. On a parallel pathway, the AWV can be validated, and more finely-tuned, via a decomposition-based evolutionary algorithm coupled with AWV, for normalized as well as scaled cases, amidst a multi-faceted non-permissive environs.

B. High-Performance Semi-Definite Programming (SDP) Solver

The described pathways converge for a constrained paradigm, which can be transformed into a convex optimization problem, via SDP solvers. The SDP solvers utilized to date have been implemented on a GNU Octave platform; signal processing and fuzzy logic packages were obtained, via Octave Forge, for use on GNU Octave. As a numerical computation platform, GNU Octave is mostly compatible with the likes of MATLAB. However, as GNU Octave is released under a GNU GPLv3 license, the source code was modified in the lab environment so as to take advantage of Compute Unified Device Architecture (CUDA) multi-threaded parallel computing accelerants for the involved SDP solvers to quickly address the various involved convex optimization problems described herein. It should also be noted that GPLv3 avoids the issue of tivoization (the instantiation of a system that incorporates software under the terms of a copyleft software license but leverages hardware restrictions or digital rights management to prevent users from running modified versions of the software on the involved hardware).

C. Reduction from Non-deterministic Polynomial-time Hardness (NP-Hard) to Polynomial Time for Signal-to-Interference-plus-Noise Ratio (SINR) Computations

Once in the convex form, which constitutes a special class, the computational complexity of the involved QCQP can be reduced from Non-deterministic Polynomial-time Hardness (NP-hard) to the desired optimality in polynomial time. Historically, this had been tested in Ilog Cplex Optimizer (a commercial software package for optimization); however, contemporary testing has migrated to AD Model Builder (ADMB) (an open source software package for non-linear statistical modeling) and Interior Point OPTimizer (IPOPT) (a software package for large-scale nonlinear optimization). Preliminary results have delineated maximized SINR for the signal detection processors (amidst interference – including narrowband jamming signals – and noise).

V. Enhancing the Maximized Signal-to-Interference-plus-Noise Ratio (SINR), via Space-Time Adaptive Processing (STAP)

Prior experimentation with STAP had been undertaken on the Phased Array System Toolbox. However, the performance of the involved complex simulations, which was essential for subsequent analysis, was suboptimal for the involved cases. As discussed above, preliminary experiments on MATLAB & Simulink segued to a Modified GNU Octave (M-GNU-O) platform. On this customized high performance, multi-threaded platform, certain insights could be quickly gleaned when testing various algorithms with regards to spatial multiplexing. For example, as transceiver polygons were removed, thereby simulating various scenarios (e.g., destroyed transceiver polygons), the array was re-formed and optimal re-configurations were re-computed in quasi-real time; this requisite software-defined paradigm — axiomatic, given the Software-Defined Radio (SDR) rubric of the various transceiver polygon approaches — underscored a fundamental point. If the utilized algorithm and platform exhibited sub-optimal performance, the associated processes would be too immature for subsequent implementation onto a programmable System-on-Chip (SoC) paradigm. Hence, the algorithmic testing on the M-GNU-O proved invaluable.

Indeed, the application of STAP can greatly enhance performance of the posited Resilient Networked Distributed Tessellation Communications (RNDTC) application paradigm, via identification of diversity paths, so as to mitigate against the multipath interference phenomenon as well as more intrusive interference measures. The determination of the diversity paths were formulated, via certain elastic functions. Furthermore, the diversity paths were validated by an AI prioritization engine [6], and exemplar Diversity Paths (DPs) can be seen in Figure 3 below [7].

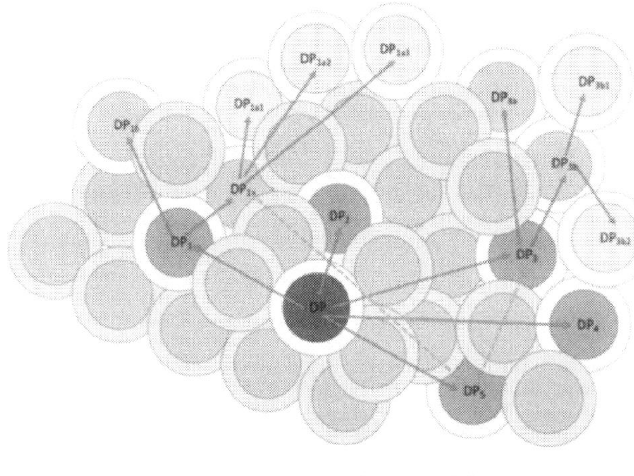

Fig. 3. Exemplar Diversity Paths (DPs)

A key factor to a robust STAP interference suppression paradigm, in addition to an advanced SDR emulation environment platform, resides in the determination of the covariance matrix, and a successful exploitation of the structure of the covariance interference matrix is addressed below.

VI. Structure Exploitation of the Covariance Interference Matrix

A. Pre-Processing

Measurement uncertainty and inaccuracy precludes success by detection processors. Let us take a given signal, which for baselining purposes is construed to be a sequence of infinite duration in the positive and negative directions (i.e., two-sided sequence), of $x = \{x_t, t=0, \pm1, \pm2, \dots\}$ on the time horizon 0, 1, …, N-1 in accordance with (1):

$$y = x_o^{N-1} + \xi \tag{1}$$

where $\xi \sim \mathcal{N}(0, I_N)$ can be representative of simple white Gaussian noise and $z_o^{N-1} = [z_0; \dots ; z_{N-1}]$; y is utilized to distinguish between two criterion: (1) nuisance noise, wherein $x \in H_0$, and H_0 is comprised of all linear combinations of d_n factors of known frequencies (i.e., the gamut of nuisance noises), and (2) intended signal plus nuisance noise signals, wherein $x \in H_1(\rho)$, and $H_1(\rho)$ is the set of all sequences x representable as $s + u$ with the nuisance noise component u belonging to H_0 and the signal component s equating to at most d_S factors (frequency agnostic), such that the uniform distance, on the time horizon in question, from x to all nuisance noise signals, is at least ρ, such as is shown by (2) [8]:

$$\min_{z \in Ho} \| x_o^{N-1} - z_o^{N-1} \|_\infty \geq \rho \tag{2}$$

The principal goal of the pre-processing algorithm is to distinguish, with a given confidence $1 - \alpha$, between (1) and (2) for as small ρ as possible. Given the sample y, a convex optimization problem is solved, and the resultant is compared with a threshold $q_N(\alpha)$, which is a valid upper bound of the $1 - \alpha$ quantile of (3) of a given tolerance, as further delineated in (4).

$$\|F_N\, \xi\|_\infty,\ \alpha \in (0,1) \tag{3}$$

$$\text{Prob}_{\xi \sim N(0,\, I_N)}\{\|F_N\, \xi\|_\infty > q_N(\alpha)\} \leq \alpha \tag{4}$$

and if Opt (y) <= $q_N(\alpha)$, the nuisance noise pathway is taken and further pre-processing must occur [8]. Conversely, if the nuisance noise has been successfully winnowed, such as shown in Figure 4 below [7], and the signal plus pathway is adopted, then the pre-processing phase advances to an initial processing phase for STAP.

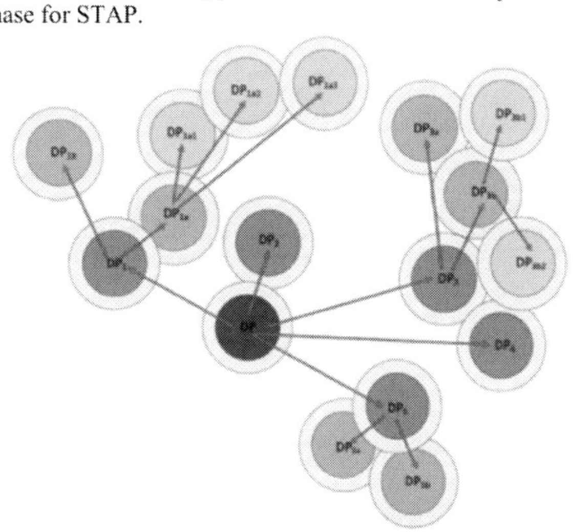

Fig. 4. Nuisance Noise Winnowing for the Diversity Paths (DPs)

It is generally accepted that the optimal STAP filter is often designed based upon being able to discern the known covariance matrix and the known Doppler angle. The principal challenge of STAP is resolving and inverting the unknown interference covariance matrix.

B. *Initial Processing*

Under ideal conditions, given a rescaled matrix, wherein the variables are rescaled, the referenced inversion is numerically stable. Under non-ideal conditions, given an ill-conditioned matrix, the inversion is numerically unstable. Presuming this non-ideal state of varied scaled variables, a viable approach vector would be to have the individual variable scales be kept distinct and disparate from the correlation matrix. Otherwise, the covariance matrix might be adversely impacted with an ill-conditioned number simply because of the varied scaled variables. As an ill-conditioned covariance matrix may amplify estimation error, an ongoing matrix regularization strategy, among other methodologies, is adopted [9].

C. *Ongoing Processing*

The real-time performance of STAP techniques often undergo a non-graceful degradation in heterogeneous environs due to the inaccurate estimation of the interference covariance matrix (R_I) from secondary data [10]; oftentimes, this degradation vulnerability is addressed by endeavoring to suppress the associated noise or clutter. In many cases, the overall STAP effectiveness is determined by the assumed relative homogeneity of the secondary data $\{y_s, s=1, 2, \ldots, N_s\}$, and generally speaking, given the availability of $N_s \geq 2MN$ homogeneous secondary data, the sample covariance matrix $R_s \triangleq (1/\ N_s) \sum_{s=1}^{Ns} y_s y_s^H$ yields a satisfactory estimate of R_I. However, for a fully adaptive STAP, the requisite secondary data constitutes such a large corpus that the associated requisite homogeneity property, amidst the intrinsic non-stationarity of the interference, is acknowledged to be impractical. To overcome such pragmatic constraint limitations, partially adaptive STAP approaches may be employed, which assume that the dominant interferences are constrained to a low-dimensional subspace; various Dimensionality Reduction (DR) STAP algorithms are available, and they are typically classified by the type of pre-processor utilized. By way of example, [beamspace] beamforming (rather than leveraging the spatial statistics of the array elements to differentiate among the signal and interference matrices, the spatial statistics of orthogonal beams — which are formed in different directions — are leveraged; this represents a shift from the higher dimension element space to the lower dimension beamspace while still achieving comparable performance) algorithms typically leverage spatial pre-processing, whereas post-doppler algorithms might leverage temporal [Doppler] pre-processing. In yet other scenarios, the structure of the clutter can be exploited to design pre-processors, which might yield the optimal minimal acceptable rank (i.e., Rank Minimization Problem or RMP) of the clutter covariance matrix [11]; the rank of the clutter covariance matrix provides insight into the expanse of the clutter paradigm as well as indicates the number of Degrees-of-Freedom (DoF) needed to achieve an effective clutter cancellation. In many cases, the involved dimensionality reduction is achieved, via various matrix rank reduction methods (wherein the approximating matrix, the optimization variable, has reduced rank compared to the given matrix, the sourced data), and the resultant lower rank matrix decomposition-based solution necessitates twice the secondary measurements as that of the rank of the clutter covariance matrix so as to achieve optimal STAP performance. In contrast to the rank reduction approach, the spatio-temporal sparsity recovery approach needs a substantially even smaller corpus of secondary data [12].

1) Rank Reduction Approach

Generally speaking, matrix decomposition problems involve a sample covariance matrix being decomposed into the sum of a low rank positive semidefinite matrix and a diagonal matrix. This equates to computing $\hat{R}_I = \hat{R}_c + \hat{R}_n$, where $\hat{R}_c$ and $\hat{R}_n$ are examined, via resolving the following Rank Minimization Problem (RMP):

$$(\hat{R}_c, \hat{R}_n) = \arg \min_{R_c, R_n} \text{rank}(\hat{R}_c), \quad (5)$$

$$\text{subject to} \begin{cases} R_c + R_n = R_s \\ R_c \geq 0 \\ R_n \text{ diagonal} \end{cases}$$

The RMP cannot be solved directly as the rank function is nonconvex and discontinuous. Hence, to make the problem convex, the rank function is replaced with the trace function and resolved by treatment as a Trace Minimization Problem (TMP):

$$(\hat{R}_c, \hat{R}_n) = \arg \min_{R_c, R_n} \text{tr}(\hat{R}_c), \quad (6)$$

$$\text{subject to} \begin{cases} R_c + R_n = R_s \\ R_c \geq 0 \\ R_n \text{ diagonal} \end{cases}$$

Since the rank function tallies the number of nonzero eigenvalues, and the trace function computes the sum of the involved eigenvalues, the equation can be reconstrued as an equivalent SDP:

$$(\hat{R}_c, \hat{R}_n) = \arg \min_{R_c, R_n} \text{tr}(\hat{R}_c), \quad (7)$$

$$\text{subject to} \begin{cases} \begin{bmatrix} W_1 & R_c \\ R_C^H & W_2 \end{bmatrix} \\ R_c + R_n = Rs \\ Rc \geq 0 \\ R_n \text{ diagonal} \end{cases}$$

Once in this form, there are numerous SDP solvers (e.g., SDPT3, which is a MATLAB/GNU Octave Semi-Definite Programming or SDP software package) available for these types of problems, and as previously discussed in Section IVB, the M-GNU-O platform has readily supported various high-performance SDP solvers.

2) Spatio-Temporal Sparsity Recovery Approach

Generally speaking, the spatio-temporal sparsity recovery approach is analogous to the rank reduction approach; in essence, the involved l_0-minimization problems are Non-deterministic Polynomial-time Hardness (NP-Hard). However, under certain conditions, such as described in Donoho's "Compressed Sensing," convex relaxation methods may be applied, wherein the l_0 norm is replaced by the l_1 norm, thereby maintaining the sparsity while also being a convex function [13][14]. There are numerous convex relaxation methods, and once again, as previously discussed in Section IVB, the M-GNU-O platform has readily supported various high-performance SDP solvers.

D. Post-Processing

As a semblance of analytical scrutinization, by way of post-processing, it is noted that while sidelobe interferences can be sufficiently suppressed by adaptive beamforming, countering interference in the mainlobe area segues to other issues, such as pattern distortion and decreased output signal with regards to the Signal-to-Interference-plus-Noise Ratio(SINR). Among others, various adaptive Kalman filter algorithms have been experimented with for coping with the unknown interference covariance matrix, which can involve [measurement] noise covariance matrices estimation (which is based upon state estimation techniques) [15]; these provide an approximation of the noise in the involved system [16]. In essence, a lower covariance value would segue to higher confidence in the detection result at time *t*, whereas a higher covariance value would segue to a higher confidence in the prior detection result at time *t-1* rather than that of time *t*.

Overall, this Section VI has articulated the leveraging of SDP solvers (and the further leveraging of optimal pre-processors). As discussed, the known structure of the clutter can be exploited to design pre-processors, which might facilitate the resolving of the clutter covariance matrix, via RMP. With regards to the known structure of the clutter, in many cases, this can be baselined over time. For example, diplomatic facilities (e.g., embassies) and their associated military annexes are relatively static; acknowledging that there is ongoing construction, renovation, and activities in the abutting areas, the structure of the clutter at relatively static locations can be better discerned with time (i.e., baselining). Accordingly, pertinent hyper-locale pre-processors can be devised.

VII. SPACE-TIME ADAPTIVE PROCESSING (STAP) HEURISTICAL VULNERABILITY EXPLOITATION AND AN EXPERIMENTAL MITIGATION FACTOR FOR THE STAP VULNERABILITY OF RESILIENT NETWORKED DISTRIBUTED TESSELLATION COMMUNICATIONS (RNDTC)

A. STAP Heuristical Vulnerability Exploitation

The described heuristic (lower covariance value → higher confidence in the detection result at time *t;* higher covariance value → higher confidence in the detection result at time *t-1)* constitutes a configuration parameter, which can be exploited, particularly when time-sensitive real-time detection systems are central to the system (e.g., You Only Look Once or YOLO v3) and Adversarial Machine Learning (ML) attacks (AMLA) are involved. The AMLA can target from among pre-processing, initial processing, ongoing processing, and post-processing (e.g., manipulation of doppler has already long been an issue [16]). Some would construe this to constitute a long-range, precision non-lethal effect, in accordance with the U.S. Army's "America's Army: Ready Now, Investing in the Future (FY19-21 Accomplishments and Investment Plan)" Multi-Domain Task Forces (MDTFs), which are "tailorable units that join Intelligence, Information, Cyber, Electronic Warfare, and Space (I2CEWS) capabilities with fires and other capabilities to deliver long-range, precision non-lethal, and as appropriate, lethal effects across joint and multi-national platforms." In the described scenario, the "Long-Range Precision Effect" is shown to be potentially operative on the STAP processing of what could be part of a mission-critical communications apparatus (as a target node). A real-world example of the import centers upon is U.S. Secretary Pompeo's announcement on 29 April 2020 that the U.S. Department of State will "require a clean path for all 5G network traffic coming into and out of U.S. diplomatic facilities at home and overseas." The described STAP heuristical vulnerability exploitation is part of that cyber-physical supply chain consideration.

B. *Experimental Mitigation Factor for the Space-Time Adaptive Processing (STAP) Vulnerability of Resilient Networked Distributed Tessellation Communications (RNDTC)*

The optimal filter is a unique member among an infinite set of consistent filters [17]. The configuration parameter or parameter tuning of the optimal filter, even after it is ascertained, can be manipulated. Tuning typically employs two approaches: Statistical Consistency Tests (SCT) (which employs statistical hypothesis testing to determine the consistency of the filter), and True Covariance Analysis (TCA) (which facilitates a computable true estimation error covariance). However, neither SCT nor TCA seem to suffice for ascertaining the true performance of the filter. Hence, AI-centric automated tuning approaches have been experimented with.

Fundamentally, Genetic Algorithms (GAs) are optimization algorithms. GAs tend to be quite efficient when a large search space is involved, the involved optimization computation can readily be parallelized, and they are of zero order (i.e., independent of the prior). GAs treat each parameter set, within the parameter space, individually. The fitness function for a given individual entity is generated by SCT, and if the individual entity is found to be consistent, its fitness is the estimated covariance norm. Alternatively, the fitness is comprised of the consistency values J. This is presented in (6) below [18].

$$\text{fitness} = \begin{cases} \parallel P \parallel & J < 0.05 \\ -J & otherwise \end{cases} \qquad (6)$$

The approach utilized was that of a GA subset entitled "Steady-State GA" (SSGA), wherein: (1) if two filters are inconsistent, their fitness value is negative, and the closer one to zero is more optimal; (2) if only one filter is consistent, the fitness value is positive, and it is construed as more optimal than the other inconsistent filter with the negative fitness value; and (3) if both filters are consistent, the more optimal filter is that with the smaller fitness value. Consequently, this re-evaluation of the filter performance enhances the reliability by removing filters that do not perform well in a consistent fashion [18][19]. In essence, the SSGA can be construed as a discrete-time dynamic system non-generational model. The value-added proposition for the experimental mitigation factor for the STAP vulnerability of RNDTC is a compression factor ζ that, in some instances, serves to squeeze the steady-state population towards an accelerated convergence. A larger compression factor ζ is indicative of a compressed convergence and corresponds to a higher magnitude jump size for the fittest proportion from one generation to the successor generator; conversely, a smaller compression factor ζ is indicative of an elongated convergence and corresponds to a lower magnitude jump size. To avoid issues of local minima (e.g., random noise), dynamically turning the compression factor ζ may provide an invaluable methodology to adjust convergence, thereby resulting in a tunable parameter that obviates the problem of premature convergence and non-optimality. In summary, the SSGA approach can indeed effectuate auto-parameter tuning so as to minimize the window for exploitation as pertains to the identified STAP heuristical vulnerability exploitation. The described work was performed in an experimentation-innovation lab in Orlando, Florida; other labs (a.k.a. "living labs") for exploring 5G-enabled defense applications and use cases are starting to emerge and multiply [20].

VIII. Preliminary Experimental Results

Simulations run atop the M-GNU-O platform have indicated that statistical consistency tests are not reliable for discerning an optimal filter. Rather, the tests yield an infinite set of consistent filters within which the optimal filter is a unique member. Preliminary experimental results indicate promise for the auto-tuning of the Steady State Genetic Algorithm (SSGA) compression factor ζ for more optimal convergence of an optimally tuned filter (or a set of near optimally tuned filters). Indeed, auto-tuning is central to this capability, and the compression factor ζ is instrumental in dictating the rate of the steady state towards convergence. Large ζ values may be indicative of earlier (i.e., premature) convergence, thereby segueing to specious solutions that have keyed in on local minima and/or noise, thereby precluding a more optimal convergence. Accordingly, one observation centers around the fact that the ability to re-tune the compression factor ζ to a lower value (i.e., <1) seems to be critical. Another observation centers around the Principal Tuning Result (PTR) for an exponentially bounded fitness, given the characteristic time λ for an overall time dependent population fitness F, which satisfies the convergence condition in (7):

$$\text{PTR} = [F_{t+1} - F_t] < F_t\,(e^{-\lambda t} - 1) \qquad (7)$$

In essence, the PTR allows for an SSGA optimization estimate for the convergent approach of the time dependent population fitness F in a quasi-analytical fashion prior to a given numerical iteration, and this is consistent with other research in the field, such as that conducted at the Sante Fe Institute [21]. Field experiments were conducted in environments, wherein the involved electrical grids (in these cases, "Smart Grids") were generating Radio Frequency Interference (RFI), via faulty electric equipment, that went beyond the prototypical radiation emissions of the usual powerlines and electric utility-related equipment (classified as "incidental radiators" by the Federal Communications Commission or FCC in the U.S.).

IX. Conclusion

In many cases, prototypical weighting techniques are utilized to attain reduced sidelobes at the expense of a more expansive and robust mainlobe [22]. In essence, some interference suppression is achieved by sacrificing the resolution of the signals. For example, the introduction of self-induced white noise (signals that mitigate against/mask other signals) could mitigate adversarial-introduced attack vectors; the white noise is generated, via receiver-based nullification endeavors, wherein the weights and phase shifts associated with a receive node or cluster of receive nodes dynamically adapt in a coalition fashion to create directional nulls. Along the vein of weight shifts, adaptive weighting techniques utilize time-varying weights so as to achieve more robust interference suppression as well as relatively higher resolution signals. Despite the advantages, adaptive techniques are computationally intensive (e.g., matrix inversion), and a variety of processing tasks are required to reduce this computational complexity. At the core, transforming problems into convex optimization problems, which can be resolved in polynomial time, and leveraging SDP solvers is a common thematic. However, the involved processes, such as STAP, reveal heuristical reliances that are subject to adversarial exploitation. Accordingly, these heuristics (i.e., configuration parameters) need to be sufficiently annealed and optimized. Accordingly, this paper proposes mitigation factors by way of AI-centric GA amidst the analysis, transformation, and synthesis amalgam. Section VIIB discussed the SSGA approach to effectuate auto-parameter tuning so as to minimize the window for exploitation as pertains to the identified STAP heuristical vulnerability exploitation. Proxy use cases (e.g., electrical grid sector) proved useful for auto-tuning experimentation as pertains to the compression factor ζ, which dictates the efficacy of the convergence upon an optimally tuned filter (or a set of near optimally tuned filters). Future work will involve furthering the exploration of the SSGA compression factor ζ and conducting more in-depth research into the SDP solver(s) atop the customized M-GNU-O platform.

Acknowledgment

This research is supported by the Decision Engineering Analysis Laboratory (DEAL), an Underwatch initiative, which has previously supported the FTA Program under the Assistant Secretary of Defense for Research and Engineering (ASDRE), via participation at certain venues (e.g., IARIA). This is part of a VT white paper series on 5G-enabled defense applications, via proxy use cases, to help inform Project Enabler.

References

[1] D. González G., H. Hakula, A. Rasila and J. Hämäläinen, "Spatial Mappings for Planning and Optimization of Cellular Networks," in *IEEE/ACM Transactions on Networking*, vol. 26, no. 1, pp. 175-188, Feb. 2018, doi: 10.1109/TNET.2017.2768561.

[2] Y. Kim, J. Lee, G. Atkinson, H. Kim and M. Thottan, "SeDAX: A Scalable, Resilient, and Secure Platform for Smart Grid Communications," in *IEEE Journal on Selected Areas in Communications*, vol. 30, no. 6, pp. 1119-1136, July 2012, doi: 10.1109/JSAC.2012.120710.

[3] H. V. K. Mendis and F. Y. Li, "Achieving Ultra Reliable Communication in 5G Networks: A Dependability Perspective Availability Analysis in the Space Domain," in *IEEE Communications Letters*, vol. 21, no. 9, pp. 2057-2060, Sept. 2017, doi: 10.1109/LCOMM.2017.2696958.

[4] Y. Benchaabene, N. Boujnah and F. Zarai, "Ultra Reliable Communication : Availability Analysis in 5G Cellular Networks," *2019 20th International Conference on Parallel and Distributed Computing, Applications and Technologies (PDCAT)*, Gold Coast, Australia, 2019, pp. 96-102, doi: 10.1109/PDCAT46702.2019.00029.

[5] "U.S. Army Cyber Warfare Field Manual (FM) 3-38," *Department of the Army*, February 2014.

[6] S. Chan and P. Nopphawan, "Artificial Intelligence-Based Approach for Forced Oscillation Source Detection and Classification," in press.

[7] S. Chan, "Prototype Resilient Command and Control (C2) of C2 Architecture for Power Outage Mitigation," *2019 IEEE 10th Annual Information Technology, Electronics and Mobile Communication Conference (IEMCON)*, Vancouver, BC, Canada, 2019, pp. 0779-0785, doi: 10.1109/IEMCON.2019.8936241.

[8] A. Juditsky and A. Nemirovski, "On Detecting Harmonic Oscillations," *Bernoulli*, vol. 21, no. 2, pp. 1134–1165, 2014, doi: 10.3150/14-BEJ600.

[9] J. Won, J. Lim, S. Kim, and B. Rajaratnam, "Condition Number Regularized Covariance Estimation," in J R Stat Soc Series B Stat Methodol, vol. 75, no. 3, pp. 427-450, June 2013, doi: 10.1111/j.1467-9868.2012.01049.x

[10] H. Yan, R. Wang, C. Gao, Y. Deng, and M. Zheng, "A novel clutter suppression algorithm with Kalman filtering," *2013 IEEE Radar Conference (RadarCon13)*, Ottawa, ON, 2013, pp. 1-4, doi: 10.1109/RADAR.2013.6586105.

[11] J. Ward, "Space-time adaptive processing for airborne radar," *1995 International Conference on Acoustics, Speech, and Signal Processing*, Detroit, MI, USA, 1995, pp. 2809-2812 vol.5, doi: 10.1109/ICASSP.1995.479429.

[12] S. Sen, "Low-Rank Matrix Decomposition and Spatio-Temporal Sparse Recovery for STAP Radar," in *IEEE Journal of Selected Topics in Signal Processing*, vol. 9, no. 8, pp. 1510-1523, Dec. 2015, doi: 10.1109/JSTSP.2015.2464187.

[13] D. L. Donoho, "Compressed sensing," *IEEE Trans. Inf. Theory*, vol. 52, no. 4, pp. 1289–1306, Apr. 2006.

[14] M. Zibulevsky and M. Elad, "L1-L2 optimization in signal and image processing," *IEEE Signal Process. Mag.*, vol. 27, no. 3, pp. 76–88, May 2010.

[15] H. Wang, Z. Deng, B. Feng, H. Ma, and Y. Xia, "An adaptive Kalman filter estimating process noise covariance," Neurocomputing, vol. 223, pp. 12-17, February 2017.

[16] D. Koks, "How to Create and Manipulate Radar Range-Doppler Plots," Defense Science and Technology Organization (DSTO)-TN-1386, Department of Defence, Australian Government, pp. i-87.

[17] J. Dunik, M. Simandl, and O. Straka, "Methods for Estimating State and Measurement Noise Covariance Matrices: Aspects and Comparison," IFAC Proceedings Volumes, vol 42, No. 10, 2009, pp. 372-277, https://doi.org/10.3182/20090706-3-FR-2004.00061.

[18] Y. Oshman and I. Shaviv, "Optimal Tuning of a Kalman Filter Using Genetic Algorithms," American Institute of Aeronautics & Astronautics Guidance, Navigation, and Control Conference, August 2000, pp. 1- 11, doi:10.2514/6.2000-4558.

[19] J. Yan, D. Yuan, X. Xing, and Q. Jia, "Kalman filtering parameter optimization techniques based on genetic algorithm," *2008 IEEE International Conference on Automation and Logistics*, Qingdao, 2008, pp. 1717-1720, doi: 10.1109/ICAL.2008.

[20] B. Vincent, "U.S. Marine Corps, Verizon Launch 'Living Lab' to Test 5G," Nextgov, 22 July 2020. [Online]. Available from: https://www.nextgov.com/emerging-tech/2020/07/us-marine-corps-verizon-launch-living-lab-test-5g/167093/.

[21] D. Noever and S. Baskaran, "Steady-State vs. Generational Genetic Algorithms: A Comparison of Time Complexity and Convergence Properties, Santa Fe Institute, pp. 15-18.

[22] L. Xin, Y. BaoGuo, and H. Ping, "Mainlobe interference suppression via eigen-projection processing and covariance matrix sparse reconstruction," IEICE Electronics Express, vol. 15, no. 17, pp. 1-8, doi: 10.1587/elex.15.20180683.

Virtual Private Blockchains: Security Overlays for Permissioned Blockchains

Samuel Onalo*, Deepak GC†, Eckhard Pfluegel‡
Faculty of SEC, Kingston University
Kingston upon Thames, Surrey, KT1 2EE, United Kingdom
email: *k1450301@kingston.ac.uk, †d.gc@kingston.ac.uk, ‡e.pfluegel@kingston.ac.uk

***Abstract*—Blockchain technology, while maturing, is still lacking features that would be considered indispensable in real-world business applications. In particular, the lack of transaction confidentiality in a public blockchain is a challenging problem. A possible solution might be the concept of a private blockchain. However, maintaining such permissioned blockchains requires resources, depends on a central authority and contradicts the original philosophy of pioneering blockchain systems such as Bitcoin. In this paper, the concept of a *Virtual Private Blockchain* (VPBC) is proposed as a mechanism to create a blockchain architecture with properties akin to those of a private blockchain, however leveraging existing public blockchain functionality. A VPBC can be set up between individuals or organisations, does not require any significant administrative maintenance, inherits all the functionality from the public blockchain, and achieves anonymity and transaction confidentiality with respect to any public blockchain node who does not belong to the VPBC. Building on this theoretical concept, it is then shown how the cryptographic technique of secret sharing can be used in order to implement a simple VPBC architecture. A proof-of-concept architecture has been created and early experiments indicate that the creation of VPBCs for potential real-world application scenarios might be feasible.**

Index Terms*—Public Blockchain; Private Blockchain; Permissioned Blockchain; Blockchain Confidentiality; Security Overlays; Virtual Private Networks; Secret Sharing.

I. Introduction

According to recent research, the adoption of Blockchain technology is steadily increasing, and major business organisations are currently investigating how to benefit from features such as immutability and public verifiability of data, decentralised architecture and (pseudo) anonymity of transactional data. As blockchain technology is gradually maturing, the quest for suitable applications is shaping the future of decentralised, networked functionality providing data integrity services and innovations in the fields of big data, cloud computing and cryptography. However, current blockchain technologies are not always able to address all specific security requirements for individual, specialist applications. For example, a public blockchain application would not be able to provide the required confidentiality to allow independent financial institutions to share sensitive data securely and anonymously.

A possible solution to this problem is the concept of a private blockchain. This is a restricted-access network, where permission has to be granted to prospective participants for transactional and administrative participation in network activities. Typically, cryptocurrencies are built on public blockchains, in which anyone can elect to join and participate. By contrast, private blockchains are targeted towards businesses and institutions who want the benefits of blockchain technology (e.g., distributed ledger consensus and immutability) but want to limit the scope of the facility, to in-house entities and trusted partners. However, maintaining such a private blockchain requires resources. Also, it contradicts the original intention of the pioneering Bitcoin technology, aiming to not rely on a central body.

The fundamental research question addressed in this paper is whether there are alternatives to the concept of a private blockchain architecture. A focus is on innovative security architectures, the application of suitable cryptographic techniques, and their use within the blockchain architecture. Furthermore, an assessment of the benefits arising from the real-world use cases of this architecture is of importance.

In this paper, the following contributions are made. First, the novel concept of a *Virtual Private Blockchain* (VPBC) is shaped, implemented and initially evaluated. A VPBC is a mechanism to create a blockchain architecture with properties akin to those of a private blockchain, however leveraging existing public blockchain functionality. Second, we show how to use the cryptographic technique of secret sharing in order to implement a simple VPBC. Finally, we devise a proof-of-concept architecture and first experiments indicate that there appear to be no major obstacles in adopting VPBCs in future real-world application scenarios.

To our knowledge, both the conceptual ideas of this paper as well as the application of secret sharing in an architecture across several blockchain systems are novel and have not been proposed in this form, in the literature to date.

This paper is organised as follows: In Section II, concepts and techniques for securing blockchain functionality are presented. Section III contains the description of the VPBC architecture, while in Section IV, an implementation and evaluation is reported. Section V relates the results of this paper to the literature, and the paper concludes in Section VI.

II. Blockchain Security

In this section, we review the basic security aspects of the blockchain. We will start with briefly recalling security concepts and techniques currently in use for achieving existing security goals in publicly available blockchain systems, with a focus on confidentiality. This will be followed by more advanced techniques improving specific dependability and security aspects of the blockchain suggested in the recent literature as conceptual contributions or used in prototype solutions.

A. Cryptographic Techniques for Blockchain Security Features

A number of cryptographic techniques are in place in mainstream blockchain applications in order to fulfil basic security requirements.

Cryptographic hash functions are used in order to ensure the integrity of the public ledger, a global record of Blockchain transactions. Based on a suitable, efficient data structure (the hash tree), even minor changes in large amounts of data can be detected and repaired if necessary. Furthermore, the principle of mining which is a digital protocol, mimicking the creation of scarce resources, implements necessary work for creating new, validated blocks by performing a pre-image attack on given hash digest values. Validation can be carried out efficiently by re-computing the digest.

The authenticity of digital messages and data is usually demonstrated or verified using digital signatures. It allows for the effective origin and message integrity as well as non-repudiation of communication between two parties. In a Blockchain, participants can sign transactions with their private keys. In Bitcoin, the concept of a wallet is implemented, controlling the spending power of a user based on a private and public key pair. Cryptocurrency transactions are not completely anonymous in nature, however, the true identities of transactors are hidden and are not provided as part of the accessible data stored on the public blockchain. The transactions are considered to be pseudonymous as the only form of identity any node on the network possesses is the wallet identity which effectively is the public key of the wallet that is owned by the node.

B. Establishing Transaction Confidentiality

More recently, a number of Blockchain systems have started addressing the lack of confidentiality for transactional information, through a variety of mechanisms. We shall present two approaches, provided by the prominent Blockchain systems Hyperledger Fabric and Multichain. These are also, the systems we have used for our first experiments towards a novel security solution, as described later on in this paper.

1) HyperLedger Fabric Channels : Hyperledger is an open-source ecosystem of blockchain services run and maintained by IBM which has developed a means of providing confidentiality by the use of a private communication "subnet". The principle is to implement so-called *Channels* [1] between two or more specific network members. A complex infrastructure of cryptographic protocols and a range of security services including confidential inter-channel communication and transactions are available. While this provides a sophisticated and powerful infrastructure for achieving the desired confidentiality on the Blockchain, it requires expertise and resources in order to deploy, configure, and manage a HyperLedger Fabric Blockchain within one or potentially several organisations.

2) Multichain Stream Confidentiality : The Multichain Blockchain system acknowledges the confidentiality loss of any raw data stored on a public ledger and proposes to address this by using a combination of symmetric and asymmetric cryptography. Any data intended to be submitted to the system is encrypted before being stored and timestamped on the chain. The password for reading the encrypted data is only made available to a subset of blockchain participants, leaving others unable to read it.

The method makes use of three blockchain streams [2], whose purposes are as follows:

- A first stream is used by participants to distribute their public Rivest, Shamir and Adleman (RSA) keys.
- A second stream is used to publish large pieces of data, bulk-encrypted using the Advanced Encryption Standard (AES) algorithm.
- A third stream provides data access. For each authorised participant, a stream entry is created which stores a security credential encrypted with the participant's public key.

While this architecture appears secure and efficient, it requires the availability of a Public Key Infrastructure (PKI) expert for effective management.

C. Advanced Blockchain Dependability and Security

In this section, the specialist topic area of using advanced cryptographic techniques for improving blockchain security is explored. This will help in illustrating the novelty of our approach in terms of how we achieve anonymity and confidentiality, using the cryptographic technique of secret sharing.

The main overall challenges for the blockchain are scalability and privacy. The first challenge is a serious reason why currently, most blockchain systems do not qualify as mainstream payment systems. They do not have enough processing power to process enough transactions per second. The second challenge – as already explored earlier – is problematic for both businesses and individuals: transactions are stored on a public database (the public ledger), which does not allow confidentiality.

Recently, the cryptographic technique of secret sharing and more generally threshold cryptography have been suggested in order to improve scalability and security aspects of blockchain security. This emerging area has so far only been explored in a small number of papers [3]–[6].

In [3] [6], the authors address the scalability of blockchain transactions by reducing the storage requirements for the public ledger, using an information dispersal scheme. A significant reduction in storage cost is achieved and furthermore, the integrity of transaction data can be improved. As an additional outcome, a reduction in energy cost due to block validation (bitcoin mining) is also achieved. Their scheme mainly focuses on reliability and redundancy, but not on security although there would be scope to do so. The key technique required for security enhancements is secret sharing, which can be seen as a variation of the information dispersal employed by the previous authors.

The paper [4] pursues this research avenue further by using a space-efficient secret sharing scheme. It differs from the previous work by not relying on encryption but solely on creating secret shares of a transaction block, and store them on different nodes altogether. This reduces storage requirements and communication costs. It also achieves confidentiality, although a rigorous security analysis is not undertaken and appears difficult due to the potential security weaknesses of the underline secret sharing scheme.

The paper [5] addresses the lack of a more sophisticated internal controls against fraud in Bitcoin. A new cryptographic threshold-signature scheme for Elliptic Curve based digital signatures is introduced. Wallets that create transactions using this signature algorithm are called threshold wallets. The major advantage of this scheme is the fact that the private key used to create the digital signature of the transaction is not required as an entire quantity, but is stored as shares in a distributed fashion. This achieves joint control of Bitcoins and extends the build-in multi-signature feature of Bitcoin, by addressing the problem of "hot storage". Two applications of the new threshold scheme are presented in the form of use cases: for businesses, to eliminate the problem with single-point of failure and for individuals, a two-factor secure Bitcoin wallet. The authors suggest that using this algorithm could be key to overcoming some of Bitcoin's biggest challenges, preventing organisations or individuals from using the system to conduct business transactions.

III. Virtual Private Blockchains

In this section, the main contribution of this paper is presented. Inspired by previous work on secure overlay architectures (see further in Section V), a blockchain architecture achieving security goals typically benefited by Private Blockchains is devised. An emphasis is on ensuring confidentiality and anonymity of sensitive transaction information that would be disclosed to all other users if it was contained in the public ledger of a traditional blockchain. These security goals are achieved by leveraging the existing Public Blockchain functionality through a suitable mechanism. The resulting Virtual Private Blockchain architecture resembles that of a traditional virtual private network, which explains the terminology "Virtual" following the original concept introduced for Online Social Networks in [7].

A. VPBC Characteristics

A VPBC has a number of interesting and appealing characteristics, both in terms of functionality and security properties.

- The term "virtual" is justified as a VPBC utilises existing Blockchain functionality and is by nature a Blockchain itself. In particular, a VPBC inherits any built-in, internal Blockchain security mechanisms.
- A VPBC is not visible to other Blockchain users that are not part of it, and it is transparent to its users. This achieves both usability and security, which is a desirable characteristic.
- Furthermore, it should be possible for users to be part of multiple VPBCs, and the impact of a VPBC on the overall Blockchain performance should not be noticeable.

Any specific VPBC implementation would have to ensure that these characteristics hold, that the precise mechanisms of inner workings would be hidden to the user, and that they do not adversely affect usability (and user experience).

We interpret the individual public blockchains as black boxes, operating in a transparent manner, with the sole purpose being the validation of transactions followed by storing them in the public ledger. The overall impact of the individual blockchains' mining process and types of consensus algorithm (proof-of-work, proof-of-stake) on the VPBC are not investigated more in detail in this paper, although this would be an interesting piece of future work.

B. Basic Idea

In order to implement a VPBC, one needs to substitute confidential transaction content with pseudo-content or, more specifically, data bits of the originally intended content through information dispersal. The precise choice of this pseudo-content will strongly depend on the particular blockchain application and will need to be carefully analysed prior to setting up the VPBC. Furthermore, a mechanism for reversing the substitution process is needed, so that other members of the VPBC can retrieve the original information. This might require exchanging secret information amongst participants of the VPBC and will have to be achieved using an out-of-bound channel, such as an email or a phone conversation. This is the equivalent of setting up a VPN in a traditional networking architecture, based on a manual configuration of keys for encryption.

The basic idea is simple, and an explanation using the Bitcoin application is straightforward. Assume Alice wants to pay Bob 100 bitcoin but would like to conceal this value to others who have access to the Bitcoin public ledger. Alice could split the amount into two parts, say $100 = 30 + 70$, send 30 bitcoin to Bob, convert the remaining 70 bitcoin to a different cryptocurrency and use the corresponding, alternative blockchain architecture to pay Bob. Subject to minor fluctuations, Bob is satisfied, having received the total amount via the two individual systems. The same idea could then be extended to using more than two blockchains, making it more difficult for an eavesdropper to reconstruct the real, original information.

While this method is effective for numerical values, it would be more difficult to apply for symbolic information. For example, if an address such as "Washington, D.C., USA" was to be split into town and country information and included in two different transactions, an attacker could potentially spot the correlation between these transactions. This could help in narrowing down search space or even to identify the used scheme. In the next section, we will present a more sophisticated approach which solves this problem.

C. Secret Sharing Approach

Expanding on the basic approach explained in the previous section, the precise cryptographic scheme that is underlying the VPBC architecture developed in this paper is the technique of *secret sharing*. The idea of secret sharing is to divide given data (the *secret* s) into n parts (the *shares*) in such a way that knowing (at least) m shares allows for reconstructing s. In an *ideal* secret sharing scheme, knowledge of less than m shares will not reveal any information on s. A secret sharing scheme with parameters m and n satisfying the aforementioned properties is also called a (m, n)-threshold scheme. A popular scheme is based on polynomial interpolation, introduced by Shamir [8].

Our VPBC architecture can now be explained as follows. Rather than using the example of Bitcoin, consider a generic public blockchain, and a requested transaction with sensitive transaction information t, requiring protection. Using a suitable ideal (m, n)-threshold secret sharing scheme, t will be shared as n pieces of information (transaction shares) $t_1, \ldots, t_n$, and these will be used for the individual transactions, executed on n independent public blockchains. Note that the resulting shares are random numbers and do not preserve any patterns that might be in the initial secret. The recipient, prior to using the scheme, has been informed about the selected blockchains. As soon as there are new transactions, a subset of m transactions (which in reality are shares of the real transaction) will be collated and the original secret transaction data can be reconstructed.

D. Security

In this section, we discuss the security of our VPBC approach. We showed that a VPBC implementation based on secret sharing is secure against any attacker being limited to accessing less than m blockchains, provided a (m, n)-threshold secret sharing scheme is used. If the secret sharing scheme is an ideal scheme, no information about the original transaction data is revealed by intercepting any of the shares. Furthermore, any collection of at the most $m - 1$ shares still does not yield any information about the original secret, in an information-theoretic sense. The security principle underlying the approach is security through obscurity. Provided that the specific transaction data protected through secret sharing is selected carefully and the resulting transaction shares appear innocuous, the technique could then be seen as a way of hiding information akin to steganography by cover modification.

In order to retrieve the sensitive information, an authorised user has to collate a collection of m transaction shares and apply the reconstruction method of the specific secret sharing scheme. In conclusion, this approach provides confidentiality under the assumption that no more than $m - 1$ blockchains would be attacked.

A number of attacks on the scheme exist, and we describe two approaches which appear the most straightforward.

1) Brute-Force Attack: In order to carry out an attack on the confidentiality of a VPBC transaction, the correct corresponding combination of transaction shares could be identified using brute-force searching across m different blockchains, users and different transactions per user. In addition, the particular secret sharing scheme would have to be known in order to reconstruct the initial transaction from the shares.

In order to gauge the feasibility of the attack, we can gather the following data: currently, there is an estimated number of about over 6900 public blockchains [9] available on the market at the time of this writing, with a tendency of this number to grow in the near future [9] [10]. This yields $n \leq 6900$ and $m \leq n$ for the secret sharing parameters, and futhermore, a number of $\binom{n}{m}$ transaction share combinations that need to be brute-forced. Denote by T the average number of daily transactions in the n participating blockchains. Then, there are $t = \binom{n}{m}T^m$ transaction combinations per day to be considered. The resulting data that needs processing is likely to be huge. For example, there are approximately $T \approx 300,000$ daily Bitcoin transactions [11]. On the other hand, the use of a $(m, 6900)$-secret sharing scheme might not be very feasible, and a balance between the level of provided protection and the computational effort for creating (and reconstructing) shares need to be found. This interesting question is planned to be investigated further by our research.

2) Deanonymisation Attack: Another way to attack this scheme would be to carry out deanonymisation (data-reidentification) techniques in order to identify users, frequently engaging with the same set of blockchains, in order to narrow down the number of required searches. While feasible in principle, it requires installing and monitoring of a maximum number of possible blockchain systems, up to the theoretical number of 6900, c.f. previous section. A criminal organisation or any other group of professional attackers could well cope with the demands of this attack, but it would be unlikely to be feasible for an individual.

On the other hand, any of these attacks resulting in a successful breach of confidentiality could be prevented by adding an out-of-band channel between individual users, for example using email or text message. If one of the transaction shares is transmitted on this channel, a successful attack purely based on processing the blockchain data would not be possible. As eavesdropping on the email message would be relatively easy, a further strengthening of the security using for example Pretty Good Privacy (PGP) or Secure/Multipurpose Internet Mail Extensions (S/MIME) should be implemented. While still possible for attackers with higher privilege (such as governments or technically more advanced cybercriminals), this improved method would be worthwhile, as it achieves a considerable strength of the security with a manageable overhead.

IV. System Simulation

One reason why Blockchain technology is enjoying growing popularity and rapid adoption is the availability of free implementations. The research described in this paper aims to provide a publicly available VPBC system, implemented as an interface for common blockchain implementation such as Multichain or Fabric Ledger, using a range of programming languages including Java and Python. This interface will allow processing transactions prior to their sending to the individual public blockchain systems. Typically, a cryptographic technique such as secret sharing will be applied in order to implement confidentiality. Efficiency and ease of use will be taken into account.

In order to investigate the feasibility of our proposed VPBC architecture, we simulated a proof-of-concept VPBC based on leveraging two Multichain blockchain systems. The two private Multichain blockchain systems (A and B) were set up on different instances of Ubuntu 12.04 LTS servers, with node A and node B representing cryptocurrency payment and digital value exchange systems (public blockchains). Multichain provides an inter-communication Application Program Interface (API), giving access to the blockchain background application. This API was used by a separate process, implementing our Virtual Private Blockchain, where the desired transaction is generated and executed via a smart contract. We may refer to this as a (virtual) node C. The client process, which can run any of the three Linux systems or a dedicated machine, generates the smart contract, performs the splitting (or more generally, the secret sharing) of the asset and creates the terms of the individual smart contracts by initiating the payment on node A and node B. The transactions on node A and node B are verified by the blockchain, and upon successful execution of both transactions, our system will report a successful conclusion/execution of the virtual transaction.

The commands below show an automated process of asset transfer on the Multichain blockchain using the bash script command and the process builder function in the Java programming language. The first instruction launches the blockchain in the background and then, using the instruction in the second line, one is able to see connected nodes with the necessary permissions to transact with the primary node. With that information, the third and fourth instructions show available assets on all connected nodes. The last two instructions implement the asset transfer and confirm the successful execution of the transaction.

```
processBuilder.command("bash", "-c", "multichaind VPBC
-dameon;
multichain-cli VPBC listtpermissions;
multichain-cli VPBC listassets;
multichain-cli VPBC gettotalbalances;
multichain-cli VPBC sendasset 1...asset1 100;
multichain-cli VPBC gettotalbalances 0;
```

V. Related Work

In this section, a brief literature review on security overlays for social network system architectures and instant messaging protocols is given. A discussion section helps to contrast this previous work with our VPBC framework presented in this paper.

A. Virtual Private Network Overlay Architectures

Several key papers [7], [12]–[16] have introduced and established the idea of improving security features of a network system architecture by creating a higher-level architecture based on a network security protocol bearing similarities to a virtual private network. While preserving the functionality of the original system, additional benefits such as sender and recipient anonymity or message confidentiality can be implemented.

In [7], the authors introduce the notion of a Virtual Private Social Network (VPSN), achieving the goal of implementing the anonymity of user-generated content in an Online Social Network (OSN). Their terminology is motivated by the similarity to a traditional Virtual Private Network (VPN), where users of the VPSN corresponds to network devices in a VPN. An implementation based on encryption and using an out-of-band channel was reported in the follow-up work [7], where the authors describe a Firefox browser plug-in called FaceVPSN.

In [12] and later [13], a different cryptographic technique is used to implement a related goal: the idea is to use steganography to hide posts in a social network by making them "socially indistinguishable" and hence difficult to detect. The need for an out-of-band is also present in this method.

An alternative architecture based on a distributed communication protocol with n channels has been proposed in [15], combining steganography with an (m, n)-threshold secret sharing scheme, applied to the plaintext message, followed by hiding the resulting individual shares in a suitably crafted carrier-medium.

In [16], a secure channel between two OSN Friends using instant social messaging is established based on a different type of distributed steganography. This implements a security control for message content facing an untrusted OSN provider. An Android mobile app prototype implementation is described, using two instant social messaging channels (Twitter and Google+).

The idea of overlay security architectures has also been applied to insecure network protocols. In [17], a secure multichannel protocol for SMS banking is developed. The cryptographic technique of steganography is used in two different information-theoretical models, inspired by the low-entropy and high-entropy approach of [13]. The resulting protocol achieves confidentiality of an SMS-banking transaction against an untrusted GMS service provider. An extended version of the protocol [18] also provides resistance against delay and replay-attacks, using cryptographic nonces.

B. Discussion

Both the idea of security overlay architectures and the cryptographic technique of secret sharing has been the initial inspiration for the work in this paper, in terms of concept and implementation.

To our knowledge, the security overlay presented in this paper is novel and unique in the context of blockchains, and there are some subtle differences compared to the previous works: a VPBC is not serving as a security control against a centralised communication service provider (such as an OSN provider). In fact, the communication setting is decentralised right from the start and remains as such. The VPBC architecture introduces several layers of the same communication model, due to the use of multiple blockchain implementations. This use of secret sharing is fundamentally different from that in [4] as, in a VPBC, shares are stored on different Blockchain implementations.

A VPBC architecture distributes the single public ledger (containing the transaction data) *vertically* onto the specific, chosen blockchain implementations while keeping the *horizontal* distribution of the public ledger as an entity, copied across all blockchain nodes, and kept in sync. Hence, a VPBC could be classified as a new type of blockchain technology bearing similarities with a Permissioned Blockchain as it is using a public ledger and a closed group of validators (the individual members of the VPBC who have to arrange membership out-of-band) while introducing a new type of ledger distribution – vertically rather than horizontally.

VI. Conclusion

In this paper, a novel Blockchain architecture is introduced by designing a security overlay, spanning across multiple Blockchain implementations. The resulting system is referred to as a Virtual Private Blockchain (VPBC) and can be interpreted as a Permissioned Blockchain with vertical (rather than horizontal) distribution of the public ledger. An evaluation of a prototype VPBC system simulation is reported.

Blockchain technology has been met with scepticism from many parties. Apart from security issues, the apparent lack of current mainstream use cases and applications, potential violations of data protection (such as the General Data Protection Regulation (GDPR)) and other shortcomings, there is also a danger of private organisations misusing data stored in private Blockchains. A VPBC might offer a solution to this problem as there is no central ledger database, offering the opportunity to exploit transaction data by a single entity for commercial purposes.

On the other hand, one drawback of the VPBC architecture is the additional overhead required for sending and validating several transactions, for each transaction on the VPBC although, in practice, this might be compensated for by the resulting security benefits. Furthermore, any VPBC – while offering attractive features in terms of confidentiality and anonymity – can also be subject of misuse. For example, illegal activities such as money laundering would be much easier to implement using a VPBC than other Blockchain architectures. As with any security solution, frequently there are ethical issues attached to its use and misuse, and developers and users alike need to remain mindful of these aspects.

In the same way as nowadays, adopters of cloud computing routinely use multiple clouds and the first multi-cloud systems have been suggested, the idea of a multi-blockchain will become more acceptable over time. Eventually, the idea of a VPBCs might become more mainstream as well. At this current moment in time, it can only be speculated what the precise future holds for the Blockchain, whether it is "virtual" or "real".

References

[1] C. Cachin *et al.*, "Architecture of the hyperledger blockchain fabric," in *Workshop on distributed cryptocurrencies and consensus ledgers*, vol. 310, no. 4, 2016.

[2] Multichain, "Stream Confidentiality," 2019, accessed 27/02/2020. [Online]. Available: https://www.multichain.com/developers/stream-confidentiality/

[3] R. K. Raman and L. R. Varshney, "Dynamic Distributed Storage for Blockchains," in *IEEE International Symposium on Information Theory - Proceedings*, 2018.

[4] H. Chen, H.-L. Wu, C.-C. Chang, and L.-S. Chen, "Light repository blockchain system with multisecret sharing for industrial big data," *Security and Communication Networks*, 2019.

[5] S. Goldfeder, J. Bonneau, R. Gennaro, and A. Narayanan, "Escrow protocols for cryptocurrencies: How to buy physical goods using bitcoin," in *Lecture Notes in Computer Science (including subseries Lecture Notes in Artificial Intelligence and Lecture Notes in Bioinformatics)*, 2017.

[6] R. K. Raman and L. R. Varshney, "Distributed storage meets secret sharing on the blockchain," in *2018 Information Theory and Applications Workshop (ITA)*. IEEE, 2018, pp. 1–6.

[7] M. Conti, A. Hasani, and B. Crispo, "Virtual private social networks," 2011.

[8] A. Shamir, "How to share a secret," *Communications of the ACM*, vol. 22, no. 11, pp. 612–613, 1979.

[9] J. Wanguba, "How Many Cryptocurrencies Are There In 2020," 2020, accessed 16/09/2020. [Online]. Available: https://e-cryptonews.com/how-many-cryptocurrencies-are-there-in-2020/

[10] Coin Market Cap, "All Cryptocurrencies," 2020, accessed 16/09/2020. [Online]. Available: https://coinmarketcap.com/all/views/all/

[11] Bitcoin.com, "Bitcoin Market Charts," 2020, accessed 16/09/2020. [Online]. Available: https://markets.bitcoin.com/crypto/BTC

[12] F. Beato, M. Kohlweiss, and K. Wouters, "Scramble! Your Social Network Data," in *Privacy Enhancing Technologies*, S. Fischer-Hübner and N. Hopper, Eds. Berlin, Heidelberg: Springer Berlin Heidelberg, 2011, pp. 211–225.

[13] F. Beato, E. De Cristofaro, and K. Rasmussen, *Undetectable Communication: The Online Social Networks Case*, July 2014.

[14] M. Conti, A. Hasani, and B. Crispo, "Virtual Private Social Networks and a Facebook Implementation," vol. 7, no. 3, 2013.

[15] C. Clarke, E. Pfluegel, and D. Tsaptsinos, "Confidential Communication Techniques for Virtual Private Social Networks," *2013 12th International Symposium on Distributed Computing and Applications to Business, Engineering & Science*, vol. 12, pp. 212–216, 2013.

[16] E. Pfluegel, C. Clarke, J. Randulff, D. Tsaptsinos, J. Orwell, and K. E. Khajuria, "A secure channel using social messaging for distributed low-entropy steganography," in *Cybersecurity and Privacy-Bridging the Gap*. River Publishers Series in Communications, 2017.

[17] O. Obinna, E. Pfluegel, C. A. Clarke, and M. J. Tunnicliffe, "A Multi-Channel Steganographic Protocol for Secure SMS Mobile Banking," in *The 12th International Conference for Internet Technology and Secured Transactions (ICITST-2017)*. Cambridge: IEEE, Dec. 2017.

[18] O. Obinna, E. Pfluegel, M. J. Tunnicliffe, and C. A. Clarke, "Ensuring Message Freshness in A Multi-Channel SMS Steganographic Banking Protocol," in *International Conference on Cyber Security and Protection of Digital Services (Cyber Security 2018)*,. Glasgow: IEEE, June 2018.

Security Requirement Modeling for a Secure Energy Trading Platform

Yasamin Mahmoodi*, Christoph Groß*, Sebastian Reiter*, Alexander Viehl*, Oliver Bringmann†

*FZI Forschungszentrum Informatik
Haid-und-Neu-Str. 10-14
D-76131 Karlsruhe, Germany
email: [mahmoodi, cgross, sreiter, viehl]@fzi.de

†Universität Tübingen
Sand 13
D-72076 Tübingen, Germany
bringman@informatik.uni-tuebingen.de

***Abstract*—The Internet of Things (IoT) paradigm has become important in many domains, ranging from smart home to medical and industrial applications. However, besides the outstanding advantages, comprehensive networking raises new security challenges. To benefit from IoT, secure embedded systems and resilient architectures are mandatory. Security-by-design is a cost efficient approach to accomplish this objective. Security requirement analysis as the first step of security-by-design plays an important role to design, develop and test secure embedded systems. This paper presents a case study to demonstrate security requirement modeling at three abstraction levels with the focus on the CIA triad (Confidentiality, Integrity, Availability). The methodology is demonstrated by applying the proposed approach to a use case from the energy domain.**

Keywords: Security analysis; IoT; Security requirement; Security-by-design.

I. Introduction

The Internet of Things (IoT) evolved into a mature technology and is nowadays used in a wide variety of application domains. Besides the numerous advantages offered by connected embedded systems, new security challenges and threats have been reported over the last years [1] [2]. The underlying embedded systems store sensitive information, such as financial data, medical data and passwords. Therefore, security issues are a critical concern.

The introduction of the IoT paradigm into the energy market, offers the opportunity to restyle the centralized energy market. This offers the opportunity to substitute centralized main energy producers with distributed decentralized small-scale energy providers. Households can install a photovoltaic system on the roof to produce their own energy and sell the rest to their neighbors. One efficient approach to sell the extra energy, which is beneficial both for seller and buyer, is the utilization of the IoT paradigm to create an automated local energy trading market. EnerDAG [3] is a platform, which provides local energy trading among neighbors employing a tangle data structure and smart contracts.

Decentralized systems are based on autonomous systems that operate on local information and work together to realize a complex task. Each system can therefore change specific information, issue non-expected transactions or try to compromise the system by other malicious behavior. Authorized nodes may try to manipulate the system in order to get financial benefits or to prevent other nodes from trading energy.

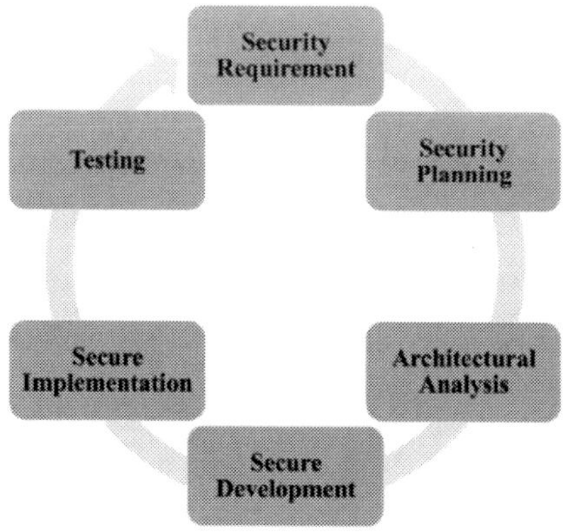

Figure 1. Secure System Development Life Cycle (SSDLC)

On the other hand, unauthorized nodes, which penetrate the system, may be able to keep nodes off the network or to use network data in order to make a Denial of Service (DoS) attack to make services non-available. Another aspect that should be considered is the anonymity of the participants. If the neighbors have access to the energy balance of other nodes, malicious neighbors can determine when people left for a vacation to break into their house. Accordingly, to get the full benefit of the comprehensively networked systems, considering security measures along the system design is inevitable.

To consider vulnerability assessment and penetration testing only on the final embedded system - security after the fact - is not an effective approach and the elimination of weak points could cost a lot of time and money. Integrating security aspects in all phases of system design - security by design - is a promising approach that lets system designers consider security from the requirements phase over the development phase to the final integration phase. The Secure System Development Life Cycle (SSDLC) [4] defines tasks, such as the definition of security requirements and assessing their risks, the planing of the security architecture, the actual design and implementation as well as task regarding testing and security assessment. An exemplary SSDLC is shown in Figure 1.

Security requirements are the foundation to design a secure system and execute security tests for each phase of the system design [5]. The better the security requirements are defined, categorized and refined, the more efficient tests can be designed and performed. Security requirements may come from different sources in various formats and abstraction levels. Managing these requirements is difficult, especially considering the fact that they may change during the system development life cycle [6].

This paper proposes three layers of abstraction for security requirements of embedded systems, which starts with general questions about security considerations at the most abstract layer and continues to explain them in more detail and finally puts them into several defined categories and deploys them to system entities. The third, most concrete security information is applied to an Unified Modeling Language (UML) model of the system with several predefined stereotypes. This procedure helps to guide the user, to keep track of the security requirements and offers the possibility to integrate them into the actual design environment. By using a well-defined interface, even an automated processing of security requirement information is possible. The paper is structured as follows: Section II-A highlights the importance of security requirement analysis in designing secure embedded systems. It mentions the three main principles that guide the information security modeling. Section III introduces the approach we applied for security requirement analysis and modeling of embedded systems. The following Section IV demonstrates the application of the methodology on enerDAG, a framework for energy trading.

II. V-MODEL FOR DESIGNING SECURE SYSTEMS

The SSDLC can be mapped to the traditional V-model [7], which provides a testing phase associated with each development phase. In Figure 2, the blue diagram represents the traditional V-model, with the system development on the right side. It starts with requirements, then it goes into the design of the system, the architecture and finally each module. Each step on the left side is directly associated with a testing phase on the right side. The V-model proposes a hierarchical perspective, which lets the designer start with a very abstract system specification and gradually add more design details. By mapping the SSDLC to the V-model design flow, the iterative nature of the SSDLC should be applied to the traditional V-model. Resulting in a repeated adjustment and refinement of the system and a repeated execution of the overall V-model.

Integrating security features and the associated validation to the overall system development process helps to discover and reduce vulnerabilities and design flaws at early stages, hence saves time and reduces costs. In Figure 2, the gray diagram depicts the SSDLC inspired, security-based V-model alongside the traditional V-model. At the right side of the diagram, security requirements alongside the other requirements of the system enable the security experts to get a comprehensive system view. As system designers go further in the development process, e.g., deriving the security architecture, more details both with regard to the design as well as to the test phases can be added. In this process, the security requirements should be refined too, and associated with components of the system design. Today's system design processes often apply a set of models, based on the UML, to specify the system

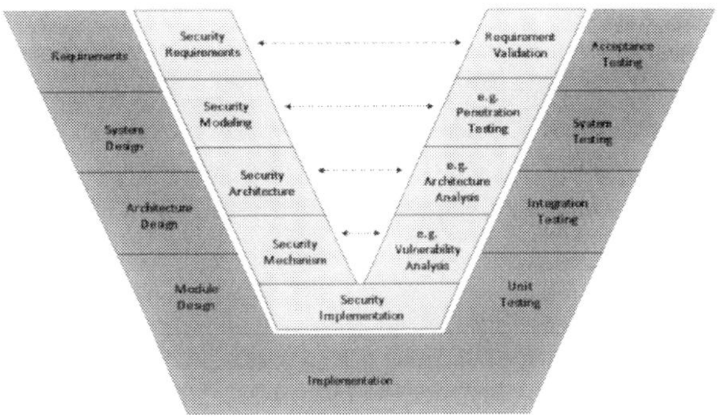

Figure 2. Security-Based V-Model

architecture as well as software features. For that reason, we propose a UML model augmented with security features as a security profile [8]. This enables the designer to refine security requirements in the same development environment as the system design. Our proposed security modeling approach provides models for security requirements and helps to discover the inherent weak points of the system architecture or chosen implementations by specifying the protection goals of the system, potential attack points, as well as additional security related documentation. Furthermore, by providing a well-defined profile the users are guided in specifying attack scenarios as well as protection goals. The UML security profile can be attached to the UML models to entitle the information about protection goals and assets, weak points and attack surfaces, as well as documentation-based information such as security mechanism and software version. These models can later on be beneficial for validation, e.g., with static analysis and vulnerability assessment. In addition, the model simplifies manual analysis, such as penetration testing, by boosting the documentation and helps identifying underlying potential design flaws, e.g., by enabling an automatic lookup in well-known security vulnerability databases.

A. *Security Requirements of Embedded Systems*

The requirement specification is the entry point of a system development process. It specifies the goals, functions and constrains of the system, and the relationship of them [9]. Requirement engineers should communicate frequently with stakeholders, system designers, developers and system analysts. A precise requirement description of the system is the basis to ensure stakeholders interests and manage the development process and budget. Bringing up security aspect into the system development process necessitates the need to integrate security requirement analyses in the first phases of the development process. Security requirement analysis is an essential step in today's system development processes, which should become the standard between stakeholder's requirement validation, development and testing. Defining security requirement categories and standards, which are pragmatic for both developers and testers, play a fundamental role. The Federal Information Processing Standard (FIPS) (The National Institute of Standards and Technology (NIST), 2010)

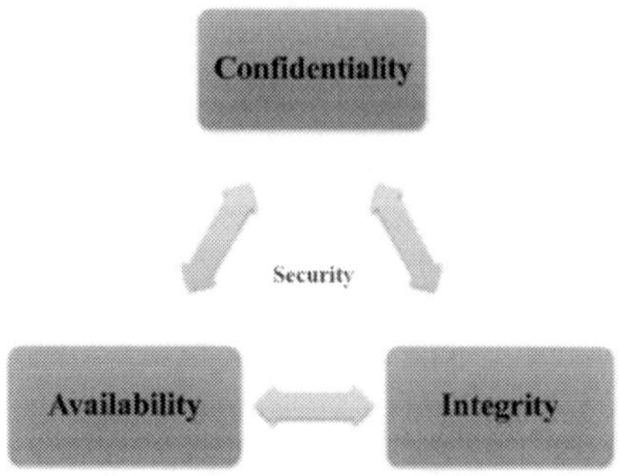

Figure 3. CIA Triad

offered three security core principles that guide the information security area:

- Confidentiality: ensures that access to the critical data is available only for authorized users.
- Integrity: assures the correctness and completeness of the data over its entire life cycle.
- Availability: makes sure that data and services are available for authorized users.

The CIA triad is shown in Figure 3.

Breaking any of the triad security principles (CIA) may lead to a level of impact, which endanger resources, information or individuals. The impact severity is define with the following three levels:

- Low: leads to limited adverse effect.
- Medium: generates serious or critical damage effect.
- High: occurs severe or catastrophic damage effect.

A security requirement modeling, which covers the CIA triad can offer a desirable standard for security requirement analysis.

III. Proposed Approach

The following section explains the proposed approach for a consistent, guided security requirements modeling. Considering the importance of security requirement analysis in designing secure embedded systems, we provide a three-level requirement modeling, which follows the sequential abstraction layers principle of the V-model. It starts with general security aspects of the system and concludes with a detailed specification of protection goals assigned to single entities in the system. The revealed information in last level is advantageous for architectural analysis as well as penetration testing. Because this last level should ensure a seamless transition into the system development process, we applied it to a traditional UML modeling approach by proposing a security profile.

The first abstraction level brings up general questions about security issues regarding the system. The stakeholders discuss about their desire system with the system designers and security experts to make a security checklist. Here is a list of the most important questions, which should be answered during security requirement analysis:

- What are the important parts of the system, which should be protected from attackers?
- Who are the potential attackers?
- Which parts are potential entry points for attackers?
- What are the effects of potential attacks on the critical data?
- Which security measures are needed?
- What is the network topology of the system and which security mechanisms will be applied to the system?
- How secure are the chosen hardware, software and technologies?
- What is required security level for the system?
- How are software updates handled?

The answers to these questions give an overall perspective about the security aspects of the system. However, this information is qualitative and subjective and in order to apply this knowledge, well-defined classifications and security metrics are needed.

In the second abstraction level, the protection goals of the system will be derived and categorized in the three classes of the CIA triad: confidentiality, integrity, availability. From this informal specification, all relevant information will be extracted in the next step.

The last abstraction level maps the information from the second layer about security requirements to a well-defined schema. The layer defines entries such as protection goal confidentiality, protection goal integrity and protection goal availability, and offers parameters to assign more details to each entry. No security mechanism by itself can protect the system completely and layered security defenses based on the nature of the protected information and weaknesses of the system are required. Untangling this issue, security experts and system designers require detailed information about the entities of the system, which should be protected, and the potential vulnerabilities and entry points. Therefore, this layer not only specifies the protection goals as well as the attack surface in a well-defined manner, it also associates each specified security entry with a system component or a sub-system. The specified data of this level should be used to decide about the design and integration of security mechanism as well as the specification of security tests. Several approaches such as [10] are already using the CIA classification to provided security mechanisms dedicated to each class and therefore integrate seamlessly into the proposed procedure.

To structure the information on the third layer in a well-defined manner, we propose to specify detailed information about protection goals, attack surfaces and documentation-based information in form of a security profile for the UML. A detailed description of the profile is present in [8]. Our security profile proposes stereotypes, which can be attached to UML modeling elements and are advantageous for both documentation and threat modeling. For security requirement modeling, we employ the protection goal category offered in our security profile. The protection goal category proposes the stereotype ≪PG.DataConfidential≫ (PG.C), which defines that the associated property should be protected against reading or predicting by an attacker. This stereotype implies confidentiality from the CIA triad. A parameter for the severity level can be added, specifying the criticality of the potential damage, if the protection goal is violated. The second stereotype of

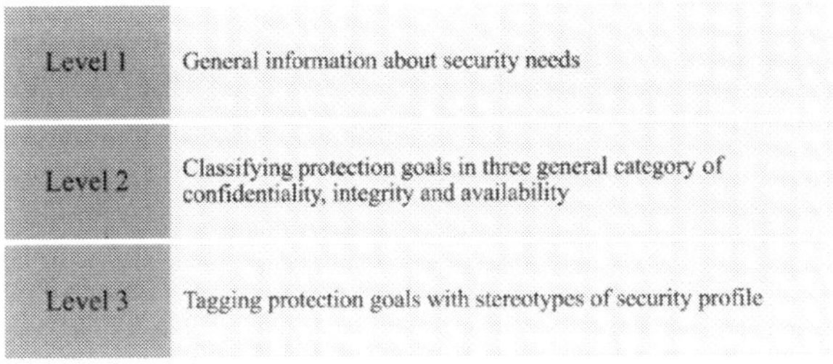

Figure 4. Three Abstraction Level Of Proposed Security Analysis Model

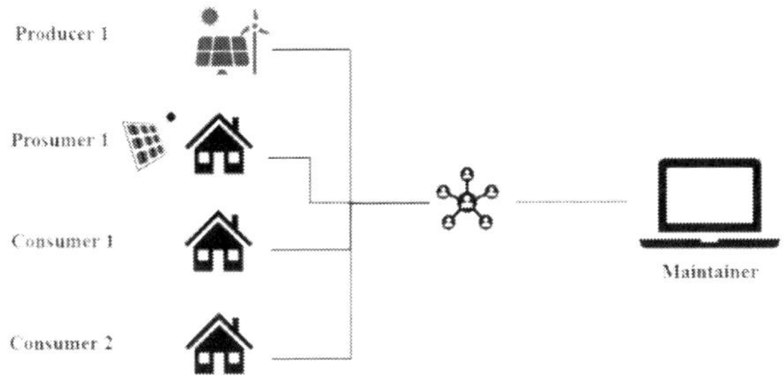

Figure 5. Model Of A Neighborhood With Different Types Of Nodes

this category. ≪PG.DataModify≫ (PG.M) indicates that the property should be protected against modification. A severity level also mentions how severe a violation of the goal is. ≪PG.DataDelete≫ (PG.D) characterizes the data that should not be deleted by an unauthorized transaction. Also a severity level was added. The stereotype ≪PG.DataAdd≫ (PG.A) indicates with its severity that this property should be protected against adding new data by an attacker. The stereotypes PG.C, PG.A and PG.D refer to the integrity of the CIA triad. The last stereotype ≪PG.ServiceAvailability≫ (PG.Ava) indicates that the stereotyped operation must be available and should not be stopped. Availability from the CIA triad is mingled with this stereotype. Figure 4 illustrates the three abstraction levels of security requirement modeling for embedded systems.

IV. Use Case

As a use case to demonstrate the security requirement analysis and modeling, we consider enerDAG (energy Directed Acyclic Graph) a local energy trading platform offered [3]. enerDAG offers an expandable platform for households to trade energy with their neighbors efficiently and securely using the tangle directed acyclic graph data structure. It is a highly distributed computing system, which applies smart contracts and majority voting for energy trading. Every household has a smart meter to measure the energy balance and a enerDAG software to communicate with other nodes and operate the contract. Each node in the neighborhood market may have a positive energy balance as energy producer or prosumer. Prosumers are households that produce energy, e.g., with photovoltaic, and also consume energy. Similarly each node can have a negative energy balance for consumer households or prosumers, if they consume more energy than they produce.

Energy trading will take place in five-minutes intervals. At the beginning of each time frame, the nodes will send their energy balance and their proposed maximum selling or minimum buying price to the network. Then, they receive the same offers from other nodes and based on an algorithm each node calculates the trade results of this contract for this time period. The contract results will then be sent to the tangle data structure and based on a majority voting will be part of the tangle. For security reasons, all the transactions are encrypted with a public encryption key of the neighborhood market as well as the private encryption key of the individual nodes.

A maintainer node registers the nodes, assembles the neighborhood and manages the market if it is necessary, as well as calculates the amount of traded energy and issues bills. Figure 5 represents a model of a neighborhood with different types of nodes.

enerDAG applies the tangle data structure, which is a directed acyclic graph that consists of transactions and their references. Each node can add transactions to the tangle and receive transactions from other nodes over the gossip protocol and insert the transactions in its view of the Tangle structure. In order to insert transactions in the tangle, the nodes have to follow the rules, e.g., by referencing at least two older transactions called tips and then publishing it to its neighbors. The enerDAG daemon, which is installed on each node, first establishes a database connection before running the main async loop forever that includes the following parts:

- *contractEngine()*: This part runs every minute and search for available contracts for execution. If it determines that a contract needs to be run, it loads and executes it via the *contactExecuter()* function. The result of a contract will be sent to the node itself for transaction handling.
- *connectionEngine()*: This part starts a server that will listen on a port for incoming messages via the *handleIncomingEvent()* function. When a transaction is received, it is processed and the correct action is taken.

A. Security requirement analysis of enerDAG

The following section highlights the proposed method applied to a security requirement analysis of enerDAG. Especially the three abstraction levels will be motivated.

1) Level one: The first abstraction level summarizes the stockholder's demand or general security needs in an informal way. Exemplary security demands of enerDAG are:

- Secure energy trading.
- Transparent transactions.
- Anonymity of the participants should be ensured.
- Non repudiation.
- The amount of energy that each node produces or consumes should be secret.
- The offered price from nodes should remain secret.
- Unauthorized user should not be able to participate in the market.
- Authorized users should not be able to cheat.
- A potential attacker may be both an unauthorized or an authorized user.

2) Level two: In the following abstraction level, the security requirements will be categorized into the three classes of the CIA triad (Confidentiality, Integrity and Availability).

- Confidentiality:
  - Energy balances of the participants.
  - Offered prices of participants.
  - The bids offered by participants.
  - Private key of the household nodes.
  - Public key of the neighborhood.
  - The transactions.
  - The seed sent by the maintainer to the household nodes.
  - List of neighbors.
- Integrity:
  - Energy balances of the participants.
  - Offered prices of participants.
  - The bids offered by participants.
  - Contract execution.
  - Majority voting.
  - The tips (least two older transactions in tangle data structure).
  - List of neighbors.
- Availability:
  - The server listening for new transaction
  - Transaction handling
  - Contract execution

3) Level three: In the last level of abstraction, we go through the software, respectively the corresponding UML model, and tag parts of the system with our proposed stereotypes, e.g., the five stereotypes to specify the protection goals of the system. This information extends the traditional UML model with security features and guides the architectural analysis and penetration testing later on. Additionally it is a good starting point for the identification of the required security mechanisms to achieve the protection goals.

The enerDAG software running on household nodes comprises of several functions, e.g., for receiving the list of neighbors from the maintainer node, handling the incoming transactions, sending the bids to the market, executing the contract and adding transaction to the tangle data structure. The maintainer node offers functions such as setting up a new node, assembling the neighborhood, sending the list of neighbors and calculating the bills for participants. With regard to the space limitations, it is not possible to explain all of the functions in detail. Therefore, we picked a few of the functions to demonstrate the utilization of the last abstraction level.

In household nodes, each time frame is five minutes. The first event in each time frame is to check if the result of the previous market execution has already been posted to the tangle and if so, to receive and to save it into the state file of the contract. Then the energy balance and the proposed price will be extracted and the bid will be structured. Afterwards, the bid will be encrypted first with the private key of the node then with the public key of the neighborhood and will be inserted into a transaction. The transaction is sent to the tangle using the neighborhood market contract's address as the receiver address. Meanwhile each node also receives the bids from the other nodes, decrypts the outer layer and puts them into the contract folder. In a next phase, each node will send its decryption key to the participating nodes and each node will decrypt the corresponding bid upon receiving this key. These two phases happen inside a 5 minute frame. The contract engine will then execute the smart contract at the end of the five minute time frame and send the results to the tangle data structure. Here we focus on the contract engine to illustrate security requirements and protection goals.

The contract engine searches through available contracts and if it finds a contract ready for execution, it provides it to the *contractExecutor()* function where the result of the contract execution is gathered, packed into a message of type *contractResult* and sent to the node itself. Then based on a majority voting the contract results will be accepted as the final results.

For the neighborhood smart contract, the *contractExecutor()* starts a loop and searches in all the contracts and find the negative energy balance (as buyers) and positive energy balance (as sellers). At the next step, it matches the best seller, sellers with lowest price, with the best buyers, buyer with highest prices, and then conduct the trade between them with the average price of both. The loop will continue until there is no energy to either sell or buy left. The list of assets and protection goals in the *Contractengine()* are represented underneath:

- *contractExecutor()* as a service should be available.
  - Asset: PG.Ava
  - Severity: Medium
  - Offered Security mechanisms: security policy (restricting sending message), IDS, firewall.
- Contract folder
  - Asset: PG.M, PG.A, PG.D
  - Severity: Low
  - Offered security mechanisms: Verifying integrity of the data using HMAC (Hash Message Authentication Code), AAA (Authorization, Authentication, Accounting) and to prevent hackers to be able to modify contract folder
- Majority
  - Asset: PG.M, PG.A
  - Severity: Medium
  - Offered security mechanisms: Encryption, hashing, verifying integrity of the data using HMAC, AAA
- Minimum selling/ maximum buying price in database
  - Asset: PG.C, PG.M, PG.A, PG.D
  - Severity: Medium
  - Offered security mechanisms:Pproper separation of Database, encryption, hashing, verifying integrity of the data using HMAC, AAA
- Validation key
  - Asset: PG.C, PG.M, PG.A, PG.D
  - Severity: High
  - Offered security mechanisms: Proper separation of Database, encryption, hashing, verifying integrity of the data using HMAC, Key management AAA
- Bid

  - Asset: PG.C, PG.M, PG.A
  - Severity: Medium
  - Offered security mechanisms: Encryption, hashing, verifying integrity of the data using HMAC, AAA

The decentralized system of enerDAG needs to validate the nodes, which are allowed to participate in the different neighborhood markets. Therefore, the energy and infrastructure providers run a node within each neighborhood that is called the neighborhood maintainer node. The maintainer sends hashed *Validation Keys* to the neighborhood nodes, sends the neighborhood list to the participants, sets up new nodes and calculate the amount of traded energy and publishes the bills. Here we focus on the function of adding a new node to show our security requirement analysis in level three.

To add a new node, the maintainer should change the complete neighbor structure of all nodes randomly in order to prevent malicious activities, e.g., by a cluster of bad nodes. The algorithm here takes each node from the database and tries to randomly assign nodes to the neighborhoods that do not have enough neighbors already. The limit is set to five neighbor nodes to allow for nice majority voting while not flooding the network with messages between nodes. The neighborhood maintainer node then sends the new neighbor list to all the nodes. At the next step the neighborhood *Validation Seed* will be generated for the new node and together with other neighborhood information, like the neighborhood encryption key, neighborhood maintainer node address and neighborhood contract address, will be sent to the node. The protection goals and assets of adding new node function are provided below.

- Neighborhood list
  - Asset: PG.M, PG.A
  - Severity: Medium
  - Offered security mechanisms: Hashing, verifying integrity of the data using HMAC, AAA
- *Validation seed*
  - Asset: PG.C, PG.A, PG.M
  - Severity: High
  - Offered security mechanisms: Encryption, hashing, verifying integrity of the data using HMAC, AAA, key management
- Neighborhood cryptography
  - Asset: PG.C, PG.M, PG.A
  - Severity: High
  - Offered security mechanisms: Encryption, hashing, verifying integrity of the data using HMAC, AAA and to prevent hackers to be able to modify contract folder
- Contract address
  - Asset: PG.C, PG.M, PG.A
  - Severity: Medium
  - Offered security mechanisms: Encryption, hashing, verifying integrity of the data using HMAC, AAA

V. CONCLUSION

Considering the importance of security requirement analysis in designing secure embedded systems, we proposed three abstraction levels for security requirement modeling in this paper, to enable a guided security consideration. The first abstraction level answers general question about security needs, considering stakeholders demands. In the second abstraction level, protection goals will be distinguished based on the information derived from the first level. Then the protection goals will be categorized in three classes, for confidentiality, integrity and availability. The last abstraction level goes into more details and classifies the exact assets of the system in five categories and protection goals: data confidentiality, data modification, data deletion, data addition and service availability. To foster the usage, we integrated the information in a classic UML based design flow, by providing a UML profile with dedicated stereotypes to specify the information. The applicability of the approach is demonstrated by modeling and transformation of security requirements for a energy trading platform (enerDAG) that enables households to create localized energy markets. We picked exemplary security requirements, modeled them on the three abstraction levels and showed the consistency and guided workflow to generate detailed protection goals and attack vectors in the use case.

ACKNOWLEDGEMENT

This work has been partially supported by the Federal Ministry of Education and Research (BMBF) within the project COMPACT (grant number 01|S17028C).

REFERENCES

[1] J. Viega and H. Thompson, "The state of embeddeddevice security (spoiler alert: It's bad)," Security Privacy, IEEE, October 2012, pp. 68–70.

[2] B. Schneier, "The internet of things' dangerous future," Jan 2017 (accessed October 2020), https://www.schneier.com/blog/archives/2017/02/security_and_th.html.

[3] C. Groß, M. Schwed, S. Mueller, and O. Bringmann, "enerdag – towards a dlt-based local energy trading platform," in 2020 International Conference on Omni-layer Intelligent Systems (COINS). IEEE, Aug 2020, p. 1–8.

[4] R. Chopra and S. Madan, "Security During Secure Software Development Life Cycle (SSDLC)," International Journal of Engineering Technology Management and Applied Sciences, vol. 3, 2015, pp. 1–4.

[5] ISO/IEC 15408-3, "Evaluation criteria for IT security – Part 3: Security assurance components," ISO, Tech. Rep., 2009.

[6] D. Mellado, E. Fernández-Medina, and M. Piattini, "SREPPLine: Towards a Security Requirements Engineering Process for Software Product Lines ," Security in Information Systems, Proceedings of the 5th International Workshop on Security in Information Systems, vol. 125, 2007, pp. 220–232.

[7] K. Forsberg and H. Mooz, "The relationship of system engineering to the project cycle." NCOSE, Chattanooga, Tennessee, 1991.

[8] Y. Mahmoodi, S. Reiter, A. Viehl, O. Bringmann, and W. Rosenstiel, "Model-guided security analysis of interconnected embedded systems," 6th International Conference on Model-Driven Engineering and Software Development, 2018, pp. 602–609.

[9] S. R. Kourla, E. Putti, and M. Maleki, "Importance of Process Mining for Big Data Requirements Engineering," International Journal of Computer Science & Information Technology (IJCSIT), vol. 12, August 2020.

[10] "A Survey of Information Security Implementations for Embedded Systems," 2017 (accessed October 2020), URL: https://www.windriver.com/whitepapers/.

Analyzing Power Grid, ICT, and Market Without Domain Knowledge Using Distributed Artificial Intelligence

Eric MSP Veith[1], Stephan Balduin[1], Nils Wenninghoff[1], Martin Tröschel[1], Lars Fischer[1], Astrid Nieße[2], Thomas Wolgast[2], Richard Sethmann[3], Bastian Fraune[3], Torben Woltjen[3]

[1] OFFIS e.V.
R&D Division Energy
Oldenburg, Germany
Email: first.last@offis.de

[2] Carl von Ossietzky University
Institute for Digitalized Energy Systems
Oldenburg, Germany
Email: first.last@uol.de

[3] Hochschule Bremen
Department for Computer Networks and Information Security
Bremen, Germany
Email: first.last@hs-bremen.de

***Abstract*—Modern Cyber-Physical Systems (CPSs), such as our energy infrastructure, are becoming increasingly complex: An ever-higher share of Artificial Intelligence (AI)-based technologies use the Information and Communication Technology (ICT) facet of energy systems for operation optimization, cost efficiency, and to reach CO_2 goals worldwide. At the same time, markets with increased flexibility and ever shorter trade horizons enable the multi-stakeholder situation that is emerging in this setting. These systems still form critical infrastructures that need to perform with highest reliability. However, today's CPSs are becoming too complex to be analyzed in the traditional monolithic approach, where each domain, e.g., power grid and ICT, as well as the energy market, are considered as separate entities while ignoring dependencies and side-effects. To achieve an overall analysis, we introduce the concept for an application of distributed artificial intelligence as a self-adaptive analysis tool that is able to analyze the dependencies between domains in CPSs by attacking them. It eschews pre-configured domain knowledge, instead exploring the CPS domains for emergent risk situations and exploitable loopholes in codices, with a focus on rational market actors that exploit the system while still following the market rules.**

Keywords*—*Cyber-Physical Systems Analysis; Distributed Artificial Intelligence; Reinforcement Learning; ICT Security; Market Design.

I. INTRODUCTION

During the last two decades, the power grid has seen an enormous development in the adoption of Information and Communication Technology (ICT) on a large scale in order to facilitate the inclusion of advanced methodologies, including Artificial Intelligence (AI)-based approaches. This increases efficiency and flexibility, which ultimately allows a higher share of renewable energy sources in the grid. However, together with a proceeding decentralization and the inclusion of energy markets, the complexity of the overall system also increased, with different factors adding to it, e.g., prosumers directly selling their Photovoltaic (PV) power or new market-based concepts for ancillary service provisioning, which need to be implemented by 2021 as per EU regulations [1].

Decentralized generation and consumption has led to the emergence of decentralized grid operation and control paradigms, many of which feature independent software agents. These Multi Agent Systems (MAS) exist for different tasks, e.g., to equalize real power generation and consumption, or to facilitate voltage control on local levels. A newer example of such a decentralized, specifically all-encompassing MAS that is aimed at including a high share of volatile, renewable energy sources is the *Universal Smart Grid Agent* system [2]–[4].

Assuming that major Internet of Things (IoT) trends will also influence the future power grid, the comprehensive use of ICT and AI technologies will, through their complexity, inevitably create an obstacle for a reliable operation of the power grid [5], [6]. At least since the cyber attack on the power grid of the Ukraine in December 2015 [7], [8], energy systems are recognized as valuable and vulnerable targets. Further attacks were seen in different stages with varying targets until and beyond 2017 [9]. These attacks demonstrate how ICT has a vital role in modern energy distribution networks. It needs to be reliable to ensure a stable power grid. However, due to the increasing ICT in modern power grids, the attack surface is getting bigger. Darknet marketplaces offer Distributed Denial-of-Service (DDoS)-as-a-Service and other attack-services for small money [10], which demonstrates that security testing is getting more important in this special domain.

Research actively addresses the numerous challenges that arise from the increased complexity and, thus, new attack vectors the emerge not only in the energy domain, but all Cyber-Physical Systems (CPSs) in general. Among them are neural control falsification, e.g., through Adversarial Learning (AL) [11]–[13], false data injection as attacks on state estimators [14]–[18], or utilizing compromised assets to actively damage the CPS [19].

In addition, a new type of attack has emerged in market-connected CPS like energy systems: The attack as a side effect of economically rational behavior. Energy markets are highly regulated in all countries. The need for regulation directly follows from the energy systems' inherent dependability on a dedicated infrastructure, like power grids, gas and heat networks. With this kind of infrastructure, a natural monopoly is given. To ensure system stability while optimizing costs, market-based approaches are regulated to realize access to this infrastructure and system stability responsibility. The adaption of regulative frameworks is late by design: Once a loophole has been found, regulation is readjusted. Even if no outright cyber-attack is staged, actors in the market might exploit loopholes while still conforming to the rules. There are a couple of known examples where this has been done and actually affected the power grid, e.g., in Germany with Inc-Dec Gaming against the zonal system with uniform pricing scheme [20], or in another case in Great Britain [21].

However, in a recent survey looking at CPSs from the perspective of AI research, we found that a large portion of research focuses on a safe inclusion of AI technologies, such as Deep Learning or decentralized control through MAS in critical infrastructures, but also emphasizes the gaps between almost fully analyzed, reliable CPS and the complexity introduced by these techniques. Additionally, there is currently no systemic analysis approach that includes AI technologies as the driver to explore and analyze unknown CPSs for safety [22]. This survey can be seen as the main motivational background for this work: Traditional methods for analyzing the operational safety of a CPS can only cover specific, partial aspects. Hence, we found extensive research into many different aspects of safe CPS operation, but no approach for systemic testing of intra- and inter-domain relationships. From the point of the analysis, this causes a fragmentation of the whole system into islands. Aggregating subsystems also means that the effects of the interaction of components, as well as the influence of market actors is not completely covered. This holds especially true for systemic vulnerabilities, in which isolated parameters are within nominal boundaries, but the overall system is being destabilized through emergent effects. On the basis of the challenges outlined above, we create an intelligent, cross-sectional software technology for analyzing complex CPS in project PYRATE. It analyzes complex CPS with interdependent components autonomously, finding vulnerabilities leading to systemic failures. The core of the software technology to be developed is based on learning software agents that interact with a model—ideally a digital twin—of a CPS, using the resulting system states as reinforcing feedback signals for full self-adaptivity to efficiently explore the search space of actions for destabilizing ones.

Our project works on two different levels: On a methodical level, we plan to develop a universal methodology to analyze weaknesses of arbitrary CPS by finding successful attack strategies. On a practical level, we apply this methodology to an exemplary scenario containing a power system, an ancillary service market, and an ICT system, to demonstrate possible applications and the effectiveness of the methodology.

The remainder of this paper is structured as follows: Due to didactic reasons, in Section II, we first introduce the three environments of our demonstrator, explain major challenges in them, and describe the co-simulation setup. Afterwards, in Section III, we follow with a description of our cross-domain learning MAS that explores a CPS in order to defeat it. The experimentation process that underpins any analysis of our technology is described next, in Section IV, followed by the post-run analysis in Section V that aims to isolate the minimal chain of actions that led to CPS failure. Finally, in Section VI, we conclude with an outlook towards the realization.

II. Environment Under Scrutiny: A Demonstrator

In the research project, a power grid, an ICT network, and a local ancillary service market are simultaneously subjected to analysis, since the goal is to analyze interdependent behavior. Since the analysis cannot be performed on real infrastructure for obvious reasons, simulation models of each of the different domains are being synchronized at run-time using a co-simulation approach.

A. Power System

In this project's demonstrator, we focus on distribution grids to show the feasibility of the approach. Today's distribution grids lend themselves very well: They contain both, distributed large and aggregateable small loads, connect the major portion of Distributed Energy Resources (DERs), and are currently subject to large-scale ICT inclusion, as well as the development of local ancillary market concepts. Furthermore, they form the smallest meaningful, mostly self-contained environment that features a complex CPS with a variety of outside influence factors such as volatile power generation from renewable energy sources.

For simulation and benchmark purposes on distribution grid level, a scenario-based benchmark environment was developed. This benchmark environment incorporates a Medium Voltage (MV) grid developed by the International Council on Large Electric Systems (CIGRE) [23], [24], time series data of one year in 15min resolution (e.g., for wind, solar radiation, or consumption) from a former research project *Smart Nord* [25], and different component models, like PV or Combined Heat and Power (CHP).

B. Ancillary Service Market

For current energy markets, regulation is mainly settled, though adaptions still can be seen quite often, e.g., for optimization reasons. When implementing new energy markets, a whole new set of regulations is needed, though: There is a lot of activity in the implementation of regional energy markets and cell-based approaches, which are still in their infancy. Thus, we can expect many upcoming iterations on the regulation sets [26]. This holds especially true for all kinds of ancillary service markets, e.g., reactive power or flexibility markets [27], [28].

In this context, even new problems arise: We found that, for grid-stabilizing ancillary service markets, regional actors and even private households could cooperatively induce problems into the grid to later get paid for eliminating these very problems. E.g., if we assume that the grid operator has to procure reactive power in a purely market-based way, private households could synchronize their load behavior in order to manipulate the local voltage level and to violate the voltage band. That forces the grid operator to announce a reactive power auction, in which generator agents would offer reactive power provision as ancillary service. Afterwards, the generator and household agents would divide profits and start a new attack. Regulation for such problems is not known at all, especially as this kind of malicious behavior is difficult to detect and proof.

Our methodology will help to systematically investigate and understand such profit-driven attacks, which will in turn allow for better market designs. For this, a local auction-based reactive power market with simple rules will be implemented as incentive for profit-driven attacks. This will allow for better understanding of possible attack vectors for profit maximization. Later, systematic comparison with more sophisticated market designs and rules will enable insights which market rules increase resilience against which attack strategies. Finally, we hope to find market designs that minimize attacks and that maximize grid stability, as well as detectability of such attacks.

C. ICT Simulation

Distributed power units are equipped with ICT to connect to wide-area networks. This enables operators to regulate and monitor distributed locations remotely, which is the foundation for implementing local ancillary service markets at the distribution grid level. The CIGRE MV model only specifies a distribution grid topology without covering the ICT domain, thus, we extend and overlay it with relevant ICT components to model a realistic multi-domain distribution grid infrastructure. Consequently, each node of the energy grid is accompanied by the corresponding representation in the ICT network that would, in reality, provide access to relevant sensors and actuators. Additionally, a communication network is built with routers and switches that connects these CPSs, arranged in multiple subnets, hence modelling a realistic ICT network.

Specific requirements arise from the multi-domain co-simulation setting: First, it needs to be efficient at simulating large networks. Second, the ICT simulation is required to create an accurate model of the reality and, therefore, compute realistic results, which is especially important when examining networks in a security context. Thus, it is necessary that existing software can be integrated with minimal modifications. Lastly, the simulation tool needs to be easy-to-use, so that also experts of the other simulated domains—who might have limited knowledge about ICT networks—can work with it after a short period of time. As there is no such simulator available that can meet all of these requirements, the *rettij* network simulator was developed. It is designed to simulate ICT components like routers, switches, clients and servers, provided as Docker containers [29] in order to represent a realistic behaviour as opposed to synthetic, simulated models. The configuration files of the ICT simulator integrate tightly with the rest of the software stack [30].

Co-Simulation

The multi-domain simulation for analysis can hardly be performed by one software tool alone. The setup of the last three sections describes three different, but intertwined, domains; each one warrants its own specific simulation software to yield realistic results [31]. In addition, specific models for power plants, wind parks, or independent market actors exist. These components are coordinated with the open-source co-simulation framework *mosaik* [32] and can therefore easily be integrated in other simulation setups relying on *mosaik*.

Figure 1 shows the complete software stack. The bottom box, labelled *co-simulation*, provides the technical view of the different simulators. Each simulator offers models, as well as attributes on these models, which form a hierarchy: The address scheme `Simulator.Model.Attribute` allows for unambiguous identification of each individual attribute and to connect them. E.g., `ARL.Attacker-1.Actuator-1` can be connected to `PowerGrid.WindFarm-1.P-Feedin` to deliver setpoints from the adaptive attacker agent to a wind farm under its control; similarly, `PowerGrid.Sensor-1.Voltage`, connected to `ARL.Attacker-1.Sensor-1`, allows the agent to measure the effects of its actions in terms of voltage values. *mosaik* synchronizes all simulators with each other and provides a common simulation clock time, the *time step*; data is transmitted to a simulator when it is *stepped*, data from its models' attributes is queried afterwards.

III. Distributed Analysis: Communication & Control

To analyze this interconnected complex system, the core tool is the application of the Adversarial Resilience Learning (ARL) methodology. ARL defines in its pure form [33] two classes of agents: *attacker agents* and *defender agents*. An instance of every class operates on a model of a CPS, i.e., both agents operate on the same shared model. However, neither attacker nor defender know of each other: They gather data from the CPS through their sensors, which retrieve the current state of the system—as far as it is observable to the respective agent—, but do not explicitly track changes induced by another party.

This specific distinction makes sense for the power grid, as well as for many other CPSs: Whether a voltage irregularity is induced by a larger PV feed-in at the end of the branch (e.g., coming from a farm) or forms a part of an attack, is hardly distinguishable, but needs to be countered in any case. Stringently, we assume that the defender needs to counter a variety of effects for resilient operation, from fluctuation in renewable feed-in to accidents to actual attacks without differentiating between them as a rule-based system would do. Therefore, neither the overall system design nor the experimenter differentiates between different causes and effects, leaving the development of strategies, as well as countering the adaption of the attacker to the defender's capability to adapt (and vice versa). That both agents learn to counter each other's strategies, thus developing them further and further, is the core of the system-of-systems learning principle of ARL [34]. Consequently, we use the attacker not just to execute actual cyber-attacks, but to represent any potentially system-harming behavior. Thus, the attacker becomes a universal analysis tool.

Focusing on the attacker, we consider a group of attacking ARL agents that form a self-organizing MAS and a single

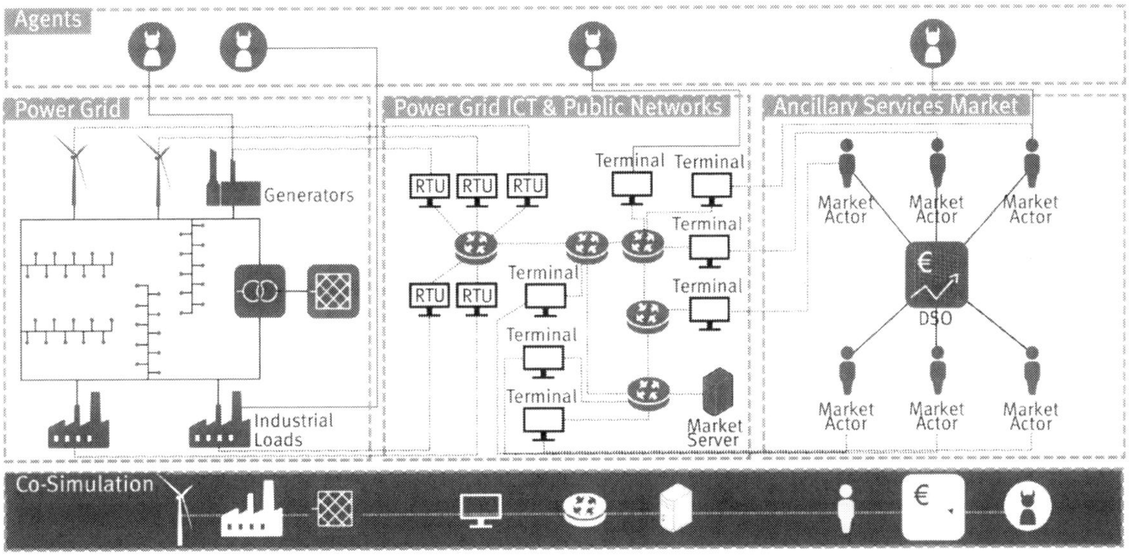

Figure 1. The Demonstrator's Co-Simulated Environments for Analysis

defender agent that represents the grid operator. All ARL agents use a modified Reinforcement Learning (RL) algorithm to explore a system that is initially unknown to them. In fact, ARL agents possess no domain-specific knowledge; their sensors and actuators contain only a description of the space for valid values. For the experimenter, these space types provide an easy way to describe types and boundaries for values; they can also be used as predicates to check whether a concrete value is a valid member of the given space. E.g., for a given value x, x is a member of the space $Discrete\{x\}$ iff:

$$Discrete\{n\} : x \in \mathbb{N}, 0 \leq x \leq n - 1 \; . \qquad (1)$$

Similarly, we can denote a box in $\mathbb{R}^n$ and check for a value x to be a member of it:

$$Box\{(l_1, \ldots, l_n), (h_1, \ldots, h_n)\} : x \in \mathbb{R}, \bigwedge_{i=1}^{n} l_i \leq x \leq h_i \; . \qquad (2)$$

Other space types are *MultiDiscrete*, *MultiBinary*, or *Tuple*. Such a space description might represent the state of a tap-changer or the feed-in of a power plant in terms of a faction of its nominal output, but this logic is completely hidden from the agent. In fact, the domain logic is the responsibility of the experimenter. As the only way for RL agents to learn is to receive feedback, the experimenter has to derive a proper reward function that covers the relevant aspects of the CPS. The reward function bridges the otherwise separated concerns, i.e., the ARL perspective that eschews domain knowledge and the CPS domain. Thus, the ARL agents remain free of any domain-specific knowledge, as the reward function is a unit-less scalar and the objective can be learned.

Because of this feature, we describe the agents as being *polymorphic*. Drawing from the analogy in software engineering, the agents' interfaces are fixed and soundly described, but do not carry any model. That means, the space types assigned to the agents' sensors and actuators form a declaration, but no definition. The agents derive this definition—i.e., their model—through exploration. Hence, they are polymorphic. This means that an abstract definition of a CPS' interface in terms of the spaces outlined above is enough to have the ARL agents explore the systems; this constitutes a fundamental difference from many modelling and analysis tools that require implicit or explicit modelling of the target domain.

As part of this new research direction, we assume that MAS are a valid approach to analyze highly decentralized systems as depicted above: They inherently allow for a representation of local knowledge and rule sets, even learned one, such as a limited view on local grid state and local control options [35]. It has already been shown that a combination with cyber-physical energy system simulation is feasible and beneficial to analyze the distributed behavior of the system, even for socio-technical system views [36]. Thus, we use MAS to represent and explore the effect of cooperative malicious actors. In this case, cooperative means that the agents act cooperatively within their defined group of malicious or unplanned malicious, simply economically rational, agents. The attackers share a reward function, which can be as easy as the amount of money gained from the market, but also be complex and encompass aspects of all domains. In any case, the reward function remains transparent to each attacker and does not convey any domain knowledge to the agents, but is defined solely at the discretion of the experimenter.

In the presented concept, the overall MAS encompasses all three domains. Individual agents represent different actors in one of the domains. E.g., in a scenario, in which the attacker MAS controls three assets in the power grid, has one entry point to the ICT network, and appears with one bidder on the market, the MAS is comprised of five agents. An example for sensor and actuator mappings is presented in Table I.

TABLE I. EXEMPLARY ARL ATTACKER MAS THAT CAN PARTICIPATE IN A REACTIVE POWER MARKET

Agent	Asset	Sensors	Actuators
a_1	PV Unit	Voltage[1], Max. Active Power[2]	Active Power[2], Reactive Power[3]
a_2	EV Charger	Voltage[1], Active Power[2]	Active Power[2], Reactive Power[3]
a_3	Load	Voltage[1], Active Power[2], Reactive Power[3]	Active Power[2]
a_4	Market	Reactive Power Commitment (relative)[3]	Reactive Power Offer (relative)[3]
a_5	ICT	Interface Utilization[2]	Manipulate Sensor Value (Apply Noise)[3]

[1] $Box\{(0.85),(1.15)\}$, [2] $Box\{(0.0),(1.0)\}$, [3] $Box\{(-1.0),(1.0)\}$

In order to develop an overall strategy, the attackers need to coordinate among themselves without a central command-&-control instance. Snapshot algorithms [37] will be used to enable the agents to interchange their local sensor data to gain knowledge of the global state. In this case, global state means the entirety of all sensors that the ARL agents have access to. Learning agents that perform decision making based on shared knowledge can then learn optimal cooperative decision making based on that knowledge. With this research direction, we thrive for the development of a domain-encompassing coordination protocol to address this holistic approach to CPS analysis.

While malicious cooperation cannot be deduced directly from regulatory or observability loopholes, beneficial cooperative behavior is analyzed as well: the defender aims to stabilize the system and prevent malicious attacks.

In our research approach, we therefore combine these agent types to act in shared environments. Thus, we hope to identify ruleset, ICT, and market designs that minimize attack possibilities and stabilize the overall system. In future work, we will define and work out the resulting multi-layer attack coordination and defense framework.

IV. EXPERIMENT PROCESS

As Figure 2 illustrates, the overall experiment process incorporates four major steps: First, a domain independent description of the CPS and its interfaces is required. The definition of such a description is called *CPS Abstract Ontology* (CPS-AO) in the context of the presented research direction. The main purpose of the CPS-AO is the definition of network topological variables and the mapping of the ARL agents' sensors and actuators to entities in the environment. Additionally, the CPS-AO defines which variables can be changed during the experiments and the valid value ranges. Furthermore, the CPS-AO takes this topology information to build up experiments. For this purposes, CPS-AO employs techniques from the domain of Design of Experiments (DoE) [38] to select only configurations that provide the strongest significance. An example for a CPS-AO configuration file can be seen in Figure 3.

Furthermore, the CPS-AO serves as an input for the so-called *experiment generator* (CPS-EG). While the CPS-AO is a domain-independent and abstract description of the system, the CPS-EG instantiates the experiment descriptions for the actual simulation, assigns values to factors, and builds execution scripts.

All so generated concrete experiments are executed by an *experiment executor* (CPS-EE) in the target environment. This provides the actual interface between the agent structure and the simulation environment. In order to enable changes, the created intermediate results will be saved so that smaller changes are possible without having to go through the entire process again. During the execution of the experiments, the states of the simulation, as well as the actions of the agents and the market results are stored and thus made available for a later weak point analysis, which will be described in the following section.

V. POST-RUN ANALYSIS METHODOLOGY

The experimenter defines a set of invariants that describe the environment's overall health. After the executor has finished the simulation run and health invariants were falsified, a *post-mortem analysis* of the defeated system shall be conducted. This CPS Vulnerability Analyzer (CPS-VA) conducts targeted evaluation of the attacks across all domains, aiming to find the smallest chain of stringent actions that defeated this system, i.e. to identify the cross-domain attack-path or kill-chain. We assume that the ARL MAS, in its exploration, conducts a lot of negligible action before staging a successful attack. Hence, identification of the minimal kill-chain is a separate analysis task.

Another goal of the research project is the development of the CPS-VA, which primarily aims to understand the produced data. It operates on data from all nodes, i.e. data from sensors and actuators. The transactions on the market, as well as states from the ICT and the power grid are collected. Then, the CPS-VA is designed to apply different analysis techniques on this data to isolate the kill-chain. For understanding the path of the kill-chain, predictive models and techniques are often not the best choice [39]. Most of the time, causality methods are more promising. Mueller, Memory, and Bartrem [40] use causal discovery techniques to discover cyber kill-chains; therefore, data is presented as a Causal Bayesian Network (CBN). Finding the right methodology to explain the experiment's outcome is also part of the development of the CPS-VA and will start as soon as first datasets are ready.

From the ICT security point of view, the task of the CPS-VA is somehow similar to what threat detection tools are designed for, but so far they only focus on ICT related data. The behaviour of the ARL agents can be treated as Advanced Persistent Threats (APT). APTs can be described as sophisticated attack processes that are often strategically-motivated and profit-focused [41]. Standard industry solutions to detect APTs are so called Security Information and Event Management (SIEM) systems. Such a system collects data from a wide variety of security applications to detect suspicious traffic and behaviour in ICT systems. To make use of this information, SIEM systems use correlation rules [42] and rise alarm in case of a anomaly detection. The CPS-VA provides

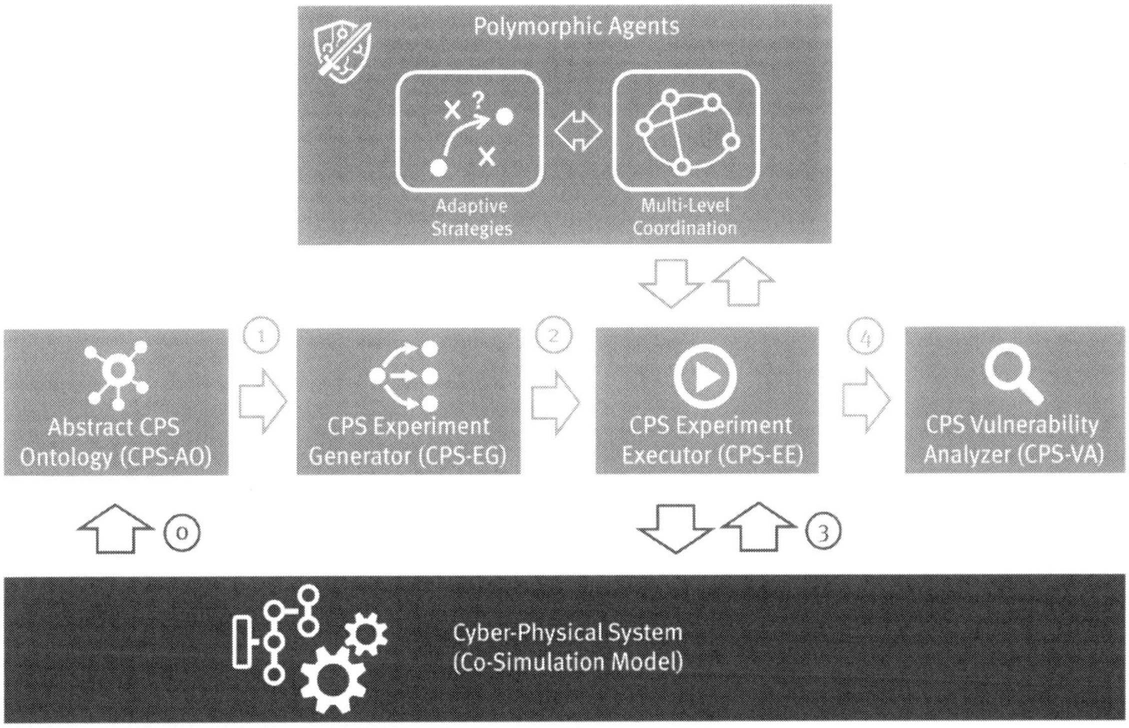

Figure 2. Experiment process of the presented research approach

```
!CPSAO
cps: !CPS # the system
  engine: # e.g. mosaik
  api: # how to instantiate
  sensors: # list of UIDs
  actuators: # list of UIDs
doe:
  runs:
  factors: # DoE inputs
  qualities: # DoE outputs
  strategy: # how to sample
  # e.g. Latin Hypercube

agents: # two or more
- !Agent
# if more than one option
# is present in the agent's
# definition, they will be
# considered for DoE
  name: # convenience
  sensors: # list of UIDs
  actuators: # list of UIDs
  strategies: # how to win
  rewards: #
- !Agent # same as above
```

Figure 3. A minimal example for a CPS-AO file. Additional parameters have been removed for the sake of brevity.

the opportunity to evaluate the idea of SIEM systems towards new applications.

First, a reasonable model from all domains is used in simulation to manually create simple correlation rules. This first step evaluates which information from the domains is necessary and how to create suitable correlation rules to generate basic knowledge for the next steps. Second, a much higher amount of relevant information for the SIEM is expected. In correlating different experiment runs from a variety of different scenarios—using, e.g., big data analytics [43]—, singular kill-chains can be derived and, thus, the respective rules be created. We expect that, starting with easy-to-observe critical states in the CPSs, an isolation path beginning on the affected components in the CPS can connect the critical states to market actors.

VI. Conclusion

Many CPS experience a broad addition of inputs, from self-driving capabilities over user inputs and IoT technologies to a broad market adoption in the case of power systems. The emergence of complex CPSs cannot be covered by traditional modelling and analysis techniques that can address only specific aspects of the overall system. In this paper, we proposed the concept for an application of distributed artificial intelligence as a self-adaptive analysis tool that is able to analyze the interdependencies between domains in CPS, covering the whole system. It eschews pre-configured domain knowledge, instead exploring the CPS domains for emergent risk situations and exploitable loopholes in codices, with a special focus on rational market actors that exploit the system while still following the rules of market.

In the future, we will demonstrate the feasibility of a cross-domain distributed analysis, documenting the experimentation system, the coordinating MAS-based exploration tool, as well as the analysis tool. With the latter, we aim to extract a reduced chain of actions leading to a cross-system exploitation, thereby isolating attack vectors and loopholes in codices. Furthermore, we expect the use of polymorphic agents to lead to new insights in the field of RL. The ARL agent interaction with the ICT, which forms a central piece of the concept, will give new valuable insights of the ICT's critical role in modern CPSs. This will enhance research towards new security tools for modern critical infrastructures.

Currently, the implementation of this framework is not yet made available to the public; however, we expect this to happen in the coming weeks. We will then publish detailed comparisons to other approaches and make the respective data available for reproducing our results.

ACKNOWLEDGEMENTS

We would like to thank Sebastian Lehnhoff for his councel and valuable inputs. This work was funded by the German Federal Ministry of Education and Research through the project *PYRATE* (01IS19021A).

REFERENCES

[1] European Union, *Directive (EU) 2019/944 of the european parliament and of the council of 5 june 2019 on common rules for the internal market for electricity and amending directive 2012/27/EU*, [retrieved: Oct, 2020], 5 June 2019. [Online]. Available: https://eur-lex.europa.eu/legal-content/EN/TXT/PDF/?uri=CELEX:32019L0944.

[2] E. M. Veith, B. Steinbach, and J. Windeln, "A lightweight distributed software agent for automatic demand—supply calculation in smart grids", *International Journal On Advances in Internet Technology*, vol. 7, no. 1, pp. 97–113, 2014.

[3] M. Ruppert, E. M. Veith, and B. Steinbach, "An evolutionary training algorithm for artificial neural networks with dynamic offspring spread and implicit gradient information", in *The Sixth International Conference on Emerging Network Intelligence (EMERGING 2014)*, International Academy, Research, and Industry Association (IARIA), IARIA XPS Press, 2014, pp. 18–21.

[4] E. M. Veith, *Universal Smart Grid Agent for Distributed Power Generation Management*. Berlin, Germany: Logos Verlag Berlin GmbH, Oct. 2017.

[5] O. Hanseth and C. Ciborra, *Risk, complexity and ICT*. Cheltenham, UK: Edward Elgar Publishing, 2007.

[6] D. Sculley *et al.*, "Machine learning: The high interest credit card of technical debt", *SE4ML: Software Engineering for Machine Learning (NIPS 2014 Workshop)*, pp. 1–9, 2014.

[7] D. U. Case, "Analysis of the cyber attack on the ukrainian power grid", *Electricity Information Sharing and Analysis Center (E-ISAC)*, 2016.

[8] J. Styczynski and N. Beach-Westmoreland, "When the lights went out: Ukraine cybersecurity threat briefing", *Booz Allen Hamilton*, vol. 12, p. 20, 2016.

[9] Reuters, *Ukrainian banks, electricity firm hit by fresh cyber attack*, Jun. 2017.

[10] A. Crawley, "Hiring hackers", *Network Security*, no. 9, pp. 13–15, Sep. 2016, ISSN: 13534858.

[11] K. Pei, Y. Cao, J. Yang, and S. Jana, "DeepXplore: Automated whitebox testing of deep learning systems", 2017, [retrieved: Oct, 2020]. arXiv: 1705.06640. [Online]. Available: http://arxiv.org/abs/1705.06640.

[12] T. Gehr, M. Mirman, D. Drachsler-Cohen, P. Tsankov, S. Chaudhuri, and M. Vechev, "AI^2: Safety and robustness certification of neural networks with abstract interpretation", in *2018 IEEE Symposium on Security and Privacy (SP)*, IEEE, 2018, pp. 1–18.

[13] S. Yaghoubi and G. Fainekos, "Gray-box adversarial testing for control systems with machine learning components", vol. 1, no. 1, pp. 179–184, 2019. arXiv: arXiv:1812.11958v1.

[14] A. Teixeira, S. Amin, H. Sandberg, K. H. Johansson, and S. S. Sastry, "Cyber security analysis of state estimators in electric power systems", *Proceedings of the IEEE Conference on Decision and Control*, pp. 5991–5998, 2010, ISSN: 01912216.

[15] H. Sandberg, A. Teixeira, and K. H. Johansson, "On security indices for state estimators in power networks", in *First Workshop on Secure Control Systems (SCS), Stockholm, 2010*, 2010, pp. 1–6.

[16] Y. Liu, P. Ning, and M. K. Reiter, "False data injection attacks against state estimation in electric power grids", *ACM Transactions on Information and System Security (TISSEC)*, vol. 14, no. 1, p. 13, 2011.

[17] S. Gao, L. Xie, A. Solar-Lezama, D. Serpanos, and H. Shrobe, "Automated vulnerability analysis of ac state estimation under constrained false data injection in electric power systems", in *Proceedings of the IEEE Conference on Decision and Control*, vol. 54, IEEE, 2015, pp. 2613–2620, ISBN: 9781479978861.

[18] L. Hu, Z. Wang, Q.-L. Han, and X. Liu, "State estimation under false data injection attacks: Security analysis and system protection", *Automatica*, vol. 87, pp. 176–183, 2018.

[19] P. Ju and X. Lin, "Adversarial attacks to distributed voltage control in power distribution networks with DERs", in *Proceedings of the Ninth International Conference on Future Energy Systems*, ACM, 2018, pp. 291–302, ISBN: 9781450357678.

[20] L. Hirth and I. Schlecht, "Market-based redispatch in zonal electricity markets", *SSRN Electronic Journal*, no. 055, pp. 1–26, 2018.

[21] C. Konstantinidis and G. Strbac, "Empirics of intraday and real-time markets in Europe: Great Britain", DIW – Deutsches Institut für Wirtschaftsforschung, Berlin, Germany, Tech. Rep., 2015, p. 21.

[22] E. M. Veith, L. Fischer, M. Tröschel, and A. Nieße, "Analyzing cyber-physical systems from the perspective of artificial intelligence", in *Proceedings of the 2019 International Conference on Artificial Intelligence, Robotics and Control*, ser. AIRC '19, Cairo, Egypt: Association for Computing Machinery, 2019, pp. 85–95, ISBN: 9781450376716.

[23] K. Rudion, A. Orths, Z. A. Styczynski, and K. Strunz, "Design of benchmark of medium voltage distribution network for investigation of dg integration", in *2006 IEEE Power Engineering Society General Meeting*, IEEE, 2006, pp. 6–12.

[24] CIGRE Task Force C6.04.02, *Benchmark Systems for Network Integration of Renewable and Distributed Energy Resources*. 2014.

[25] L. Hofmann and M. Sonnenschein, "Smart Nord—final report", *Hartmann GmbH*, 2015.

[26] C. Weinhardt *et al.*, "How far along are local energy markets in the DACH+ region?: A comparative market engineering approach", in *Proceedings of the Tenth ACM International Conference on Future Energy Systems, e-Energy 2019, Phoenix, AZ, USA, June 25-28, 2019*, ACM, 2019, pp. 544–549.

[27] F. Lilliu, M. Vinyals, R. Denysiuk, and D. R. Recupero, "A novel payment scheme for trading renewable energy in smart grid", in *Proceedings of the Tenth ACM International Conference on Future Energy Systems, e-Energy 2019, Phoenix, AZ, USA, June 25-28, 2019*, ACM, 2019, pp. 111–115.

[28] S. C. Chau, J. Xu, W. Bow, and K. M. Elbassioni, "Peer-to-peer energy sharing: Effective cost-sharing mechanisms and social efficiency", in *Proceedings of the Tenth ACM International Conference on Future Energy Systems, e-Energy 2019, Phoenix, AZ, USA, June 25-28, 2019*, ACM, 2019, pp. 215–225.

[29] The Docker developers, *Docker website*, [retrieved: Oct, 2020]. [Online]. Available: https://www.docker.com/.

[30] T. Woltjen, G. Gritzan, P. Kathmann, and R. Sethmann, "Simulationsumgebung für IKT-Netze zur Cyber-Abwehr", in *Tagungsband AALE 2020*, VDE Verlag, 2020, pp. 233–239, ISBN: 978-3-8007-5180-5.

[31] S. Balduin, M. Tröschel, and S. Lehnhoff, "Towards domain-specific surrogate models for smart grid co-simulation", *Energy Informatics*, vol. 2, no. 1, p. 27, 2019.

[32] The mosaik Developers, *Mosaik website*, [retrieved: Oct, 2020]. [Online]. Available: https://mosaik.offis.de/.

[33] L. Fischer, J.-M. Memmen, E. M. Veith, and M. Tröschel, "Adversarial resilience learning—towards systemic vulnerability analysis for large and complex systems", in *The Ninth International Conference on Smart Grids, Green Communications and IT Energy-aware Technologies (ENERGY 2019)*, vol. 9, 2019, pp. 24–32.

[34] E. M. Veith, N. Wenninghoff, and E. Frost, *The adversarial resilience learning architecture for ai-based modelling, exploration, and operation of complex cyber-physical systems*, 2020. arXiv: 2005.13601 [cs.AI].

[35] Y. Shoham and K. Leyton-Brown, *Multiagent Systems - Algorithmic, Game-Theoretic, and Logical Foundations*. Cambridge, MA, USA: Cambridge University Press, 2009, ISBN: 978-0-521-89943-7.

[36] I. Praca, H. Morais, C. Ramos, Z. Vale, and H. Khodr, "Multi-agent electricity market simulation with dynamic strategies & virtual power producers", in *2008 IEEE Power & Energy Society general meeting*, Piscataway, NJ: IEEE, 2008, pp. 1–8, ISBN: 978-1-4244-1905-0.

[37] K. M. Chandy and L. Lamport, "Distributed Snapshots: Determining Global States of Distributed Systems", *ACM Transactions on Computer Systems (TOCS)*, vol. 3, no. 1, pp. 63–75, 1985, ISSN: 07342071.

[38] J. P. Kleijnen, "Design and analysis of simulation experiments", in *International Workshop on Simulation*, Springer, 2015, pp. 3–22.

[39] G. Shmueli, "To Explain or to Predict?", *Statistical Science*, vol. 25, no. 3, pp. 289–310, Aug. 2010, [retrieved: Oct. 2020], ISSN: 0883-4237. arXiv: 1101.0891. [Online]. Available: http://projecteuclid.org/euclid.ss/1294167961.

[40] W. G. Mueller, A. Memory, and K. Bartrem, "Causal discovery of cyber attack phases", *Proceedings - 18th IEEE International Conference on Machine Learning and Applications, ICMLA 2019*, pp. 1348–1352, 2019.

[41] A. Ahmad, J. Webb, K. C. Desouza, and J. Boorman, "Strategically-motivated advanced persistent threat: Definition, process, tactics and a disinformation model of counterattack", *Computers & Security*, vol. 86, pp. 402–418, Sep. 2019, ISSN: 01674048.

[42] A. Ambre and N. Shekokar, "Insider Threat Detection Using Log Analysis and Event Correlation", *Procedia Computer Science*, vol. 45, no. C, pp. 436–445, 2015, ISSN: 18770509.

[43] A. a. Cardenas, P. K. Manadhata, and S. P. Rajan, "Big data analytics for security", *IEEE Security & Privacy*, vol. 11, no. 6, pp. 74–76, Nov. 2013, ISSN: 1540-7993.

International Academy, Research, and Industry Association (IARIA)
412 Derby Way
Wilmington, DE 19810

ISBN 978-1-7138-2163-2

CURRAN ASSOCIATES INC.
proceedings.com